SANDY GUNN

SANDY GUNN

OPERATION OVERLORD
—D-DAY—
DAY BY DAY

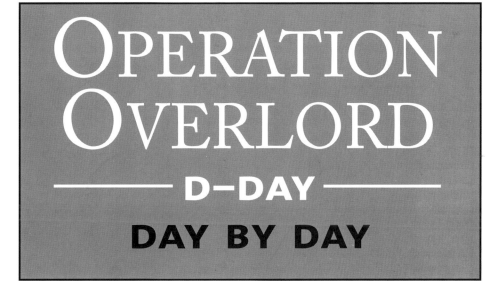

OPERATION OVERLORD

─ D-DAY ─

DAY BY DAY

ANTHONY HALL

Grange
BOOKS

This edition published in 2003 by
Grange Books
Grange Books plc
The Grange
1-6 Kingsnorth Estate
Hoo
Near Rochester
Kent, ME3 9ND
www.grangebooks.co.uk

ISBN 1-84013-592-1

Printed in U.A.E

Editorial and design:
The Brown Reference Group plc
8 Chapel Place
Rivington Street
London
EC2A 3DQ
UK
www.brownreference.com

Senior Editor: Peter Darman
Editors: James Murphy, Mark Hawkins-Dady
Picture research: Andrew Webb
Design: Jerry Udall
Maps: Bob Garwood
Production Director: Alastair Gourlay

PICTURE CREDITS
All images from the Robert Hunt Library

PAGE 1: *B-17 Flying Fortresses newly arrived in Great Britain from the United States (note the absence of any nose art or mission markings) await deployment to a frontline bombing wing.*

PAGE 2–3: *A railway marshalling yard comes under attack from Allied bombers. The concerted pressure to deny German forces freedom of movement was incessant before D-Day.*

THESE PAGES: *British troops take cover from enemy fire on Sword Beach.*

CONTENTS

INTRODUCTION

D-Day, June 6, 1944, has sometimes been referred to as the day of decision in the war on Hitler's Germany: a period of 24 hours when the outcome of the conflict hung in the balance, as Allied forces tried, in one almighty assault, to land on the beaches of Normandy, break the German Army behind its Atlantic Wall, and open the Second Front in Europe.

The stakes were indeed high. Failure to win a bridgehead on that day could have had catastrophic repercussions. Defeat might have led to a reassessment by the United States of its war aims around the world, and even a transfer of its forces to the Pacific. In Great Britain, exhausted after five years of total effort, it could have raised the possibility of a collapse of the will to fight on. On the Eastern Front, failure might be have been taken by Stalin's Soviet Union as proof that the British and Americans, having delayed the

invasion for nearly three years, were not committed to defeating the Nazis, and that the Red Army would have to beat Germany alone – and take sole charge of postwar Europe. This was a task that, by June 1944, the Soviet Union was more than capable of achieving, having 11 armies advancing west on a single front, from the Baltic to the Black Sea.

The progress of the war, and any postwar settlement, thus rested in the balance on that June day. Failure was certainly a possibility, though Allied commanders and politicians dared not mention it openly for fear of under-mining military and civilian morale. The Supreme Allied Commander, General Dwight D. Eisenhower – a man who knew just how detailed the invasion plans were and how powerful the Allied military effort was – knew it. He even drafted a personal statement on the day before the invasion, to be

released to the press in the event of a defeat, accepting responsibility for it.

It was because the risk of failure had to be reduced to the minimum that the invasion was so meticulously planned and preparations took so long to complete. Success on D-Day was the culmination of 26 months of planning and training, and of innovative military technology that was to advance the art of amphibious warfare to a new level – bringing forward, as it did, new types of landing craft, specialist armoured vehicles and unique concepts such as the Mulberry temporary harbours.

The need to establish the most favourable strategic conditions for the invasion also dictated the course of Allied war effort. From January 1942, at the conclusion of the first Anglo-American summit conference between Roosevelt and Churchill, in Washington, DC, it was decided that an invasion of Occupied Europe and Germany should

◀ *US GIs drag their half-drowned comrades ashore after their landing craft was sunk off Utah Beach. Many soldiers were not so lucky, and drowned before even reaching the shore.*

▶ *Gold Beach viewed from an approaching British landing craft. Littered with obstacles, and rigged with booby-traps and explosives, the beaches were treacherous places.*

◄ *Under a withering hail of German bullets, mortars and artillery shells, US troops surge onto Utah Beach on D-Day.*

be the first priority of the new alliance. All Allied operations against the Third Reich from then on were meant, ultimately, to lead to that end.

As a result, the defeat of the U-boats during 1943 and 1944 allowed the safe passage across the Atlantic of over one million US troops and millions of tonnes of arms and supplies for the pre-invasion build-up. The joint Royal Air Force (RAF) and US Army Air Forces' (USAAF) strategic bombing campaign of Germany put the German Luftwaffe (Air Force) on the defensive, increased fighter production at the expense of bombers, and drew aircraft

away from France and back to defend the Reich.

Even the invasions of Sicily and the Italian mainland in 1943 played their part in the overall scheme. Advocated and heavily promoted by the British, these operations were initially resisted by the US Joint Chiefs of Staff precisely because they diverted men and resources into the Mediterranean and away from the invasion build-up. Nevertheless, Sicily and Italy did serve as the proving grounds for large-scale amphibious operations, the cooperation of air, naval and ground forces, and combined Allied chains of command – all of which were later vital to the success of D-Day.

By the time General Eisenhower was appointed Supreme Allied Commander, in December 1943, the concentration of the Allied war effort on opening the Second Front had reached a very high pitch. Thus it was that the final planning, training and execution of the operation, by then codenamed "Overlord", took barely five months,

from the arrival in London of General Montgomery as commander of Allied ground forces – January 2 1944 – to the sailing of the invasion fleet from the south coast of England – June 5 .

During those few hectic weeks there were crises, of course, and the occasional loss of nerve. The fickle English weather played havoc with the sailing schedules and delayed the invasion by a day, while logistical plans were jeopardized because of a shortage of LSTs (Landing Ships, Tanks), the ocean-going vessels essential for the transport of vehicles and tanks.

There was also a dangerous crisis of confidence in some quarters, about the huge numbers of casualties that the first units ashore might suffer. Press reports in the spring of 1944 came up with figures as high as 90 percent killed or wounded. Even senior commanders, such as Air Chief Marshal Leigh-Mallory, were not immune. The air chief officially raised his doubts with Eisenhower, as late as May, that the airborne assault, particularly by the two US divisions, might result in a 50 percent casualty rate.

The answer to Leigh-Mallory's fears came, in part, from the commander of the US 82nd Airborne Division, General Ridgeway, who assured Eisenhower that his division knew the importance of its task and would do its job. It was such qualities of determination that typified the fighting men who won the bridgehead on D-Day, and who, through their leadership and courage, would silence the doubts and tip the balance on that historically decisive day.

December 1943

▲ Field Marshal Erwin Rommel (right) on one of his many inspections of the coastal defences in France. In December 1943 he was made commander of Army Group B under von Rundstedt, and was also made Inspector General of the coastal defences.

This month the leaders of the Soviet Union, Great Britain and the United States – Stalin, Churchill and Roosevelt, the "Big Three" – met in Tehran to agree on the summer 1944 timing for the invasion of northwest Europe. Following on from this meeting, President Roosevelt announced that General Dwight D. Eisenhower would be supreme commander of the Allied Expeditionary Force of the cross-Channel invasion, with General Sir Bernard Montgomery, hero of North Africa, the Commander of Allied Ground Forces.

▶ A German artillery position on the French coast in late 1943. Though the German High Command had no idea of precise dates, they were aware that an attempted invasion by the Allies was inevitable.

TUESDAY, DECEMBER 7

COMMANDERS, *ALLIES*

President Franklin D. Roosevelt, on his way back to the United States from the Allied leaders' conferences in Tehran and Cairo, breaks his journey at Tunis, in North Africa, to meet US Army General Dwight D. Eisenhower, the commander of Allied forces in the Mediterranean. The president tells Eisenhower that he has been chosen to be Supreme Commander of the Allied Expeditionary Force now being formed in Britain. This force will launch the campaign, codenamed Overlord, to liberate Hitler's Europe, and it is scheduled to begin on May 1, 1944. One of Eisenhower's first actions as Supreme Commander is to appoint US Lieutenant-General Walter Bedell Smith as his chief of staff.

Two of Eisenhower's subordinates for Overlord have already been appointed by the Combined Chiefs of Staff in Washington, DC, and are now in post in Great Britain. They are Royal Air Force (RAF) Air Chief Marshal Trafford Leigh-Mallory, commander-in-chief Allied Expeditionary Air Forces, appointed in November; and the Allied naval commander Admiral Bertram H. Ramsay, Royal Navy, who has been working on plans for the naval and amphibious element of Operation Overlord, codenamed Neptune, since his appointment in July.

SUNDAY, DECEMBER 12

GERMAN DEFENCES, *FRANCE*

Field Marshal Erwin Rommel arrives in France to review defence preparations. He is on an inspection tour of the western coast, from Denmark to the Spanish border, ordered by Hitler and the Army High Command, the Ober-kommando der Wehrmacht (OKW) in November. Rommel will review the progress of the fixed defences of the "Atlantic Wall" and the preparedness of German Army units. He sets up his headquarters at Fontainebleu, southeast of Paris, and begins work north of the River Seine. This coastal sector of the Pas de Calais, from Le Havre to Ostend, is held by the Fifteenth Army,

▲ **US President Franklin D. Roosevelt (seated, second from left) and British Prime Minister Winston Churchill are accompanied by Chinese leader Chiang Kai Shek (seated, far left) at the Cairo Conference of December 1943.**

▼ **The vast network of concrete bunkers, pillboxes and gun emplacements that made up the Atlantic Wall stretched across 2720km (1700 miles) of France's Atlantic coastline. It was built on the express orders of Hitler himself, who took great delight in following the construction.**

▶ British divers ride a human torpedo during a training exercise in the Solent, off southern England. The Combined Operations Pilotage Parties were to play a key role in gathering intelligence on the geography of the landing beaches.

commanded by General Hans von Salmuth. It is the stretch of French coast closest to Great Britain, and the most likely target for an Allied invasion.

SUNDAY, DECEMBER 19

GERMAN DEFENCES, *FRANCE*

In Paris, Rommel meets with Field Marshal Gerd von Rundstedt, the commander of Oberbefehlshaber West (OB West), which controls the German Army in France and the Low Countries. Although Rommel has no role within the OB West chain of command, his recommendations for the defence of France go direct to Hitler, so von Rundstedt must take them into consideration. The field marshals agree that the Pas de Calais is the most likely invasion point, and that it is unlikely that the Atlantic Wall will be strong enough to hold the Allies on the beaches. A counterattack by armoured divisions will be needed, but the two men disagree on how to organize it. Von Rundstedt wants to counter-attack inland, away from any navy bombardment, using a large armoured reserve. Rommel knows that such a reserve will come under concentrated Allied air attack. He wants a mobile reserve to hit the Allies near the beachhead. In order to hold the Allies long enough to give the reserve time to move in, coastal defences will have to be improved rapidly.

▶ A British diver in his specialized equipment. This included a rubber "dry suit", a buoyancy aid and breathing apparatus. By modern standards the equipment was very primitive.

FRIDAY, DECEMBER 24

COMMANDERS, *ALLIES*

British General Bernard L. Montgomery, of the Eighth Army in Italy, is appointed commander of the 21st Army Group. Its head-quarters (HQ), based

▲ General, later Field Marshal, Bernard Law Montgomery was made commander of the invasion forces, following the fame he had gained from fighting against Rommel in the North African desert between 1942 and 1943.

in Great Britain, will be charged with planning and executing the amphibious assault and initial stages of the land battle in France. General Montgomery will report directly to General Eisenhower, who will retain overall command of all the Allied forces in Europe.

MONDAY, DECEMBER 27

COMMANDERS, *ALLIES*
Montgomery flies to Algiers to meet Eisenhower. It is their first discussion about the organization of the Allied armies for Overlord and Montgomery's precise role. They agree that after the landings Montgomery will establish a forward tactical 21st Army Group HQ in France to control the battle. In effect, he will be Overlord's land forces commander until there are sufficient US Army forces in France to create their own army groups.

THURSDAY, DECEMBER 30

COMMANDERS, *ALLIES*
Montgomery leaves the Eighth Army HQ in Italy for Great Britain and his 21st Army Group command.
RECONNAISSANCE, *COASTS*
Steps are already being taken by the Allies to identify and chart potential landing beaches in Normandy. This secret work is undertaken by the Combined Operations Pilotage Parties (COPP), based in Portsmouth. These units

▶ *Field Marshal Gerd von Rundstedt (front). He had been responsible for the building of the Atlantic Wall and the organizing of German defences from 1942 until Rommel arrived to perform this duty.*

▲ *A V-1 flying bomb. The first weapon of its kind ever built, this primitive self-propelled cruise missile was targeted on London. The first V-1 fell on the East End seven days after the Allied invasion.*

include Royal Navy and British Army personnel who specialize in covert reconnaissance. They operate from canoes or miniature submarines and have already worked successfully on the coasts of Sicily and mainland Italy.

Two of COPP's swimmers, Major Scott Bowden and Sergeant Ogden Smith, are on a mission tonight to survey an area of beach opposite the village of La Rivière. They are dropped by launch to swim 365m (400 yds) to shore. Once there, they use augers to take samples of beach sand to bring back. This is vital work. Planners must be told whether potential landing beaches are stable enough to hold the weight of vehicles and armour.

GERMAN DEFENCES, *FRANCE*
There are proposed changes to the German chain of command in France. So far Rommel's task here has been as advisor to Hitler and OKW regarding defence preparations; he has no control

▲ *A reinforced concrete artillery battery, part of the Atlantic Wall network. This particular one was named after Dr Fritz Todt, the Reich Minister for Munitions who was killed in a plane crash in 1942.*

over field units within OB West. Both von Rundstedt and Rommel realize that this situation is a waste of Rommel's experience, so von Rundstedt recommends to Hitler that a new army group be established in northern France and the Netherlands, under OB West control but commanded by Rommel – in effect, putting Rommel in charge of defence preparations.

FRIDAY, DECEMBER 31

PLANNING, *OVERALL STRATEGY*
On his way to London, Montgomery stops off in Morocco to visit Winston Churchill. The prime minister is convalescing in Marrakech after a bout of pneumonia contracted after the recent Allied conferences. He gives Montgomery a copy of the only invasion plan the Allies have so far. It has been drawn up by Lieutenant-General Sir Frederick E. Morgan's COSSAC (Chief of Staff to the Supreme Allied Commander) planners. They have been working on it since April. Montgomery informs Churchill that his initial opinion is that the plan is too limited and would be unable to land

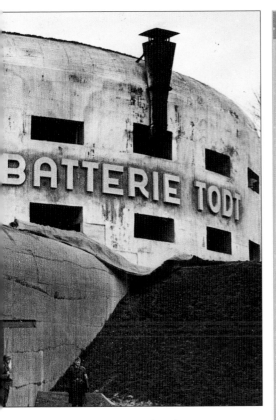

STRATEGY & TACTICS

THE INITIAL INVASION PLAN BY COSSAC

Lieutenant-General Sir Frederick E. Morgan was appointed Chief of Staff to the Supreme Allied Commander (COSSAC) by the Allied Combined Chiefs of Staff (CCS) on 26 April, 1943. As there was no Allied Supreme Commander appointed for Europe at the time, Morgan's task was strictly that of a planner. He was to present the Combined Chiefs with an operational scheme for a landing on the continent of Europe and the advance into Germany.

Morgan established a small Anglo-American staff in Norfolk House, St James's Square (off Piccadilly), London, and set about the task. The plan was presented to the British Chiefs of Staff on July 15, and approved in outline in August, during the Allied conference between Churchill and Roosevelt in Quebec.

It was the COSSAC plan that identified the Bay of Seine and the area of the Calvados coast of Normandy as the preferred site for the landings. The plan envisioned a limited assault by one corps comprising three divisions, landing along a 16km (25-mile) front on three beaches between the River Vire in the west and the River Orne to the east.

A key objective would be the town of Caen, to be seized on D-Day by an airborne assault of at least one division. Then, an advance west, into the peninsulas of Brittany and Cherbourg, would seize ports enabling US Army forces to land directly from the United States. Further advances would be made south to the River Loire and west to the River Seine.

The scale of the 1943 plan was limited by the serious shortage of landing craft and shipping available that year. However, three important elements were to survive the wholesale revisions made by General Montgomery in January 1944: the choice of the Calvados coast; the importance of Allied air superiority over France; and the use of artificial harbours, codenamed Mulberry. The latter were essential because the Calvados coast had no big ports for landing supplies.

▲ *Two of the concrete blocks that would make up part of the Mulberry artificial harbours.*

sufficient troops to break out into France or repel a counterattack. With only five months left before the proposed invasion date, Montgomery realizes his first priority must be a complete revision of the plan.

GERMAN DEFENCES, *FRANCE*
Rommel submits his first report to Hitler on probable Allied intentions for the invasion, based on his assessment of Allied reactions to the coming campaign of V-1 flying bomb attacks,

on London, scheduled to begin in June: "The focus of the enemy landing operation will probably be directed against the Fifteenth Army sector,

largely because it is from this sector that much of our long-range attack [by V-1s] ... will be launched. With difficult sea conditions, it is likely that the enemy's main concern will be to get the quickest possible possession of a port or ports capable of handling large ships ... It is most likely that the enemy will make his main effort ... between Boulogne and the Somme estuary and on either side of Calais, where he would have the best support from his long-range artillery, the shortest sea route for the assault ... and the most favourable conditions for ... his air arm."

◀ *Christmas Day 1943. US General Eisenhower (left), General Alexander (centre) and Churchill (right) pose for a photograph. Churchill was recuperating after a bout of pneumonia.*

January 1944

▲ Hitler and Field Marshal von Rundstedt (right) pore over a map of Europe. By 1944 Hitler had begun to interfere in detailed military planning.

Bernard Montgomery, commander for the ground invasion, drastically revised the Overlord plan for the liberation of Europe. Across the English Channel, Rommel was promoted to command Army Group B. As part of the invasion preparations, Operation Carpetbagger was launched to deliver weapons and equipment to resistance fighters in Europe. In Italy, meanwhile, Allied forces landed at Anzio but quickly became bogged down. Back in Great Britain, Allied chiefs invented a bogus army stationed in England, the First US Army Group, to confuse German intelligence. And Allied bombers attacked German production plants.

SATURDAY, JANUARY 1

GERMAN DEFENCES, *FRANCE*
From Führer Headquarters in Rastenburg, East Prussia, Hitler agrees to von Rundstedt's proposal that Rommel should command a new army group to be known as Army Group B. It will encompass three major forces: General Hans von Salmuth's Fifteenth Army, defending the coast from Antwerp in Belgium to the River Orne in Normandy; General Friedrich Dollman's Seventh Army, holding a sector covering both Normandy and Brittany from the Orne to the River Loire; and the Netherlands occupation forces of LXXXVIII Army Corps, commanded by General Hans Reinhard.

▼ Allied troops practice a large-scale amphibious assault on an English beach. A complicated operation such as D-Day required ceaseless rehearsals.

▲ German fallschirmjäger, or paratroopers, race south to reinforce the German line at Anzio, south of Rome, following the Allied amphibious assault in January 1944.

Army Group B will remain subordinate to von Rundstedt's OB West. Confusing the German chain of command further is the fact that all panzer units in northern France are presently under the separate command of General Geyr von Schweppenburg's Panzer Group West. Von Schweppenburg reports to OB West regarding training

and organization, but any commitment of armoured units to combat operations by von Rundstedt must have Hitler's personal permission. Rommel will assume his command of Army Group B on January 15.

SUNDAY, JANUARY 2
COMMANDERS, *ALLIES*
General Montgomery arrives in London to take up his post as commander 21st Army Group. Admiral Ramsay, who has been working on naval invasion plans for the past five months, airs a rather pessimistic view to Sir Alan Brooke, Chief of the Imperial General Staff, that Monty's arrival has come "two months too late".

General Eisenhower arrives in Washington, DC, from North Africa, for a short visit to his family before he flies to London to take up his post as Supreme Commander. While in Washington, "Ike" will hold several meetings with General Marshall and President Roosevelt. Of particular concern to Marshall is the British attitude to Operation Anvil, the proposed invasion of southern France, earmarked to coincide with Operation Overlord. Marshall is worried that the British seem more concerned with keeping forces in Italy than using them in an assault on France's Mediterranean coast.

▲ Field Marshal Sir Alan Brooke, Chief of the Imperial General Staff. He had been promised command of Overlord, but Roosevelt insisted Eisenhower get the job.

MONDAY, JANUARY 3
PLANNING, *OVERALL STRATEGY*
At 09:00 hours, within hours of his arrival from Morocco, General Montgomery convenes the first Overlord planning conference at the headquarters of 21st Army Group, located in St Paul's School in Hammersmith, West London.

▲ *A British X-craft, number 25, on exercise in British waters. These mini-submarines were vital tools in the reconnaissance of the landing beaches. Manned by three operatives, they were uncomfortable and cramped.*

For this meeting Montgomery summons the COSSAC staff from Norfolk House to hear, for the first time officially, their plan of operations for Overlord. Unfortunately for these officers, Montgomery has already read the plan, having been given sight of a copy by Churchill in Marrakech three days previously. This has given Monty ample time to form the opinion that, in his own words, it is "thoroughly bad". However, he allows the planners to make their presentation first before making his own views felt.

Montgomery tells them that he disagrees with their whole proposal. The three-division assault over three beaches is too narrow. It would lead to congestion at the bridgehead, with only one corps HQ being used to control the whole front. No landing is being attempted on the Cotentin Peninsula although the capture of Cherbourg is vital. Monty also disagrees with the emphasis placed on the early capture of Caen. "What was needed," he told them, "was not so much a town, so much as a bridgehead, and a port. What was more, the whole scale of the invasion needed looking at."

▶ *A German artillery battery opens fire on Allied forces at Anzio. Despite an easy landing in the face of German unreadiness, the Allies faced a bitter struggle as the Germans regained their composure and began to counterattack.*

Having demolished their detailed work of nine months, he sends the COSSAC staff back to Norfolk House to reconsider the plan and report back the following day. What he wants to see is an extension of the assault front on both flanks, taking it west into the Cotentin and northwest towards Dieppe.

Montgomery's next task is to begin the complete reorganization of the 21st Army Group HQ. As he finds it in January it is not an organization fit to command combat troops, and Montgomery swiftly acts to rectify the situation. Whole sections, such as the Chemical Warfare Directorate, are abolished and half the existing staff officers are dismissed. In their place Montgomery brings in trusted officers from his former Eighth Army command, including chief of staff Major-General "Freddie" de Guingand.

TUESDAY, JANUARY 4

PLANNING, *OVERALL STRATEGY*
Montgomery holds his first meeting with Allied naval commander Admiral Ramsay at Norfolk House. Later in the day, at 21st Army Group HQ, the general meets with COSSAC planners once again. The officers have worked overnight and studied the feasibility of an extension of the assault front on both flanks. They conclude that extending the initial assault into Brittany and towards Dieppe would be impractical, and Montgomery agrees; but the COSSAC staff concur with the general that a landing on the east coast

▲ *With dense cloud formations below, Boeing B-17 Flying Fortresses of the US Eighth Army Air Force head towards Germany to bomb submarine pens near the town of Bremen.*

of the Cotentin Peninsula is essential, to secure Cherbourg. The conference will conclude tomorrow.

TRAINING, *AMPHIBIOUS ASSAULT*
The first major amphibious exercise for American troops begins at Slapton Sands, Devon. Exercise Duck I involves headquarters units of US V Corps and 29th Infantry Division, together with elements of the 175th Regimental Landing Team and 1st Engineer Special Brigade. About 16,000 assault troops are involved, embarking on landing craft from ports along the south coasts of Cornwall and Devon. Duck I has been in preparation since November 1943.

A convoy including 14 LCT (Landing Craft, Tanks), 57 LCM (Landing Craft, Mechanized), escorted by four British destroyers, simulate an opposed landing. The assault troops overcome "enemy" coastal defences, including pillboxes and (simulated) minefields, and then move inland to establish a defensive perimeter against attack by armour. While the assault teams practice combat, support units are refining their own tasks. Quartermaster units experiment with loading and unloading equipment on newly designed pallets, while engineers try out new techniques for laying beach roads. Despite the months of planning and the thousands of troops involved, the US Ninth Army Air Force cannot supply aircraft on the opening day because of other priorities.

WEDNESDAY, JANUARY 5

ORDER OF BATTLE, *US FORCES*
The US Strategic Air Forces in Europe are established in the UK under the

▲ *General Omar C. Bradley, commander of the US First Army. Quiet, polite and popular among his men, he would play a crucial role in the D-Day landings.*

▶ *Iron girders are cemented into the ground along the Atlantic Wall as a means of preventing Allied tanks and other vehicles from moving inland.*

command of Lieutenant-General Carl Spaatz. He is to coordinate operations of the US Eighth and Ninth Army Air Forces in Great Britain and the US Fifteenth Army Air Force in Italy. Although he is independent of Eisenhower's command of Overlord, his cooperation will be essential for the success of the invasion, particularly because he has operational control of the B-17 and B-24 squadrons of VIII Bomber Command.

PLANNING, *STRATEGY*

This is the final day of Montgomery's review of the COSSAC invasion plan. These meetings are later recalled by one of COSSAC's senior planning officers, Major-General K.G. McLean:

"On the third day we reduced his demand to extending to 'Sword' beach [on the left flank] ... and to the Cotentin. He decided not to use airborne for Caen, but to land on the Vire [River] and the neck of the Cotentin. He didn't believe in the Mulberry [harbours], stressed Cherbourg heavily, which we didn't. This is particularly why he wanted the Cotentin. On the third day Monty took the line we must have more [landing] craft. He said it must be a five division front – or no show, 'Give me this or get someone else ....'"

Finally, the planners are told to go away and draft a wholly new invasion plan, to involve a five-division assault flanked by two airborne landings. The assault area is to be on a 30km (50-mile) front, stretching from the River Orne to the east coast of the Cotentin.

The conclusions reached at this first Overlord conference will form the basis of all the invasion plans agreed upon in the coming months. One decision, however, will prove to have far-reaching implications for the battle of Normandy later in the year. The capture of Caen, the region's biggest town and communications hub, will no longer be guaranteed as a D-Day objective.

In three days Montgomery has galvanized the planning operation and injected a much-needed sense of urgency. He has also identified the fact that so far Overlord has not been given the resources it needs, and that if an invasion is to go ahead at all it must have first call on one of the most important Allied strategic resources: landing craft.

FRIDAY, JANUARY 7

GERMAN DEFENCES, *FRANCE*
General Alfred Jodl, the chief of operations for the German Army High

▼ *Rommel, front, third from left, oversees preparations for the coming invasion. Four types of beach obstacle are visible, including the "Belgian Gate" and "Czech Hedgehogs" made of welded steel girders. The wooden obstacles are pointing inland to snare landing craft moving back on an outgoing tide.*

◀ *General Montgomery arrives in London in January to meet with other invasion commanders.*

Command, the OKW, is on a tour of inspection of the Western defences. He is deeply concerned by their poor state of readiness. He identifies several major problems. These include the transfer of experienced combat units and officers to the Eastern Front and the use of the Western theatre of operations as an area for re-equipping and reorganizing units after tours of duty in Russia. He notes in his diary: "The best people have been removed. The officers are good and the men are good, but they cannot act. Re-equipment is producing chaos." Despite the current lack of combat-ready divisions in the West, Jodl puts his faith in the construction of Hitler's Atlantic Wall.

MONDAY, JANUARY 10

AIR CAMPAIGN, *TARGET PLANNING*
The Allied Expeditionary Air Force sets up its Bombing Committee, to agree on the targets on the continent to be raided in support of the invasion. SHAEF and the Supreme Commander, however, have no control over the strategic bombers commanded by Air Marshal Harris and General Spaatz.

Until there is a change in the Allied chain of command these two bomber chiefs will answer to the Combined Chiefs of Staff only. The consequence of this is that the bomber chiefs will regard SHAEF's targeting requests as a low priority.

▲ *The senior officers of Royal Air Force Bomber Command plan a large-scale raid on German positions. In the centre, wearing dark-rimmed glasses, is the Commander-in-Chief of Bomber Command, Air Chief Marshal Sir Arthur Harris, or "Bomber" Harris.*

TUESDAY, JANUARY 11

◄ *Churchill returns to London from Egypt. Greeting Churchill are two future Prime Ministers: Clement Attlee (shaking hands) and Anthony Eden (far left).*

TUESDAY, JANUARY 11

ORDER OF BATTLE, *US FORCES*
The headquarters units of the US 4th Armored Division arrive in Great Britain by ship from Boston. This is the first American armoured division to arrive in Great Britain, and will be organized into General Omar C. Bradley's US First Army. The division will not land in France until July.

AIR CAMPAIGN, *FACTORY BOMBING*
As part of a strategy to seriously reduce the numbers of German fighter aircraft available to meet the invasion, bombers of the US Eighth Army Air Force attack three fighter production plants in central Germany.

PLANNING, *AIR, SEA AND LAND*
General Montgomery holds an Overlord planning meeting at St Paul's School, the 21st Army Group HQ. Those present include Admiral Ramsay and the Allied Air Force Commander Leigh-Mallory. For the first time the commanders of the two armies that will actually make the invasion assault are also present: General Omar C. Bradley, commander of the US First Army, and General Miles C. Dempsey, commander of the British Second Army.

RECONNAISSANCE, *COASTS*
The COPP beach reconnaissance parties have revealed a potentially serious problem with some of the landing beaches. Samples taken from along the Calvados coast by COPP swimmers have shown the presence in some areas of peat and clay. This could be disastrous. A report for 21st Army Group by geologist Professor J.D. Bernal describes possible repercussions if the presence of peat and clay proves widespread: "A large part of the area between Asnelles and la Riviere will prove impassable even to lightly equipped infantry without vehicles."

The response to Bernal's report is immediate and far-reaching. Further COPP missions are ordered in order to gather more beach samples, and an intelligence operation is mounted into occupied France. French geologists are

◀ *The commander of a British X-craft stands atop the conning tower as the vessel gets under way.*

STRATEGY & TACTICS

THE BODYGUARD STRATEGY

The object of Bodyguard was to conceal the timing and location of the invasion from the Germans by drawing their attention away from Normandy and the landing beaches. At the same time it was to fool Hitler into dispersing his forces around Europe, so that when the invasion occurred he would have insufficient troops in France to repel it.

The deceptions were both military and diplomatic. Militarily they were designed to convince the enemy that the invasion would strike the Pas de Calais region of France. They also exploited Hitler's fears of an Allied attack on Norway and the Balkans. In diplomatic terms, the aim was to undermine Hitler's trust in his allies Hungary, Romania and Bulgaria by suggesting their possible defection to the Allied side, thus persuading Hitler to keep units, especially armour, in or near these countries instead of in the West. Bodyguard schemes shared the characteristic of a successful lie: they had just enough truth in them to make their stories plausible.

◀ *Bodyguard exploited Hitler's distrust of his allies, especially in Eastern Europe. He responded quickly when they appeared ready to defect from the Axis. This is a Tiger II tank in Budapest, Hungary, following the German takeover of the country in March 1944.*

sent into Paris to find geological maps of Normandy. Four volumes are secured and smuggled out, to be studied by the Inter-Services Topographical Department, in Oxford. Bernal's warnings prove pessimistic, although the chance of armoured vehicles sinking into some of the landing beaches remains a possibility that must be lived with.

TRAINING, *AMPHIBIOUS ASSAULT*
US V Corps headquarters issues a critique of Exercise Duck I, completed last week. Although the exercise was

▼ *German Panzergrenadiers move to their next objective in Italy. Note the heavy camouflage applied to the German halftrack personnel carrier.*

the first amphibious operation undertaken on a large scale by American troops, V Corps' report is highly critical. Embarkation of troops was slow and the organization of supplies needs improving. During the assault the landing craft became disorganized and landed out of order. Once on the beach, the troops were overloaded with equipment, and were too slow and bunched together under simulated fire. Corps commander General Gerow goes so far as to wonder whether any of them would have made it off the beach alive. Support units come in for equal criticism. Vehicles were landed and not unloaded, troops and vehicles used the same roads resulting in traffic jams inland, there was a lack of radio equipment, security was very bad and camouflage was poor.

V Corps HQ concludes that a lot of work needs to be done and much improvement shown, at all levels.

THURSDAY, JANUARY 13

GERMAN DEFENCES, *FRANCE*

General Jodl continues his inspection of coastal defences in France. He finds preparations in Cherbourg – one of the largest ports on the Atlantic coast and an obvious Allied invasion objective – to be in a state of chaos. As a result of

▼ *Dozens of B-17 Flying Fortresses newly arrived in Great Britain from the United States await deployment to a frontline bombing wing.*

Jodl's findings, Cherbourg and other major ports on the coast are fortified on the landward side and their port facilities wired for demolition.

PLANNING, *ARMY*

Montgomery convenes a meeting of senior British and American army corps and divisional officers at 21st Army Group HQ. With the imminent arrival from the United States of the Allied Supreme Commander, Eisenhower, Monty describes the organizational structure of the Supreme Headquarters,

▲ *Sub-Lieutenant Robinson of the British Royal Navy looks out on the world through the periscope from the confines of his X-craft. He was the commanding officer of the vessel.*

Allied Expeditionary Force (SHAEF) and his own role within it. The general also describes how he intends to run the coming land battle and what he expects of his chief subordinate officers. He places particular emphasis on integrating the work of the various

▲ *B-24 Liberators fly over the Normandy coast, France. They had a 2272kg (5000lb) payload, usually consisting of 10 500lb bombs, or five 1000lb bombs.*

command staffs within 21st Army Group and the importance of Allied air superiority to the land campaign.

COMMANDERS, *ALLIES*
General Eisenhower flies into Great Britain from Washington, DC. He arrives late at night in secret, and without any ceremony is driven straight to London and his quarters near Berkeley Square.

FRIDAY, JANUARY 14

COMMANDERS, *ALLIES*
Eisenhower makes his visit to Norfolk House where SHAEF HQ is to be

▶ *A British Churchill tank, specially designed to rescue other armoured vehicles that have got into difficulties.*

▲ *Massive Allied LST (Landing Ship, Tank) assault vessels at Anzio. Dozens of craft like these were desperately needed for the invasion of northern France.*

established initially. In the coming weeks the Supreme Commander will divide his time between here and his personal office at 20 Grosvenor Square.

General Montgomery leaves London in his own specially converted HQ train to visit and address units of V and VII Corps, US First Army. As he is now officially in command of US Army troops, this is a morale-boosting public-relations exercise, and the first of several such tours in which Monty will speak to groups of up to 5000 men at a time.

AIR CAMPAIGN, *TARGET STRATEGY*
As part of the campaign to reduce the threat German fighters pose to the invasion, Air Chief Marshal Arthur Harris, head of RAF Bomber Command, is ordered by the Combined Chiefs of Staff to concentrate his raids on fighter production plants and ballbearing factories. He agrees reluctantly, but voices the opinion that his bombers would be better employed attacking German cities, particularly Berlin.

SATURDAY, JANUARY 15

ORDER OF BATTLE, *COMMAND*
Today is the formal end of COSSAC. Most of its staff will be absorbed into

Supreme Headquarters, Allied Expeditionary Force (SHAEF) in the coming four weeks. The former head of COSSAC, General Frederick Morgan, will now become one of the deputies to SHAEF's chief of staff, Bedell Smith. General Eisenhower will fill other key appointments with officers who have served his earlier commands in North Africa and the Mediterranean. These will include RAF Air Chief Marshal Sir Arthur Tedder, who was former Commander-in-Chief, Mediterranean Allied Air Forces. He is to be appointed as Deputy Allied Supreme Commander.

SUNDAY, JANUARY 16

COMMANDERS, *EISENHOWER*
It is announced by BBC radio that General Eisenhower is now the Allied Supreme Commander in Europe. SHAEF holds a press conference to give details to the newspapers of the free world.

MONDAY, JANUARY 17

RECONNAISSANCE, *COASTS*
As part of the increased reconnaissance by COPP of proposed landing beaches

▶ *Allied shipping at anchor off the coast of Italy. While vital to the overall strategy of liberating Europe, the amphibious operations in the Mediterranean placed a great strain on the Allied shipping fleets.*

TUESDAY, JANUARY 18

along the Calvados coast, Royal Navy midget submarine *X-20*, under Lieutenant-Commander Wilmott, begins a secret mission. On board are two COPP swimmers, Major Scott Bowden and Sergeant Ogden Smith, who completed a similar mission 17 days previously. Tonight Wilmott surfaces the *X-20* just 350m (380yds) from the shore of occupied France, and Bowden and Ogden swim ashore to take the first of a series of geological samples. The mission will go on for the next three days.

ORDER OF BATTLE, *US FORCES*
Eisenhower appoints General Omar N. Bradley, commander US First Army, as the future commanding officer of all US armies in the field. The appointment will take effect after the invasion, and only when the battle for Normandy has been won and US forces are in a position to strike towards Germany. Before this time US forces will operate under the control of Montgomery's 21st Army Group.

TUESDAY, JANUARY 18

COMMANDERS, *EISENHOWER*
After the public announcement of Eisenhower's arrival in Britain as Allied Supreme Commander, the general meets the press for a photo session.

▲ *Like bees leaving the hive, Landing Craft, Assault, each carrying about 30 infantrymen, leave their transport vessels, known as Landing Ship, Infantry, and head for the shore.*

Winston Churchill arrives back in London from Marrakech, Morocco, after convalescing from a bout of pneumonia. The prime minister has been out of the country since he left for the Cairo and Tehran conferences the previous November. He is now extremely keen to be brought up to speed with all current invasion plans and preparations.

ORDER OF BATTLE, *US FORCES*
Eighteen thousand men of the US 4th Infantry Division, under the command of Major-General Raymond O. Barton, set sail from New York for England.

WEDNESDAY, JANUARY 19

FRENCH RESISTANCE, *RESOURCES*
The Committee for National Liberation today formerly appeals to the Combined Chiefs of Staff for a large increase in the amount of arms and supplies being sent to Resistance groups. The Germans have been very successful in finding arms caches in recent months. There is also a request by the British Special Operations Executive (SOE), the secret organization responsible for sabotage and subversion, for an increase in airlift capacity. At present there are only 23 Halifax bombers available to drop agents and supplies into the whole of

northern and northwest Europe. SOE wants a substantial increase in aircraft if its agents and the Resistance groups it supports are to play a full role in the coming invasion.

THURSDAY, JANUARY 20

COMMANDERS, *TEDDER*
Today, Air Chief Marshal Tedder officially assumes his duties as Deputy Supreme Commander at SHAEF.
DECEPTION, *ORGANIZATION*
Eisenhower attends his first meeting to discuss Overlord's deception plans.

▲ *A Churchill gun carrier armoured vehicle, complete with "Snake" equipment. The tubes are line-charges, to be placed and detonated for mine clearance.*

Codenamed "Fortitude North" and "Fortitude South", they form part of a much wider campaign of covert deception, known as "Bodyguard", which operates throughout Europe. Briefing the Supreme Commander is Colonel John H. Bevan of London Controlling Section (LCS), the secret department responsible for deception,

▶ *A dummy Sherman tank, made of wood and cloth. These were used to confuse any German reconnaissance aircraft gathering intelligence on the invasion.*

which operates within Winston Churchill's own Joint Planning Staff. US commanders generally have little time for these devious plots and intrigues, but Churchill has always been very enthusiastic, and in fact Fortitude/Bodyguard has been an integral part of Overlord since June 1943, when Normandy was first chosen as the invasion site. Soon SHAEF will have its own department for deception, known by the anodyne title Committee of Special Means (CSM). Eisenhower will take overall responsibility for these schemes and will monitor their progress, but operationally they will remain under the control of LCS/CSM.

FRIDAY, JANUARY 21

RECONNAISSANCE, *COASTS*

The midget submarine *X-20* returns successfully from its mission to survey the Normandy landing beaches. The two COPP swimmers involved, Bowden and Ogden Smith, bring back detailed information on beach geology, the position of rocks, and tidal ranges. Their findings are passed to the Inter-Services Topographical Department and Admiral Ramsay. Although they report firm beaches and few obstacles, Ramsay still has doubts as to the viability of some of the landing sites, and orders more survey missions.

PLANNING, *SEA, AIR AND LAND*

At Norfolk House, Eisenhower convenes the first conference of senior Neptune/Overlord commanders. All three services are involved. Among those present are Tedder, Ramsay, Leigh-Mallory, Montgomery, the chiefs of staff de Guingand and Bedell Smith, and the senior staff of 21st Army Group, as well as General Morgan and former COSSAC planners.

The meeting begins with a description of

◀ *An innovative tank design incorporating a flamethrower on a tank chassis. Known as a "Crocodile", it could spew flames up to a range of 150m (492ft).*

COSSAC's 1943 invasion plan. Montgomery then presents his proposed revisions to it, explaining the need for a larger invasion front of 30km (50 miles). He details the need to include the east coast of the Cotentin Peninsula as a landing site and argues for an increase in the number of assault divisions, from three to five, with an airborne drop of two further divisions.

Initial reaction from the navy and air force officers present is that they do not have the resources to carry out such an operation. Air Chief Marshal Leigh-Mallory explains that he would need an extra eight fighter squadrons to cover the extended assault area and that the proposed airborne drop would need at least another 200 transport aircraft. Admiral Ramsay says that he would need to assemble two more naval assault forces, including bombardment ships, transports, escorts and minesweepers. He also explains that the new plan would exacerbate the serious shortage of landing craft already being experienced. To ease this shortfall Montgomery agrees to limit the numbers of vehicles transported with each assault division, from 3000 to 1450. It means that the assault units will be less mobile on D-Day, but goes some way to making sure that the navy can land all five divisions.

Time is needed to build more landing craft and train the necessary air crews for the airlift, and this brings the May 1 invasion date into question. It is agreed that a new date for D-Day of 31 May be proposed to the Combined Chiefs of Staff.

This is the earliest date when the tides will be high enough and there will be sufficient moonlight. If this slips, optimum conditions for the assault will fall next on 5, 6 and 7 June.

Despite the considerable reservations voiced by Leigh-Mallory and Ramsay, Eisenhower agrees that Montgomery's plan will be submitted to the Combined Chiefs as the new Neptune/Overlord invasion plan.

▼ *General George S. Patton. He was the "commander" of a phantom US army, the First US Army Group, which was part of the Allied deception plan.*

SATURDAY, JANUARY 22

GERMAN DEFENCES, *EUROPE*
The Allies make a two-division amphibious assault on Anzio, south of Rome. It is the last large-scale seaborne attack on German-held territory before Overlord, and its progress is watched carefully by SHAEF planners in London. Initially, it is a remarkable success. An armada of 250 ships land 50,000 British and American troops and 5000 vehicles almost unopposed. The landings are a boost to SHAEF, because they reveal the appalling state of German military intelligence. Two days before the landings the OKW Intelligence Section in Berlin confidently reported that "there are no indications that any major undertaking in the Mediterranean area is imminent."

The Anzio operation also reduces the number of first-class German units, particularly panzergrenadier and falschirmjäger (paratroop) divisions, available to meet the invasion of France. OKW transfers movement orders for five divisions from the Channel coast to Italy within days. For months the British have advocated continued support for the Italian campaign for exactly this reason. Their faith now seems justified. By March there will be 24 German divisions fighting in Italy.

▲ *Hundreds of M4 Sherman tanks are stockpiled ready for the coming invasion. Although no match for German armour, the Sherman tank was fast and reliable.*

◀ *A US tank commander prepares to lob a hand-grenade from his M3 Stuart light tank during a training exercise in England. The M3 was virtually obsolete and used only for reconnaissance.*

SUNDAY, JANUARY 23

PLANNING, *RESOURCES*
Eisenhower and Bedell Smith draft a long telegram to the Combined Chiefs of Staff in Washington, DC, informing them of the conclusions of the 21 January commanders' conference. It explains Montgomery's revised invasion plan and lists the additional landing craft and warships SHAEF needs to implement it. They include an extra 47 LSTs (Landing Ship, Tanks), 144 LCTs (Landing Craft, Tanks), 72 LCI(L)s (Landing Craft, Infantry, Large), together with 24 more destroyers and an extra 5 cruisers. The telegram also advocates the new D-Day target date of 31 May and makes a plea to end what Eisenhower sees as the current under-resourcing of Overlord. He states bluntly that Overlord is the moment of crisis for the entire European war and that British and American governments must ensure the resources for success.

WEDNESDAY, JANUARY 26

ORDER OF BATTLE, *US FORCES*
The US 4th Infantry Division arrives in Great Britain after a nine-day ocean voyage from New York. The 4th Infantry is organized into VII Corps, US First Army, and is earmarked to be one of the assault divisions on D-Day.

The 4th Infantry is the tenth US Army division to arrive in Great Britain. The past five months have seen the arrival of the 1st, 2nd, 5th, 8th, 9th and

28th Infantry Divisions, the 101st Airborne and the 2nd and 4th Armored. They all join the 29th Infantry Division, which has been in England since October 1942.

COMMANDERS, *PATTON*

US General George S. Patton flies into a US Army Air Force base in southern England from the Mediterranean. He arrives without any ceremony and is driven directly to central London for a meeting with Eisenhower. Patton has not held a combat command since the summer of 1943, when he publicly slapped a shell-shocked soldier during the Sicily campaign. Now Eisenhower tells him his career is to be revived and that after the invasion he is to command the US Third Army for its breakout from the Normandy bridgehead. He will be under the command of General Bradley.

The Third Army is currently still being formed in the United States, and until it is activated in France Patton's task will be to lend his high public profile to a Fortitude South deception

DECISIVE WEAPONS

79TH ARMOURED DIVISION

This British Army division was at the forefront of developments in armoured warfare technology. It was established in April 1943, under Major-General Sir Percy Hobart, with the sole task of creating specialist armoured vehicles to defeat German fixed defences, and then to work out the best techniques of using them in combat. As such, the division had training bases as well as technical workshops around the country. Sea trials and practice launches of the famous DD (Duplex-Drive) Sherman amphibious tanks took place at Stokes Bay, on the Solent, near Portsmouth. The division had its own stretch of coast at Linney Head in South Wales to practice landing drills and combat techniques. The headquarters in Suffolk, which both Eisenhower and Sir Alan Brooke visited in January 1944, was by far the biggest base. On a barren area of heathland, different kinds of German-style coastal defences were built on the basis of aerial reconnaissance photographs, and then methods were found to overcome them. Sea walls were bridged, bunkers demolished, ditches filled and minefields cleared.

▲ *The top-secret DD Sherman tanks and their crews practice waterborne travel in calm waters.*

▼ *The "Big Three" at Tehran, 1943. Stalin's (front, left) approval for the D-Day plan was vital, as the Allies needed Soviet forces to launch a simultaneous thrust that summer.*

plan, part of Operation Bodyguard. He will make personal appearances around Great Britain, avidly followed by the press, in his role as commander of an invasion army known as the First US Army Group (FUSAG) being organized along the east coast of England, and threatening the Pas de Calais. FUSAG, in fact, will be fake and will consist of Patton, bogus radio traffic and a lot of busy-looking staff officers at an HQ building in Knutsford, Cheshire. They will create the impression of a vast force, consisting of 11 armoured and infantry divisions in four army corps. To complete the deception, the east coasts of Kent and Essex will appear to be alive with the movement of men and equipment, most of which will be dummy or put on for show.

Patton gratefully accepts command of the Third Army and agrees to his role in the FUSAG deception. Personally, however, he is disappointed and frustrated that he will miss out on perhaps the greatest single event of the war. He will not be involved in the invasion planning and neither will he lead a combat unit on D-Day itself.

THURSDAY, JANUARY 27
RECONNAISSANCE, *COASTS*
From today, all cross-Channel raiding stops. The previous summer was

▼ *A Royal Air Force (RAF) Halifax bomber is prepared for take-off at an airfield in southern England. The lack of rear guns indicates it may be a glider tug.*

▲ *The ruins of a German factory that was one of the principle producers of fighter aircraft for the Lutfwaffe. Note the plethora of bomb craters.*

marked by an upsurge in commando activity, which gathered valuable intelligence on German defences. Now that the invasion is definitely on, the priority will be to avoid drawing attention to the French coast. The Germans must not be given any reason to strengthen their defences. The only cross-Channel operations authorized until the invasion will be the reconnaissance missions undertaken by the Combined Operations Pilotage Parties (COPP).

ORDER OF BATTLE, *ARMOUR*
General Eisenhower and the Chief of the Imperial General Staff, Sir Alan Brooke, travel to the headquarters of the British 79th Armoured Division, near Orford in Suffolk. Met by division commander Major-General Sir Percy Hobart, they see demonstrations of the specially designed vehicles he is developing for the invasion. Brooke's diary records:

"Hobart collected us at 9 a.m. and took us first to his HQ where he showed us his models and his proposed assault organization. We then went to see various exhibits such as the Sherman tank for destroying tank mines, with chains on a drum driven by the engine, various methods of climbing walls with tanks, blowing up minefields and walls, flamethrowing Churchill tanks, wall-destroying engineer parties, floating tanks, teaching men how to escape from sunken tanks, etc, etc. A most interesting day, and one which Eisenhower seemed to enjoy thoroughly."

FRENCH RESISTANCE, *RESOURCES*
Churchill holds a meeting in response to recent calls from the French Committee for National Liberation and SOE that more transport aircraft and supplies be made available to Resistance groups. The meeting includes representatives of SOE, two members of General de Gaulle's Free French HQ in London and Air Chief Marshal Charles Portal, Chief of the Air Staff. The French are promised that two

▶ *US infantry soldiers paddle across a stream using a craft that they have constructed from branches and twigs, during an invasion exercise in England.*

US Army Air Force bomber squadrons will be made available for clandestine air drops in the coming weeks. The SOE also provides an assessment for the prime minister of future Resistance capabilities. It predicts that with a fresh supply of weapons, and after a period of retraining during the spring, there will be little problem in launching a substantial campaign of sabotage to coincide with the invasion.

The meeting results in an intensification in the number of clandestine air sorties over France and a very marked increase in the supplies dropped for the Resistance.

▶ *US troops practice using a "bangalore torpedo" – a long line-charge used for clearing mines and obstacles such as barbed wire.*

◄ A U-boat lies disabled after it had been attacked in the Atlantic. The curtailing of the U-boat threat was essential to the success of the Allied invasion fleet.

FRIDAY, JANUARY 28

LOGISTICS, *TANKS*

After General Eisenhower's visit to the headquarters of the 79th Armoured Division, the Supreme Commander is approached by divisional commander Major-General Hobart for help. Hobart has had 900 of the amphibious Duplex-Drive (DD) Sherman tanks on order from British manufacturers since July 1943. However, not one tank has so far has been delivered. Impressed by what Hobart and his division are attempting to achieve, Eisenhower takes a hand, and soon an engineer is on his way to the United States with technical drawings. From now on factories in the United States will become involved with the conversion of DD tanks. They will have them built and delivered by May.

SUNDAY, JANUARY 30

DECEPTION, *BODYGUARD*

Two of the officers responsible for the Bodyguard deception plan fly to Moscow to ask for Soviet cooperation. Bodyguard will not work without the active participation of the Russians. It is vital that the Soviet summer offensive coincides with Overlord. While Churchill broached the subject to Stalin at the Tehran Conference in November–December 1943, there are doubts in London that the Russians will be willing to alter their own plans to suit Overlord. Making the hazardous trip from Scotland, crammed into the bomb bay of a B-24 Liberator, are Colonel Bevan of London Controlling Section (LCS) and his assistant Lieutenant-Colonel Baumer, US Army.

▼ *US troops during a training exercise in England. The terrain in the invasion area included many small farm holdings, so practice in urban warfare (note the buildings) was essential experience.*

MONDAY, JANUARY 31

DECEPTION, *BODYGUARD*

Colonels Bevan and Baumer arrive in Moscow. They have not risked carrying the Bodyguard plan with them, but have all 10 pages transmitted by coded telegram to the British embassy. Ambassador Sir Archibald Kerr will today present it to Soviet Foreign Minister Molotov, leaving Bevan and Baumer to wait for a response.

OPERATION BOLERO, *US FORCES*

"Bolero" is the codename for the build-up of US forces and equipment in Great Britain in preparation for the invasion of Europe. In progress since January 1942, only now is it producing significant results. With the Allied campaigns in the Mediterranean downgraded and the U-boats in the Atlantic largely beaten, US resources in the UK by the end of January 1944 stand at 937,308 troops and 3,553,755 tonnes (3,497,791 tons) of arms and supplies. These totals will almost double in the next 12 weeks.

PLANNING, *STRATEGY CONFIRMED*

Eisenhower receives a telegram from the Combined Chiefs of Staff in Washington, DC. In this, they agree to Montgomery's revised invasion plan and the new proposed date for D-Day of May 31. It is understood, however, that the precise timing will depend on fair weather and calm seas in the English Channel. Montgomery's plan will now be worked up into SHAEF's official Initial Joint Plan for "Neptune", the codename for the first phase of Overlord, which includes the Channel crossing and the amphibious and airborne landings.

GERMAN DEFENCES, *FRANCE*

Under orders from Rommel, the new commander of Army Group B, the strenghtening of French coastal defences begins. Time is short and there are hundreds of miles to cover. Heavy reliance is being placed on the laying of minefields, both anti-tank and anti-personnel, and on the construction of thousands of improvised beach obstacles to destroy enemy landing craft. These are being built along the line of low tide and are often made from crudely cut timber topped with mines. Rommel understands that time is running out, but remains optimistic: "the enemy will have to adapt himself at the last moment to this new form of defence, which is certain to take a heavy toll of his landing craft."

▼ *A section of the Atlantic Wall, with obstacles for denying the movement of vehicles. Tank traps and strongpoints were established up to 3.2km (2 miles) inland.*

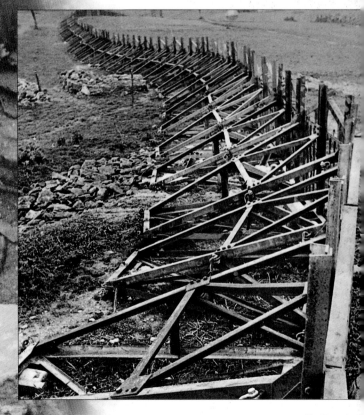

February 1944

Production of vehicles and equipment for the invasion was stepped up as Allied troops continued training for D-Day across Great Britain. Initial results were not promising, though. The embarkation areas along the south coast of England were sealed off from public access, and the first plans for the top-secret "Mulberry" harbours were shown to Allied chiefs.

▼ *The Supreme Command of the Allied Expeditionary Force poses for a press corps photograph.*

COMMANDERS, *PRESS RELATIONS*
The commanders of the Allied Expeditionary Force to Europe are today introduced to the world's press. Under tight security, 60 newspaper photographers and newsreel cameramen are taken by closed truck to a secret London location (in fact Norfolk House), for a photo session with, they are told, "certain members of the Supreme Command". Present for this photo session are Eisenhower, Tedder, Bedell Smith, Montgomery, Ramsay, Leigh-Mallory, and General Bradley of the US First Army. The session lasts for barely 15 minutes and is a low-key affair. The officers sit around three bare trestle tables and gesture at a large unmarked map of Europe. No talking is allowed. This public-relations exercise, however, sends the clearest message yet to friend and foe that the invasion and liberation of Europe is imminent.

PLANNING, *THE IJP*
SHAEF issues the Initial Joint Plan (IJP) for Operation Neptune, following its approval by the Combined Chiefs of Staff. The plan provides a broad

framework on which Admiral Ramsay's naval command and the staffs of the US First Army and British Second Army will draw up their own detailed operational plans. SHAEF requires these completed by the end of February.

Those officers who are briefed on the full extent of the IJP, and who will be involved in its further development and implementation, are given a special security clearance, allowing them to see material classified as "BIGOT". This is the most secret information on Overlord and deals with the big three questions: Where?, When? and How?

THURSDAY, FEBRUARY 3

LOGISTICS, *US NAVY*

The US Navy now has at least 18 major bases in Great Britain, including a hospital, 11 amphibious training centres and 6 supply depots. Most are located along the south coast of Devon and Cornwall and were established between August and December 1943. They are run from the Landing Craft and Bases Europe Command, located in Falmouth, Cornwall. The biggest US Navy base in Great Britain is currently

▼ *British troops practice overcoming a barbed-wire beach obstacle. Using ladders, mats or even their own bodies, the soldiers prepared ways to get off the exposed beaches and into cover.*

STRATEGY & TACTICS

THE INITIAL JOINT PLAN

The IJP directed the Allied navies to land five assault divisions on D-Day along a front stretching from the east coast of the Cotentin Peninsula to the estuary of the River Orne northeast of Caen. The five assault beaches were codenamed Utah, Omaha, Gold, Juno and Sword. To consolidate this bridgehead, reinforcements after D-Day were to be landed steadily. Nine divisions were to arrive by D+3, and a total of 20 divisions were to be in France by D+20.

The US First Army was to be responsible for the landings on Utah and Omaha. The IJP proposed that the division from Utah would advance immediately north to capture the port of Cherbourg. From Omaha, forces would move west, crossing the River Vire to take the town of Periers, and then advance to Lessay on the west coast of the Cotentin, a distance of some 40km (25 miles). Its task would be cut off the peninsula and protect the rear of the division attacking Cherbourg. By D+20 American forces should have been advancing into Brittany to take the port of Brest, reinforced by the armoured divisions of General Patton's US Third Army

British and Canadian units of the British Second Army would assault the three eastern beaches, Gold, Juno and Sword. Forces from Gold would then strike south,

reaching the Caen–Bayeux road, 7.5km (5 miles) away, and east to link up with the Americans from Omaha. Forces from Juno Beach would also advance south to the Caen–Bayeux road and secure ground northwest of Caen. The division from Sword would advance 19km (12 miles) inland to capture Caen and secure airfields located southeast of the town.

The invasion front would be protected on the flanks by an airdrop of two divisions, to be made in the early hours of D-Day morning, about seven hours before the beach assaults. One US airborne division would drop behind Utah to secure the roads leading inland, across a large area of flooded country, while a British airborne division would drop into the area northeast of Caen, between the estuaries of the rivers Orne and Dives, to secure the river crossings.

This initial plan for D-Day would prove, in reality, to be far too ambitious. It assumed that the assault divisions could breach the German coastal defences, land and organize sufficient forces, and then make advances inland of over 19km (12 miles), all in one day. To achieve this the IJP relied too much on the element of surprise, the speed of the Allied ground forces and the total absence of all German armoured units between Caen and the Cotentin Peninsula.

the main supply base at Exeter, Devon, which has 176 buildings over 170 acres, housing 2352 officers and men.

FRIDAY, FEBRUARY 4

LOGISTICS, *TANKS*
American factories begin converting Sherman tanks into the amphibious Duplex-Drive (DD) variant. By April, 300 of them will be ready for delivery to the British 79th Armoured Division.

MONDAY, FEBRUARY 7

PLANNING, *THE IJP*
The Initial Joint Plan for Neptune, distributed on February 1, is already coming under scrutiny. One of its early critics is the Supreme Commander himself. General Eisenhower suggests today that the number of airborne divisions committed to the assault be increased and that a third division be dropped the day after the landings (D+1). Leigh-Mallory's air staff object to

▼ *Top-secret Duplex-Drive (DD) Sherman tanks on exercise. These specially designed vehicles were regarded as the best way of getting armour onto the beaches.*

his proposal on the grounds that they have insufficient air crews to transport three divisions in two days.

TUESDAY, FEBRUARY 8

INTELLIGENCE, *U-BOATS*
Today the submarine tracking section of the Royal Navy's Operational Intelligence Centre, based in Whitehall,

▲ *Thousands of Allied artillery pieces and traversing wheels. As factories produced materials for the assault, vast supply areas were needed to store the equipment.*

London, publishes an assessment of the current number of German U-boats in operation along the French coast. Although they have been driven from

the Atlantic sea lanes, in the view of the author of the assessment, Captain Rodger Winn, they still pose a serious threat to the Allied invasion: "a total of 175 to 200 U-boats," he states "will be used to prevent or impair landings." Action will have to be taken to neutralize this threat.

PLANNING, *LOGISTICS*

SHAEF today addresses the important subject of logistics. It issues the Joint Outline Maintenance Project/Administrative Plan, the framework for the future logistic support of its American and British armies on the continent.

The plan is complex and exhaustive. The areas of policy it covers include: the maintenance of combat forces; the control of base areas and reserves; movement and transportation; road building; airfield construction; hospital depots; bulk petrol and water supplies; ordnance stores; vehicle workshops; welfare of personnel; medical services; casualty evacuation; and burials. The plan even addresses the logistics of printing and stationery supplies.

To control every aspect of the movement and build-up of troops and supplies before, during and after the invasion, five inter-service organizations will be established. The Build-up Control Organ (BUCO) will coordinate and control the overall build-up plan. Prior to the invasion, the

▲ *Troops of the British Special Air Service (SAS) practice their climbing techniques on a rockface in Scotland.*

Movement and Control Section (MORCO) will direct the movement of men and vehicles from concentration areas in southern England to their embarkation ports. The Turnaround Control Organization (TURCO) will ensure the rapid turnaround of supply ships in the ports of England and France. The Combined Operations Repair Organization (COREP) will deal with the repair of damaged transport vessels and landing craft, while tugs will be controlled by the Combined Operations Tugs Organization.

WEDNESDAY, FEBRUARY 9

ORDER OF BATTLE, *SAS*

The Special Air Service (SAS) sets up its new headquarters at Sorn Castle in Ayrshire, Scotland. The SAS is being reorganized into an Anglo-French brigade for Operation Overlord, and is currently under the command of British I Airborne Corps. The brigade now consists of 1 SAS Regiment, 3 French Parachute Battalion, 4 French Parachute Battalion and the Belgian Independent Parachute Company. As it will be working with French Resistance groups behind the lines, the brigade also has two liaison headquarters, the HQ, French Demi-Brigade, and 20 Liaison HQ, SAS. There are plans for 2 SAS Regiment to join the brigade after its transfer from the Mediterranean. (SEE MARCH 17)

WEDNESDAY, FEBRUARY 9

SECURITY, *ENGLISH COAST*

In Whitehall, the Cabinet's Home Defence Committee, which includes the prime minister, meet to discuss a request from SHAEF and the Ministry of Home Security to seal off the southern coast of England from the public as a security measure. It is along this coast that all the major invasion ports and troop embarkation points are located, and security officials want to stop visitor access from outside. As a SHAEF assessment warns: "If the enemy obtains as much as 48 hours warning

▼ *Allied landing craft await D-Day. The original assault plan called for the use of thousands of craft, but the shipyards could only provide a third of the number.*

of the location of the assault area, chances of success are small, and any longer [period] spells certain defeat."

Most Cabinet members and the Chief of the Imperial General Staff, Sir Alan Brooke, approve of the measure; Prime Minister Winston Churchill is against the idea, saying that "we must beware of handing out irksome for irksome's sake", and in a heated debate blocks its imposition for now.

However, on the recommendation of MI5 Churchill does approve a travel ban to and from Ireland. The Republic, which is neutral, has refused to sever diplomatic links with Germany and Japan, and is viewed as a security risk.

▶ **Hundreds of Allied tanks and other vehicles are stockpiled, ready for deployment. The vast planning needed for D-Day required the finest logistical minds.**

◀ **B-17 Flying Fortresses of the US Eighth Army Air Force over France. A concerted effort was made by Allied command to degrade enemy capabilities.**

JUNE 6

D-DAY SECURITY. LIEUTENANT-COMMANDER DALZEL-JOB, ROYAL NAVY INTELLIGENCE.

Patrick Dalzel-Job served as a lieutenant-commander in the Royal Navy's 30th Advanced Unit (30 AU), an intelligence force that operated with Royal Marine Commandos ahead of the frontline troops to capture enemy prisoners, documents and equipment. He landed on Utah beach on 10 June (D+4). In his 1991 memoir he recalled the security surrounding Overlord in the months beforehand and his own position.

"Before D-Day, we were all issued with special passes, which 'by command of General Eisenhower' authorized us to do practically anything, anywhere, adding in block capitals, 'THE BEARER OF THIS CARD WILL NOT BE INTERFERED WITH IN THE PERFORMANCE OF HIS DUTY BY THE MILITARY POLICE OR BY OTHER MILITARY ORGANISATION'. We knew almost everything about the plans for the D-Day landings well in advance, excepting only the date and precise landing places. That vital information came to my knowledge in an odd way. Its classification was one stage higher than 'Top Secret' and was called 'Bigot'. One day someone asked me casually whether I was bigoted, I said that of course I was, and he then chatted away quite openly. Needless to say, I kept it all to myself, but it was useful information ... I was 'bigoted' a few days later."

"Arctic Snow to Dust of Normandy", by Patrick Dalzel-Job, Barnsley: Leo Cooper, 2002.

The German legation in Dublin was still in direct radio contact with Berlin up until the end of 1943, when pressure from Washington persuaded the Irish to shut down the transmitter. The problem of Ireland is made more complicated by the fact that an estimated 150,000 Irish nationals are in Great Britain working as labourers in Overlord preparation areas. The travel ban will come into effect in March.

AIR CAMPAIGN, *TARGETING*

Eisenhower receives a proposal from his air chief, Leigh-Mallory, for a bombing campaign targeting the French railway system. It is the work of Professor Zuckerman, who developed a similar plan for Italy. The object of the scheme, soon to be known as the Transportation Plan, is to attack rail lines, junctions and bridges in such a way as to isolate Normandy from the French rail system, making it impossible for the Germans to transport their armoured divisions directly to the invasion beachhead.

The idea is sound but senior Allied figures raise objections. Churchill is very concerned about the French civilian casualties it will inflict in the weeks prior to the invasion, while the bomber chiefs, Harris and Spaatz, do not want their aircraft pulled from the strategic objective of bombing German

cities. Spaatz also wants a higher priority given to tackling German oil production. Nevertheless, Eisenhower gives his approval to the plan.

THURSDAY, FEBRUARY 10

LOGISTICS, *LANDING CRAFT*
In a move to find SHAEF all the landing craft it has requested, the Combined Chiefs of Staff signal the headquarters,

◀ *Allied commanders, including General Bradley (second from left) and Rear-Admiral Alan G. Kirk (far left), watch a mock amphibious assault before D-Day.*

Mediterranean Theatre of Operations, that all LSTs (Landing Ship, Tanks) no longer required in theatre are to be returned to Great Britain. To finalize landing craft numbers, General Marshall has sent two of his senior planners to London.

FRIDAY, FEBRUARY 11

ORDER OF BATTLE, *US FORCES*
The invasion force builds. From New York, the US 5th and 6th Armored Divisions sail for Great Britain, to be joined by the 30th Infantry Division from Boston.

STRATEGY & TACTICS

THE VISITORS BAN

When Churchill first blocked the idea of sealing off the south coast from the public, he did so for political reasons. He was willing, however, to be persuaded of its importance on security grounds and asked that he be given – on one sheet of paper – a list of the kinds of thing the public should not see. It promptly arrived after the Cabinet security meeting of February 9, and it reveals the huge scope and variety of invasion preparations. It also shows that there were few locations between Suffolk and Cornwall not involved in Neptune and Overlord.

IMPORTANT ITEMS WHICH IT IS UNDESIRABLE FOR VISITORS TO SEE
Most Secret Equipment
Mulberry, Phoenix and Bombardon
Probably the greatest single factor of surprise in the operation.
Construction Sites – Portsmouth, Stokes Bay, Alverstoke, Southampton, Hayling Island, North Point [Hampshire], Rainham, Tilbury, Erith [southeast London].
Mulberry Group Training Sites:
Mulberry – Christchurch and East of Selsey.
Phoenix – Christchurch Bay.
Bombardon – Weymouth Bay and Ringstead.
PLUTO [Pipeline under the Ocean] including REL, DUMBO, SOLO and BAMBY:
Construction Sites – Tilbury, Lydd, Dungeness, Rye, Hamble, Fawley, Lepe, Gurnard, Shanklin and Sandown.
Training Area – Christchurch to Lymington.
R.G.: DD TANKS: C.D.L TANKS AND OTHER MOST SECRET MILITARY ASSAULT EQUIPMENT TRAINING AREAS:
King's Lynn, Sheringham, Great Yarmouth (Broads Area), Ipswich, Colchester, Maldon, Sandwich, Dover, Folkestone, St. Leonards, Beachy Head, Hove, Storringham, Havant, Fareham, Southampton, Beaulieu-Fording-

bridge, Broadstone, Swanage, West Lulworth, Dorchester, Budleigh Salterton, Paignton, Kingsbridge, Ivybridge, Penrhyn.
COMBINED OPERATIONAL TRAINING AREAS:
There are 28 of these areas from The Wash to Lands End of which Southwold Beaches, Studland Bay and Stuart Bay are major training and rehearsal areas.
HARDS:
There are 56 separate hards and 10 more under construction in sheltered waters from The Wash to Penzance for the embarkation of AFVs, guns and vehicles. Each accommodates one to four landing ships or equivalent in landing craft, and are designed to supplement port facilities.
EMBARKATION AREAS:
Great Yarmouth, Ipswich, Felixstowe, Tilbury, Gravesend, Deal, Dover, Folkestone, Hythe, Hastings, Newhaven, Shoreham, Portsmouth, Gosport, Southampton, Stanswood Bay,

Beaulieu, Lymington, Poole, Weymouth, Portland, Torquay, Brixham, Dartmouth, Plymouth, Devonport, Fowey, Falmouth.
MARSHALLING AREAS:
Measuring about 20 miles by 10 miles behind the Embarkation Areas and contain camps where the final briefing of troops assault divisions, supporting troops (tanks, etc) and immediate follow-up divisions will take place.
SECRET NAVAL STORES FOR THE ASSAULT:
There are 28 civil firms between The Wash and Lands End which hold these stores.
DECOYS
There are 96 Air Decoys within 10 miles of the coast from The Wash to Lands End, which represent air fields, large fires, dummy dockyards, etc. Many more lights representing dummy hards are being installed.

▼ *Civilians were forbidden from entering cordoned-off areas, or liaising with troops stationed in them.*

SATURDAY, FEBRUARY 12

COMMANDERS, *EISENHOWER*
In Washington, DC, the Combined Chiefs of Staff draw up General Eisenhower's directive as Supreme Commander, Allied Expeditionary Force. This document constitutes the order officially confirming Eisenhower in his post and in eight points details his tasks and responsibilities.

SUNDAY, FEBRUARY 13

ORDER OF BATTLE, *US FORCES*
The main units of the US Third Army Headquarters sail from New York for Great Britain.

LOGISTICS, *LANDING CRAFT*
The "Landing Craft Conference" is held in London to finalize the numbers of vessels needed for the invasion. Present are two of General Marshall's senior planning officers from Washington, General John E. Hull and Rear-Admiral

Charles M. Cooke. They meet at Norfolk House with SHAEF staff and two of the US Navy's senior officers in Great Britain, Rear Admiral Alan G. Kirk, who will command the Western Task Force, and Rear-Admiral John L. Hall, currently responsible for the amphibious training of all US forces.

▲ *Various landing craft and vehicles, including an LCT (Landing Craft, Tank) on the far right, practice loading supplies onto the shore.*

▼ *Another top-secret Allied development, the rocket ship. It was capable of firing high-explosive rockets over a vast area.*

◄ *General Sir Alan Brooke, Chief of the Imperial General Staff. He spearheaded the British preparations for D-Day, and was Churchill's principal military advisor.*

It is agreed that seven more LSTs should be sent from the United States and that the British should transfer another 21 LSTs and 20 LCI (Landing Craft, Infantry) from the Mediterranean. There should also be an increase in the weight loaded into each vessel.

MONDAY, FEBRUARY 14

COMMANDERS, *EISENHOWER*

In London, Eisenhower receives his directive from the Combined Chief of Staff (CCS). This directive states that he will be responsible directly to the CCS, but that he should also work directly with British and American Chiefs of Staff for logistical support. It defines his task as follows:

"You will enter the Continent of Europe and, in conjunction with the other United Nations, undertake operations aimed at the heart of Germany and the destruction of her armed forces. The date for entering the Continent is the month of May, 1944. After adequate Channel Ports have been secured, exploitation will be directed towards securing an area that will facilitate both ground and air operations against the enemy."

This directive, however, gives Eisenhower no authority at all over the strategic bomber force of General

Spaatz and Air Chief Marshal Harris. It is an oversight that will cause the Supreme Commander problems in the coming weeks as he tries to employ the bomber force in a tactical role to assist Overlord's ground campaign.

ORDER OF BATTLE, *US FORCES*
The US 82nd Airborne Division arrives in England and moves into camps near Leicester, 120km (75 miles) north of London. The division left the Mediterranean in November 1943, and in the space of 10 weeks has moved from Sicily to North Africa, to Northern

▼ *British troops in transit to the south coast. They are on board one of the London Underground trains.*

▲ *German Grand Admiral Karl Dönitz (second from left). Despite his reluctance, he was ordered by Hitler, in 1944, to guard Norway against possible Allied invasion.*

Ireland and from there to England. The 82nd is now the second US airborne division in theatre, the 101st Airborne having arrived direct from New York in September 1943.

DECEPTION, *BODYGUARD*
In Moscow, meetings begin with the Soviets to discuss the Bodyguard deception plans. Colonels Bevan and Baumer, who brought the plans over from London in January, meet with two Soviet generals and a representative of the Soviet foreign ministry. It is vital to secure Russian cooperation. Talks will continue for the next two weeks.

WEDNESDAY, FEBRUARY 16

GERMAN DEFENCES, *FRANCE*
From his headquarters at Wilhelmshaven, Germany, U-boat commander Grand Admiral Karl Dönitz today orders the transfer of 10 submarines from the French coast to Norway. With these boats he establishes Centre Group to guard the North Sea

approaches. His action comes at the insistence of Hitler, who remains convinced that Norway is an Allied invasion target.

THURSDAY, FEBRUARY 17

PLANNING, *AIRBORNE ASSAULT*
Major-General Richard Gale, commander of the British 6th Airborne Division, based in Wiltshire, receives orders from 21st Army Group. Gale is to prepare operational plans for air landings on the left flank of the invasion beaches. These are to include three specific pre-dawn attacks: the capture of bridges over the River Orne and Caen Canal near the village of Bénouville, the destruction of bridges further east over the River Dives, and the destruction of the coastal battery

FRIDAY, FEBRUARY 18

▶ *A British Supermarine Seafire on board an aircraft carrier. The Seafire provided the invading troops with air cover.*

near Merville, 2.4km (1.5 miles) from the coast. Gale assigns the River Orne attack to Brigadier Nigel Poett's 9th Brigade, while the two other objectives become the responsibility of Brigadier James Hill's 3rd Parachute Brigade.

FRIDAY, FEBRUARY 18

HOME FRONT, *GREAT BRITAIN*
If there is any complacency creeping in among the Allied high command that the war is as good as won and that they can plan Overlord in peace and quiet, it ends tonight. The German Luftwaffe (Air Force) begins a new series of air raids on London. In what will become known as the "Little Blitz", the attacks go on for the next five nights, leaving 961 civilians dead and over 1700 injured. The German air raids will continue into late March.

► *Field Marshal Erwin Rommel surveys coastal defences in northern France. He threw himself into the task of organizing German defensive preparations.*

SATURDAY, FEBRUARY 19

PLANNING, *MEDITERRANEAN*
Despite the fact that Overlord is now meant to have priority in the European theatre this year, rows continue among the Allies about operations in the Mediterranean. A meeting today, between the British Chiefs of Staff and Eisenhower, Bedell Smith and Tedder of SHAEF, reveals serious disagreements about a possible attack on southern France – Operation Anvil – to coincide with the Normandy assault. The British emphasize the need to keep units in Italy, while SHAEF (and the Americans) want these forces diverted to the south of France. Sir Alan Brooke records in his diary: "If they had had any sense they would have realised that the situation in Italy now makes such an operation impossible." Such disagreements will divert valuable time and energy from Overlord.

TRAINING, *MEDICINE*
Exercise Crackshot begins. This is the first training exercise for medical troops and

involves hospitals in southern England. The task is to assess the best methods of admitting and discharging large numbers of wounded soldiers. No invasion units are involved. Crackshot continues until Friday 25th.

WEDNESDAY, FEBRUARY 23

ORDER OF BATTLE, *US FORCES*
The build-up of US troops in Great Britain moves into high gear. Lead units of the US 6th Armored Division arrive in England, the third US armoured division to arrive in four weeks. It will be organized into XX Corps, part of Patton's Third Army. Today also sees the arrival of the US 30th Infantry Division, sailing from Boston. It is organized into XIX Corps; part of Bradley's First Army.

THURSDAY, FEBRUARY 24

ORDER OF BATTLE, *US FORCES*
The US 5th Armored Division begins to arrive in England. It will be assigned to V Corps, First Army.

FRIDAY, FEBRUARY 25

PLANNING, *MEDITERRANEAN*
The debate over the future of Operation Anvil reaches the Combined Chiefs of Staff, who attempt to find a

◄ *A US Army Air Force ground crew prepare a B-17 for another bombing mission. These aircraft had a payload of up to 3635kg (8000lb) of bombs.*

compromise solution. They agree that an attack on the south of France might have to be postponed until after Overlord is established in Normandy, and that the shipping previously earmarked for Anvil can be switched to the English Channel. The debate, however, rumbles on.

TRAINING, *PILOTS*
Overlord will see an unprecedented degree of cooperation among land, sea and air forces, and today begins the training near Portsmouth of a select group of Royal Navy pilots from 3 Naval Fighter Wing. Flying the fast,

▼ *A convoy of American fighter-bombers and their transport trucks forms a surreal sight as it winds its way through an English town prior to D-Day.*

manoeuvrable Supermarine Seafires, these men have been chosen to work over the beachhead as airborne spotters, targeting and correcting naval gunnery coming in offshore in support of ground forces. They will be trained in tactical reconnaissance and army cooperation.

SATURDAY, FEBRUARY 26

PLANNING, *HEADQUARTERS*

Admiral Ramsay's staff begins to move the Allied naval headquarters from Norfolk House, in central London, to Southwick House, 11.2km (7 miles) north of Portsmouth Dockyard. It is from here that Ramsay will oversee the embarkation of the assault forces and the Channel crossing. By May both SHAEF and 21st Army Group will have advance headquarters here.

▼ *German troops on the Eastern Front in February 1944. As the Soviets drove the Wehrmacht back, Hitler was forced to take units from the West to reinforce the East.*

DECEPTION, *FORTITUDE*

SHAEF issues a directive on the Fortitude deception plans. Fortitude North – directed at occupied Norway – will be the responsibility of the General Officer Commanding, Scotland, while Fortitude South – the deceptions targeting Normandy and northern France – will be the responsibility of Montgomery, Ramsay and Leigh-Mallory. Eisenhower will retain control of the implementation of Fortitude plans, which must be coordinated through SHAEF's deception staff, the Committee for Special Means – Ops B.

MONDAY, FEBRUARY 28

GERMAN DEFENCES, *FRANCE*

The armies in the West continue to be stripped of their strongest units as Hitler reinforces the collapsing Eastern Front. Today, the Führer cancels the transfer to France of two armoured divisions, 21st Panzer and Panzer Lehr, instead redirecting them east for the planned occupation of Hungary.

SECURITY, *AIR TRAVEL*

The Home Defence Committee recommends new security measures to the Cabinet and Winston Churchill. It proposes tight restrictions on civil flights to the Irish Republic. The Aer Lingus service from Liverpool to Dublin should be stopped, and the only remaining flights should be those of British carrier BOAC. The air service between Aberdeen and neutral Sweden should also be interrupted as soon as possible. The object is to control all access to and from Great Britain.

TUESDAY, FEBRUARY 29

LOGISTICS, *MULBERRY*

The British Chiefs of Staff are shown scale models of the Mulberry artificial harbours currently under construction at sites near Portsmouth, Southampton and the Thames estuary. Two complete harbours will be towed, in sections,

▶ *German troops in Russia in early 1944. Allied deception was remarkably successful in convincing the Führer that an attack was coming in the East.*

across the Channel immediately after the assault and established off the Normandy coast. One will supply the US sector, the other the British and Canadians. Mulberry is designed to have enough capacity to receive up to about 12,200 tonnes (12,000 tons) of equipment and 2500 vehicles per day.

SECURITY, *MEDIA*

The British government finally imposes a press ban, warning British newspapers to stop speculating about the timing, location and size of an invasion. A similar request is made in the United States. Given the importance of the invasion to the outcome of the war, the press cooperate.

March 1944

A s Rommel was kept busy preparing German defences in France, US aircraft joined in the bombing of Berlin. The Soviet Army broke through in the Ukraine, and the Wehrmacht entered Hungary at the "invitation" of Admiral Horthy to counter Soviet moves. Meanwhile, Allied bombers continued to target the French infrastructure to hinder German movements.

▼ US paratroopers prepare to board C-46 Curtis Commando aircraft during a training exercise in southern England.

SECURITY, *COASTS/TRAVEL*
The Cabinet's Home Defence Committee meets again. It endorses the proposal for a visitor ban along the south coast, recommended on February 28, and suggests extending it to other areas of the country, including Milford Haven in Wales, Portishead on the Severn Estuary near Bristol and the estuaries of the Forth, Tay and Clyde in Scotland. It also recommends a ban on all diplomatic communications by the British representatives of neutral and friendly countries prior to the invasion – except, of course, the United States.

HOME FRONT, *GREAT BRITAIN*
Churchill holds the first weekly meeting of the government's Overlord Preparation Committee. Its brief is far-reaching and covers every aspect of Overlord as it affects the Home Front. Present are 12 ministers, responsible for labour, health, war transport, food, fuel and power, plus representatives of the War Office, Air Ministry and Admiralty. Among their first discussions are proposals to clear civilian hospitals

▼ Russian soldiers in early 1944. Across the Eastern Front, Soviet units attacked the Germans and kept them occupied.

▲ *Russian self-propelled artillery pieces crash their way through the forests of western Russia in March.*

of patients, in order to make room for the thousands of military casualties expected on D-Day.

THURSDAY, MARCH 2

PLANNING, *IJP REVISIONS*

The Initial Joint Plan (IJP) issued by SHAEF in February is now being worked up in detail by individual commands. In an early revision, US First Army asks SHAEF for a second airborne drop to be made in support of its landings. One airborne division is already earmarked for a drop west of Utah beach, but First Army now asks

▲ *The C-47 Dakota was the air workhorse of the Allied forces. As well as delivering supplies, it dropped paratroops.*

for another airborne division to be landed in the centre of the Cotentin Peninsula around the village of St Sauveur-le-Vicomte. This would be made during the early hours of D+1, after the transport aircraft have completed their D-Day operations.

FRIDAY, MARCH 3

The chances of this request being accepted are good. There are now two US airborne divisions available in the UK, the 82nd and 101st, and Allied air command reports to SHAEF that the numbers of trained air crews available to fly them is increasing. This had been the main hurdle to planning large-scale airborne operations for D-Day.

FRIDAY, MARCH 3

DECEPTION, *BODYGUARD*
In Moscow, the Soviet–Allied talks over Operation Bodyguard come to a successful conclusion. The Soviets agree to participate fully. Their role will be threefold. They will begin their summer offensive after Overlord has begun, and will make every appearance of preparing attacks on northern Norway and the Black Sea coasts of Romania and Bulgaria.

▼ *A logistically important railway bridge just outside Paris lies in ruins following an Allied bombing raid.*

SATURDAY, MARCH 4

PLANNING, *HEADQUARTERS*
SHAEF HQ begins a move out of Norfolk House. The building is too small, and recent German air raids on central London have convinced Eisenhower that a new location is needed. It is moving to a former Eighth Army Air Force headquarters in Bushy Park, in the suburbs of southwest London. The move will be completed by Monday, but plans have already been made to create a forward HQ at Southwick House, near Portsmouth.

MONDAY, MARCH 6

AIR CAMPAIGN, *RAIL TARGETS*
Tonight, RAF Bomber Command carries out the first raids on French rail targets to test the feasibility of Zuckerman's Transportation Plan. The 261 Halifax bombers attack the rail centre of Trappes, southwest of Paris, and knock out the entire electrified line from Chartres to Paris. The bombers return without loss. There have been doubts that these strategic aircraft can bomb accurately enough to hit such small targets at night, but Bomber Command finds these results very encouraging. One of Harris's staff officers reports that "it is appreciated that this new-found ability to saturate with bomb strikes a given area of approx 500 x 1,000 yards square constitutes a weapon of war of enormous power".

Raids on French rail targets will continue over the next three weeks, with attacks on the nights of March 13-14, 15-16, 23-24, 25-26 and 26-27.

DECEPTION, *FORTITUDE NORTH*
As part of Fortitude North, Colonel R.M. MacLeod arrives in Edinburgh to establish the headquarters of the phantom British Fourth Army. The deception is designed to give the impression that an Allied attack on Norway from Scotland is imminent. It is created by MacLeod and a staff of 30, who generate enough radio traffic between Edinburgh, Stirling and Dundee to convince the Germans that there is a force of 250,000 men, complete with armoured division and tactical air support, being organized to strike across the North Sea.

▲ *A reconnaissance photo of the railway yards at Juvisy-sur-Orge before an attack by aircraft of RAF Bomber Command. Such installations were key targets for Allied bombers leading up to D-Day.*

TUESDAY, MARCH 7

SECURITY, *PRESS REPORTS*
The invasion poses a huge problem for the security services: for those involved it is the secret everyone wants to talk about, but which no one is allowed to mention in public.

In this climate of frustrated gossip someone is bound to say something and today's security breach comes via the *London Evening News*. Despite undertakings not to publish such speculation, the newspaper reports the Canadian minister of munitions as predicting major Allied operations will take place "within the next three or four months". The story is shown to Churchill, who sends a stiffly worded personal telegram to the Canadian prime minister, reminding him that ministers should not make any reference to the "timing, scope or direction of forthcoming operations".

FRIDAY, MARCH 10

GERMAN DEFENCES, *FRANCE*
Rommel's Army Group B headquarters moves from Fontainebleau to the castle of La Roche-Guyon, northwest of Paris. It will now be closer to the coast and the OB West HQ at St Germain.
SECURITY, *COASTS*
After weeks of discussion, Churchill finally agrees to the ban on the movement of civilians to and from the south and east coasts.

MONDAY, MARCH 13

SHAEF, *INSIGNIA*
SHAEF's insignia patch comes into use. Designed by Colonel Norman Lack and Corporal Doreen Goodall, it shows a flaming sword on a field of sable over which are the rainbow colours of the United Nations' flags. It will be worn by all in Eisenhower's HQ, a staff that will grow to over 16,000 by May 1945.

FRIDAY, MARCH 17

ORDER OF BATTLE, *BRITISH FORCES*
The 2nd SAS Regiment arrives from North Africa and joins SAS Brigade.
AIR CAMPAIGN, *RAIL TARGETS*
In raids designed to assess the feasibility of Zuckerman's

SUNDAY, MARCH 19

▶ *Hungarian soldiers discuss the news of the German invasion of their country. Hitler's decision to invade his former ally may have been prudent, but it alienated the Hungarian armed forces.*

Transportation Plan, B-26 Marauder medium bombers of the US Ninth Air Force today hit the rail yards at Creil, north of Paris, in the first of three raids. They will return there next week and attack again on Monday and Thursday.

SUNDAY, MARCH 19

GERMAN DEFENCES, *FRANCE*

At his Berchtesgaden mountain retreat, Hitler holds a strategy conference with his senior commanders from the West, including von Rundstedt and Rommel of OB West, the Luftwaffe's Field Marshal Hugo Speerle, commanding Luftflotte (Air Fleet) 3, and Admiral Theodore Kranke, in charge of Navy Group West.

In a private meeting with the Führer, Rommel attempts to extend his authority at von Rundtedt's expense. He asks to command all armoured and motorized units in the West, as well the First and Nineteenth Armies in the South of France. This would consolidate

Rommel's authority and solve the impasse with von Rundstedt over the formation and use of a large armoured reserve to counter the invasion.

Hitler compromises: Rommel will receive the 2nd, 21st and 116th Panzer Divisions as an Army Group B reserve,

▼ *German Panzer IV tanks and their crews, shown here moving into position in southern France.*

with von Schweppenburg's Panzer Group West still in control of organization and training. Hitler also establishes an OKW reserve under his personal control. This consists of the 1st SS Panzer, 12th SS Panzer, Panzer Lehr and the 17th SS Panzergrenadier Divisions. It seems as if, while the Allies are working hard to create a unified chain of command, Hitler is doing his utmost to divide that of OB West.

In developments that further disperse his armoured forces, Hitler today orders the invasion of Hungary, his former ally. It is a pre-emptive strike to ensure the country's continued allegiance and the supply of oil from her oilfields. The Führer has no forces near the country, and

STRATEGY & TACTICS

THE OCCUPATION OF HUNGARY

The German occupation of Hungary in 1944 coincided with Soviet advances in the East, as communist forces were only 272km (170 miles) from the Hungarian border. In 1941 Hungary had become an active Axis power, taking part in offensives against Yugoslavia and Russia. It had also been supplying Germany with much-needed materials, such as oil. In 1944, Hitler, seeing that the loss of Hungarian oil would harm the German war effort, coerced the Hungarian Regent, Admiral Horthy, into agreeing to the occupation of his lands by German forces, ostensibly to guarantee Hungarian "integrity". Though a military strategy, Hitler also imposed Nazi political systems, forced the deportation of Jews and took control of Hungary's oil.

MONDAY, MARCH 20

GERMAN DEFENCES, *FRANCE*

As a consequence of the Sunday strategy meeting, Hitler issues his own assessment of Allied intentions for the coming year, which begins: "It is evident that an Anglo-American landing in the West must come. How and where it will come no one knows."

He acknowledges the strategic significance of the French Atlantic ports, and, in a decision that will have serious future repercussions – for US operations against Cherbourg and for Overlord's whole reinforcement plan – he designates them as a fortresses. They must be held, he says, "to the last round of ammunition, the last tin of rations, until every last possibility of defence has been exhausted".

He orders that: "The enemy's entire landing operation must under no circumstances be allowed to last longer than a matter of hours or, at the most, days ...." But he believes that "once the landing has been defeated, it will under no circumstances be repeated by the enemy", citing the Allies' war weariness and the devastating effect of heavy Allied casualties as factors.

Hitler concludes, as the senior Allied commanders do, that the coming struggle in the West will be decisive: "The destruction of the enemy's landing attempt means more than a purely local decision on the Western

▲ *A young German crew man their Marder III self-propelled anti-tank gun. A Czech chassis with a German 76mm gun, it saw action mainly on the Eastern Front.*

has had to transfer Panzer Lehr and the assault guns from four frontline divisions in the West. Only the direct intervention of OKW has stopped the deployment of the 21st Panzer Division as well, which is ordered back to France.

Hitler's move is motivated partly by a Bodyguard operation, which leaked news of Hungarian government peace approaches to the Allies.

WEDNESDAY, MARCH 22

▶ *Bletchley Park, England, location of the top-secret Allied code-breaking centre, Station X. It was responsible for deciphering Axis signals, and it is most famous for breaking the German Enigma codes.*

Front. It is the sole decisive factor in the whole conduct of the war and hence in its final result."

WEDNESDAY, MARCH 22

GERMAN DEFENCES, *FRANCE*
From his HQ at Wilhelmshaven, Grand Admiral Dönitz orders the establishment of the U-boat Gruppe Landwirt (Farmer Group). These 15 boats, based among the French ports of the Bay of Biscay, are to patrol the western approaches to the English Channel.

THURSDAY, MARCH 23

COMMANDERS, *INSPECTION*
Eisenhower and Churchill begin a two-day inspection of US troops, including units of the 101st Airborne Division, based around Newbury, Berkshire.

FRIDAY, MARCH 24

PLANNING, *MEDITERRANEAN*
The Combined Chiefs of Staff decide that because Operation Neptune has priority over the use of landing craft, the invasion of southern France will not be launched simultaneously with Overlord. Instead it will be postponed until at least July 10, when landing craft used in the English Channel should be available for transfer to the Mediterranean.

SATURDAY, MARCH 25

GERMAN DEFENCES, *FRANCE*
Despite his recent declarations of the importance of the war in the West, Hitler continues to strip OB West of frontline divisions to bolster the Eastern Front. Today, II SS Panzer

◀ *Churchill (left) and Eisenhower (centre) inspect glider and parachute troops of the US Army, after witnessing a mass paratroop drop.*

Corps, consisting of the 9th and 10th SS Panzer Divisions, are ordered east, towards Hungary. With this transfer, there will be no fully operational armoured divisions in France.

TRAINING, *BEACH ASSAULTS*
The first training exercise for US VII Corps has been completed. Called Exercise Beaver, this simulated attack on "Utah Beach" includes units of the 101st Airborne, though for this exercise they are driven to their objectives, rather than dropped by parachute.

SUNDAY, MARCH 26

AIR CAMPAIGN, *E-BOAT TARGETS*
Over 300 B-26 Marauders of the US Ninth Army Air Force attack the base of an E-boat flotilla at Ijmuiden, on the Dutch coast. These vessels – known by the Germans as S-boats – have a speed of 36 knots and are armed with twin torpedoes. They are a serious threat to the Allied invasion fleet and efforts are underway to clear them from the Channel. The Germans have five flotillas of E-boats, based in Ijmuiden, Ostend, Boulogne and Cherbourg, operating about 30 vessels.

Air raids this far north along the coast are also part of a concerted effort to draw German attention away from Normandy. For every raid west of the River Seine, two are launched to the north of it.

WEDNESDAY, MARCH 29

COMMANDERS, *CRERAR*
The Canadian general Henry Crerar arrives in London from Italy. He is to command the Canadian First Army on its activation in France – planned for around D+90.

▲ *A B-26 Marauder of a US Army Air Force flies over northern France following a bombing mission.*

AIR CAMPAIGN, *PANZER TARGETS*
The ultra-secret radio intelligence base Station X, at Bletchley Park, decrypts the movement order from Berlin to II SS Panzer Corps in France. Bomber Command targets the assembly point of the 10th SS Panzer Division and tonight raids the rail junction at Vaires, outside Paris. Bombs hit munition stores and kill 1200, including the administrative staff and key technical personnel. The division is temporarily crippled.

FRIDAY, MARCH 31

RECONNAISSANCE, *BATTERIES*
The French coast is now under constant aerial reconnaissance by specially converted Mk XI Spitfires and P-51 Mustangs, fitted with horizontal and vertical cameras. Recent photographs reveal a disturbing and dramatic rise in the number of German gun batteries in the Normandy assault area. In eight weeks numbers have risen from 16 to 49. It seems Rommel's arrival in France is having an effect.

▲ *A German Kriegsmarine S-boat arrives in harbour. These fast torpedo boats were a serious threat to invasion preparations, and they became key targets of Allied bombing raids.*

April 1944

Bomber Command stepped up its attacks on French railways and bridges, and all leave was cancelled for Allied soldiers as D-Day loomed nearer. Admiral Dönitz ordered his U-boat captains to take "extreme measures" against any invasion fleet. Allied troops continued to practice amphibious assaults.

LOGISTICS, *MULBERRY*
The Bombardon sea barriers undergo their first, and successful, sea trials, off Weymouth Bay. The floating concrete boxes withstand 2.4m (8ft) seas for 10 hours.

SECURITY, *COAST/FREE FRENCH*
The visitors ban comes into effect. Its terms are strict. No civilians will be allowed into an exclusion zone extending 16km (10 miles) inland from the coast, and residents will only be permitted to travel a few miles from their homes. The zone covers a stretch of coast from the River Humber to Penzance, as well as Milford Haven, Portishead and estuaries of the rivers Forth, Tay and Clyde.

The need to maintain strict security is also having a serious impact on the Allies' relationship with the Free French. SHAEF fears that the ciphers used by de Gaulle's Committee of National Liberation are compromised, and there are concerns about its communist members. From today the Combined Chiefs of Staff order that no information about Neptune/Overlord be passed to the committee. In effect,

▼ *A German Tiger tank of the Totenkopf (Death's Head) Division. The Tiger was one of the most powerful weapons in the German armoury, and was skillfully employed during the fighting in Normandy.*

▶ *The ruins of a German synthetic oil factory, following a bombing raid by RAF and US Eighth Army Air Force aircraft.*

France is to be invaded without its self-appointed provisional government being informed.

SUNDAY, APRIL 2

HOME FRONT, *GREAT BRITAIN*
The Chiefs of Staff obtain Churchill's agreement to reorganize Britain's anti-aircraft defences to protect the invasion fleet. Selected batteries will now be moved from civilian areas to the embarkation ports. It is a risk, as the German air raids on cities continue. In March, civilian casualties from raids over London, northeast England and south Wales were 279 killed and 633 injured.

MONDAY, APRIL 3

DECEPTION, *FORTITUDE NORTH*
From Edinburgh, Colonel MacLeod's Fourth Army deception scheme begins.

▼ *General Somervell (left), CO of US Army Service Forces, confers with Generals Eisenhower (right) and Devers (centre).*

TUESDAY, APRIL 4

► *An immense column of smoke rises above the important rail junction at Busigny, northern France, as an A-20 Havoc passes over the target area.*

It is helped by MI5's double-agents, who leak false information to Berlin that a group of Russian liaison officers have arrived in Scotland to plan the Anglo-Soviet invasion of Norway. The Germans believe the lie. The Norway occupation army will be reinforced to 13 divisions, 1 panzer division and 6000 SS troops, and an air raid will be launched on MacLeod's HQ.

The deception also benefits Overlord. The Scottish estuaries of the Forth, Tay and Clyde are beginning to fill with warships, mostly cruisers and battleships. These will form part of the two bombardment groups tasked with supporting the landings. MacLeod's Norway operation creates a perfect cover story for their presence.

TUESDAY, APRIL 4

AIR CAMPAIGN, *CIVILIAN DEAD*
After the recent successful air raids on French rail targets, the British War Cabinet discusses the full implementation of Zuckerman's Transportation Plan. The plan calls for raids on 72 separate locations: 39 are in western Germany and 33 are in France. Marshalling yards, repair depots and rail junctions are all targeted, and most are in, or near, major towns and cities. This leads to serious debate about the

▼ *Waffen-SS troops at an English Channel observation post train their machine gun on the sea. Note the distinctive SS camouflage smocks.*

civilian casualties the French raids will cause and whether this should influence the choice of targets. Air Chief Marshal Portal, Chief of the Air Staff, estimates as many as 40,000 dead and injured. Churchill also has severe reservations, and even Eisenhower voices concern: "Considering that they are all our friends," he writes, "this might be held to be an act of great severity, bringing much hatred on the Allied air forces." The unhappy fact is that bombing remains one of the Allies' most effective weapons, and for the greater good – the liberation from Nazi domination – the bombing of French targets will continue.

COMMANDERS, *EISENHOWER*
Eisenhower writes to his friend General Brehon Somervell in Washington, describing the current mood at Allied headquarters:

" ... tension grows and everybody gets more on edge. This time, because of the stakes involved, the atmosphere is probably more electric than ever before ... we are not merely risking a tactical defeat; we are putting the whole works on one number. A sense of humour and a great faith, or else a complete lack of imagination, are essential to sanity."

TRAINING, *COMMUNICATIONS*
Exercise Spandu takes place. This is the first of the Allied armies' signal exercises and it tests the radio communications among US First Army, British Second Army, Canadian First Army and the 21st Army Group.

THURSDAY, APRIL 6

GERMAN DEFENCES, *FRANCE*
Hitler confers with OKW Operations Staff. The continued lack of information about the invasion target leads to an outburst from the Führer. He pours scorn on the very idea that an assault will take place and calls the Allied preparations, "a bare-faced piece of play-acting". However, a calmer mood

prevails. Defences, he says, must be concentrated between the River Seine and the Belgian border. However, he is not blind to the other possibilities and orders that Normandy should be reinforced immediately, though not to the detriment of the Pas de Calais. These reinforcements will consist of infantry divisions. The bulk of his armour is still committed in the East.

SECURITY, *LEAVE CANCELLATION*
All service leave is suspended until further notice. This order is issued by the Inter-Services Security Board, the committee responsible for

▲ *As preparations for D-Day continued, the war on the Eastern Front dragged on. Here, German Tigers ford a shallow stream in Russia.*

implementing all security measures at military installations in Britain.

FRIDAY, APRIL 7

AIR CAMPAIGN, *COMMAND*
Eisenhower receives a new directive from the Combined Chiefs of Staff: "The US Strategic Air Force and British Bomber Command will operate under the direction of the Supreme

STRATEGY & TACTICS

D-DAY OBJECTIVES

During Exercise Thunderclap the army and corps commanders explained the objectives that the assault divisions were expected to achieve on D-Day.

On the right flank, behind Utah beach, the 82nd Airborne Division was to secure both banks of the River Douve around the village of St Sauveur-le-Vicomte. The division would be operating up to 16km (10 miles) from the coast. The 101st was to be dropped to the south and west of the 82nd Airborne. It was tasked with the capture of four roads leading inland from Utah over an area of flooded marshland, which would secure the routes for the 4th Infantry Division. To the south, the division was to capture and hold three crossings of the River Douve north of the town of Carentan.

On the left flank, behind Sword Beach, the British 6th Airborne Division was to land in an area east of the River Orne, north of Caen. The division would seize the crossings over the Orne and the Caen Canal and destroy a large German battery near Merville. Further to the east it would attack and destroy the bridges over the River Dives. The division was to secure a series of villages holding the left flank, including Ranville, Le Mesnil, Breville and Le Plein.

From Utah, the 4th Infantry would secure the four beach exits and the road running north to Cherbourg and push west towards Ste Mère-Eglise. From Omaha, the 29th Division was to take the villages of Vierville and St Laurent-sur-Mer and move south towards Formigny and the main road from Carentan to Bayeux. Meanwhile on its right, 1st Division would

secure Colleville-sur-Mer, Le Grand Hameau and advance east towards Port en Bessin, to link up with the British coming from Gold Beach. From Gold, the British 50th Division would move south to Bayeux and west towards Arromanches. From Juno, the Canadian 3rd Division would move east to take Courseulles and Bernières, and south to take the village of La Rivière and the crossings of the rivers Seulles and Mue that carried one of the main roads east from Bayeux towards the Caen Canal. From Sword, the British 3rd Division would take Ouistreham on the Orne estuary and advance south to take Caen at least up to the north bank of the River Odon.

The landings would be supported by commandos and US Army Rangers, tasked to destroy German coastal strongpoints, which infantry and armour would bypass.

At Omaha a Ranger force of two battalions would destroy the German positions west of the landing area and attack a gun battery on the cliffs of the Pointe-du-Hoc. From Gold, 47 Royal Marine (RM) Commando would take Port en Bessin and make contact with the Americans. From Juno, 4th Special Service Brigade would move inland to capture Douvres and make contact with forces from Sword, while 48 (RM) Commando would attack Langrune-sur-Mer. From Sword, 41 (RM) Commando would secure Lion-sur-Mer, while 1st Special Service Brigade would advance south to Bénouville, to reinforce the troops at the Orne river bridges and make contact with 6th Airborne.

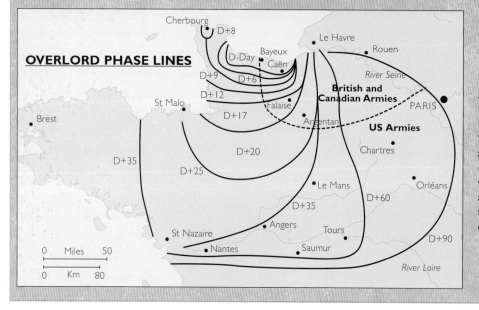

OVERLORD PHASE LINES

◀ *The projected Allied advance from D-Day to D+90, drawn up by the staff at 21st Army Group.*

Commander in conformity with agreements between him and the Chief of the Air Staff [Leigh-Mallory], as approved by the Combined Chiefs of Staff."

This gives the Supreme Commander some control over the strategic bomber force, which he has hitherto lacked.

ORDER OF BATTLE, *US FORCES*
The US 79th Infantry Division sails from Boston.

PLANNING, *OFFICER BRIEFING*
On this Good Friday, at the 21st Army Group HQ, in St Paul's School, west London, Montgomery, Leigh-Mallory and Admiral Ramsay begin the biggest ground-forces briefing undertaken so far. Known as Exercise Thunderclap, it involves officers from all the field

armies, and will, in Montgomery's words, "put all senior officers and their staffs completely into the whole Overlord picture". The exercise will go on for two days.

The day begins with Leigh-Mallory and Ramsay explaining the air and naval plans. Montgomery then takes over. Using a huge, scale model of Normandy he outlines his plan for the battle of the bridgehead. This, he says, will not be a fight for towns, but a battle to secure a lodgement area big enough, and secure enough, to allow the build-up of men

▼ *A British commando landing party comes ashore under intense fire. Each commando unit went on a three-week course to practice landings for D-Day.*

and resources for an armoured thrust into France. Rommel's response, he warns, will be to "hold his mobile divisions back from the coast until he is certain where our main effort is being made. He will then concentrate them quickly and strike a hard blow. His static [infantry] divisions will endeavour to hold on defensively to important ground and act as pivots to the counterattack."

Generals Bradley and Dempsey, the commanders responsible for the assault phase, then introduce themselves and their respective corps commanders. From US First Army Bradley presents General Joseph Lawton Collins, VII Corps, and General Leonard T. Gerow, V Corps. General Dempsey, of British Second Army, presents Lieutenant-General Sir John Crocker, I Corps, and General Gerard Bucknall, XXX Corps.

The divisions chosen to make the D-Day assault are: Utah Beach, US 4th Infantry Division, VIII Corps; Omaha Beach, US 29th Infantry and 1st Infantry Divisions, V Corps; Gold Beach,

British 50th (Northumbrian) Infantry Division, XXX Corps; Juno Beach, Canadian 3rd Infantry Division, I Corps. Sword Beach; British 3rd Infantry Division, I Corps. The flanks of the landing area will be secured by the US 101st and 82nd Airborne on the right and the British 6th Airborne on the left.

SATURDAY, APRIL 8

PLANNING, *WAR GAMES*

The second day of Exercise Thunderclap sees the invasion plan war-gamed: the army, corps and division commanders are thrown a series of worst-case scenarios to work their way out of. After today, detailed planning will be devolved to officers at brigade, regiment and battalion level: units of this size will do the fighting on D-Day. They are small and mobile enough to be landed in a matter of hours, but big enough to take and hold ground – though only

▲ *British troops wade ashore from an LCI (Landing Craft, Infantry) during a training exercise "somewhere in southern England".*

▲ *B-17 Flying Fortresses of the US Eighth Army Air Force continue to pound German positions and installations throughout France in preparation for D-Day.*

with the element of surprise and assuming German Panzers do not counterattack in force.

Also today, SHAEF HQ issues the draft Joint Fire Plan, the schedule for bombardment of the Normandy coast prior to the landings. With timetables and targets for warships, fighter-bombers and medium bombers, it is part of the naval and air force plans.

COMMANDERS, *HEADQUARTERS*
Montgomery's forward, mobile HQ is established, staffed by 20 officers and 200 men to oversee the Normandy battle. It is set up initially in the grounds of Southwick House, Admiral Ramsay's forward HQ near Portsmouth.

The main 21st Army Group HQ will remain at St Paul's School to coordinate reinforcements and liaise with the navy and air force commands.

Sunday, April 9

AIR CAMPAIGN, *RAIL TARGETS*
As part of the Transportation Plan, tonight aircraft of RAF Bomber Command attack rail targets in northern France, hitting Lille, Villeneuve and Laon.

Monday, April 10

OPERATION NEPTUNE, *ORDERS*
Admiral Ramsay's HQ begins to issue the Operation Neptune Naval Orders. The result of nine months' work, they are huge in size and exhaustive in detail. They run to 1100 pages, divided into 22 separate sections, including appendices and annexes. Every aspect

of the cross-Channel operation is covered. Section ON1, Appendix VII Annex B, for example, sets down the assault areas, beach sectors, and includes detailed maps; ON4, describes how the invasion

STRATEGY & TACTICS

OPERATION NEPTUNE

Admiral Ramsay's orders of April 10 organized an invasion fleet of 4126 amphibious landing craft, supported by 1141 warships and over 224 cargo vessels. It was divided into five forces, U, O, G, J and S – one tasked for each beach. Each was made up of up to 16 separate convoys. There would also be two follow-up forces, B and L, carrying the first reinforcements, with three and five convoys respectively

Forces U and O sailed from Dartmouth and Weymouth, and were tasked for the US beach sectors. They were organized into the Western Task Force, commanded by Rear-Admiral Alan G. Kirk, US Navy. The remainder were tasked for the British and Canadian sectors, and organized into the Eastern Task Force, commanded by Rear-Admiral Sir Philip Vian. Force G sailed from Southampton, J from Portsmouth and S from Shoreham. Follow-up Force L would sail from the Thames estuary and Felixstowe, while Force B would sail from Plymouth. These follow-up forces would arrive between the afternoon of D-Day and the morning of D+1.

All forces would converge through four designated routes to Point Z, 13km (8 miles) southeast of the Isle of Wight, from where the fleet would assemble in an area 8km (5 miles) in radius, codenamed Piccadilly Circus. Minesweepers would then sail south to clear five channels, one for each task force, with each channel having two lanes to provide a clear run for slower and faster vessels to the Normandy coast.

The assault landings would be given fire support from 106 warships, including 6 battleships, 23 cruisers and 73 destroyers, organized into two bombardment groups.

▶ *The American battleship USS* Texas, *underway in the Channel. She was tasked with bombarding positions off Omaha Beach.*

fleet will assemble mid-Channel; ON6 covers minesweeping; ON18 details navigation and weather. The orders are to remain sealed until Allied Navy HQ orders them opened.

AIR CAMPAIGN, *GUNS*
Reconnaissance has discovered increased numbers of German gun batteries in the assault area. These are now targeted for air attack. The first raid, by Marauders of the US Ninth Air Force, is on eight batteries housed in concrete casemates near Le Havre. But bomber commanders doubt such small targets can be accurately targeted from high altitude.

AIR CAMPAIGN, *RAIL*
Tonight, bombers return to attack Lille, Villeneuve and Laon. By the end of tonight's raid, the RAF will have dropped over 8000 tonnes (8130 tons) of bombs on these three rail centres.

TUESDAY, APRIL 11

GERMAN DEFENCES, *FRANCE*
Grand Admiral Dönitz sends a message to the U-boat

◀ *British soldiers on a large training exercise. The soldier in the centre is carrying the Bren light machine gun, the others are carrying Lee Enfield bolt-action rifles.*

▶ *British Covenanter tanks advance during training. These tanks were plagued with mechanical problems, and were used for training only, never seeing combat.*

captains of Group Landwirt (Farmer) in France. In terms that resound with desperation he exhorts his men to take extreme measures against the coming Allied invasion, going so far as to suggest suicide attacks. "Every vessel taking part in the landing," he writes, "even if it has but a handful of men or solitary tank aboard, is a target of the utmost importance which must be attacked regardless of cost." He goes on: "Every boat that inflicts losses on the enemy while he is landing has fulfilled its primary function, even though it perishes in so doing."

my view it is the Germans who will suffer very heavy casualties when our band of brothers gets among them."

opinion that the strategic bombers would be better used attacking the German aircraft industry.

WEDNESDAY, APRIL 12

PLANNING, *ALLIED CASUALTIES*
Churchill sends a telegram to President Roosevelt, detailing Montgomery's Exercise Thunderclap briefing. The prime minister is full of optimism: "I do not agree with the loose talk ... on both sides of the Atlantic about the unduly heavy casualties ... we shall sustain. In

THURSDAY, APRIL 13

AIR CAMPAIGN, *RAIL TARGETS*
The Cabinet Defence Committee approves the implementation of the Transportation Plan. Only two of the proposed French rail targets are rejected. For some members of the committee, however, doubts remain. The CIGS, Sir Alan Brooke, voices the

FRIDAY, APRIL 14

PLANNING, *ARMOUR*
Following the conclusions drawn from the Exercise Thunderclap war games, Montgomery completes his tactical instructions to generals Bradley and Dempsey. After the initial landings, he writes, the speed of the attack must be maintained. Armoured units must

STRATEGY & TACTICS

INVASION AIR COVER

All the time during its cross-Channel journey the invasion fleet would be under air cover. Leigh-Mallory's plan called for the deployment of up to 171 squadrons during D-Day alone – including 3700 fighter aircraft. These would also provide cover over the landing beaches, a ground-attack role (supporting the ground troops) and escorts for bombers. All this activity would be coordinated with the help of the Fighter Direction Tenders, which sailed with the fleet. There were three of these communications vessels, one each for the American and British sectors, and another in reserve. Medium bombers, meanwhile, would attack the German coastal defences, providing an initial attack wave before the start of the naval bombardment, which would then continue right up until the time of the landings.

It was essential for the progress of the tactical air campaign for airfields to be established in Normandy as soon as possible after the initial landings. The air plan calls for three emergency landing strips to be set up on D-Day, to be followed by two British and two US "refuelling and rearming" strips by D+4. By D+14 there were planned to be 18 Allied airfields in operation in the lodgement area. To tackle this work, five airfield construction groups of the British Royal Engineers and 18 US aviation construction battalions were earmarked for France.

▶ *A B-26 Marauder provides air support for the invading forces. Medium bombers concentrated on German beach defences.*

concentrate and move quickly inland to establish secure positions ahead of the main body. These will create bases, which any German counterattack will have to deal with first.

AIR CAMPAIGN, *AIR SUPERIORITY*
Eisenhower declares that one of the main prerequisites for the successful launching of Overlord has been fulfilled: the Allies have air superiority over Europe. This is due mostly to the success of Operation Pointblank, the round-the-clock attacks on German targets by strategic bombers. These have all but destroyed the Nazi aircraft industry, crippled the production of synthetic oil, and, since January, have been responsible for the deaths of an estimated 1700 German fighter pilots.

SATURDAY, APRIL 15

ORDER OF BATTLE, *BOMBERS*
The Allies' strategic bomber force comes under Eisenhower's direction. It is not the full control that some wanted; the Combined Chiefs of Staff directive (April 7) is a compromise. The

◀ *A German factory, manufacturing Messerschmitt Bf 109 fighters, comes under attack from bombers of the US Eighth Army Air Force.*

Supreme Commander's control over the bombers is temporary, lasting only "until Overlord is established." This gives Overlord's operational needs precedence during the invasion, but maintains the independent commands of Harris and Spaatz.

Eisenhower appoints his deputy, Sir Arthur Tedder, to coordinate operations by bomber forces and Leigh-Mallory's Allied Expeditionary Air Force.

PLANNING, *AIR OPERATIONS*
Leigh-Mallory issues his Overall Air Plan for Operation Neptune. This fulfils six main functions: to maintain air superiority over the assault area; to provide reconnaissance; to disrupt enemy communications and supplies; to support the amphibious landings and land battle; to attack German naval forces; and to provide airlift for the airborne divisions, to be supplied by IX Troop Carrier Command, US Ninth Air Force, and the RAF's 46 and 38 Groups.

The Allied Expeditionary Air Force will command two separate air forces: the British Second Tactical Air Force, under Air Marshal Sir Arthur Coningham, and the US Ninth Air Force under Lieutenant General Lewis Brereton. These commands will fly light and medium bombers, day and night fighters, fighter-bombers and reconnaissance aircraft.

PLANNING, *COASTAL COMMAND*

As Leigh-Mallory begins finalizing his plans for the Allied Expeditionary Air Force, the RAF's Coastal Command, under Air Chief Marshal Sir William Sholto, is putting the final touches to its own battle plan. Coastal Command's vital task will be to guard the northern and western flanks of the invasion fleet from U-boats, in Sholto's words, "putting the cork in the bottle".

▲ *Sunderland Flying Boats search out German U-boats in the Atlantic. Vital in winning the Battle of the Atlantic, they also guarded the invasion fleet.*

▼ *The American battleship USS Arkansas. She was tasked with providing naval gunfire support for the US forces attacking Omaha Beach.*

To patrol the western approaches to the Channel – an area of 51,800 square kilometres (20,000 square miles) from southern Ireland to Brest – Coastal Command has 29 squadrons of 19 Group, approximately 350 long-range Liberators, Sunderlands and Wellingtons. To the north 16 Group will patrol from Kent, while 15 and 18

Groups will range over the North Sea, flying from Scotland and Iceland. But the greatest responsibility falls to 19 Group over the western approaches, in watching the U-boats known to be in the Bay of Biscay. Its commander, Air Vice Marshal Baker, plans a massive projection of force, Operation Swamp. The whole area will be divided into 12 rectangular patrol areas and continually swept with airborne radar. These sets, known as ASV IIIs, can detect submarines on the surface at a distance of 19km (12 miles).

PLANNING, *OPERATION NEPTUNE*

A crisis looms after the British Admiralty study Admiral Ramsay's plan. To fulfil its need for extra warships to cover a five-beach assault, the Royal Navy will have to adjust its commitments in every theatre of the war. Ships will have to be taken from the Atlantic convoy escorts, the Home Fleet will have to give up many of its destroyers, reinforcements will not be sent to the Far East, and ships will have to be recalled from the Mediterranean. And still there won't be enough vessels for the whole of Operation Neptune.

▲ *A Sunderland Flying Boat attacks a German U-boat with depth charges and machine-gun fire. Shortly after this photograph was taken, the U-boat sank.*

To cover some of the shortfall, Admiral Ernest King, of the US Joint Chiefs of Staff, agrees to reinforce the US Navy warships available for Neptune with three battleships, *Nevada, Texas* and *Arkansas*, as well as another 2 cruisers and 22 destroyers. Most of this extra support is earmarked for the Western Task Force, and specifically Omaha Beach.

In a separate development, Neptune's requirements mean the necessary employment of over half of Britain's coastal vessels, about 610,000 tonnes (600,000 tons) of shipping, for the initial lift on D-Day. As coastal vessels carry the bulk of important goods, such as coal, to British cities, this will mean some unavoidable hardship for the civilian population.

SUNDAY, APRIL 16

ORDER OF BATTLE, *US FORCES*
The lead units of the US 79th Infantry Division arrive in the England. The division will be organized into VII Corps, First Army, and is scheduled to land in Normandy on D+8.

▲ *Troops of the 1st Polish Brigade. Though it did not feature in D-Day, the 1st Polish Armoured Division did see action around Falaise during August 1944.*

LOGISTICS, *LANDING CRAFT*

Despite the "Landing Craft Conference" held in February, and the postponement of Operation Anvil, there are still not enough LSTs (Landing Ships, Tanks) in Great Britain to carry all the necessary vehicles. The problem is fast becoming a crisis, with just seven weeks left until the planned invasion date. Churchill is to send a personal message to the US Chief of Staff, General Marshall, asking for his help and reminding the general what the judgement of history might be if the

problem isn't solved. "How it is", the prime minister writes, "that the plans of two great empires like Britain and the United States should be so much hamstrung and limited by a hundred or two of these particular vessels will never be understood by history ....The absence of these special vessels may limit our whole war effort on our left flank, and I fear we shall be accused unjustly of not doing our best, as we are resolved to do."

MONDAY, APRIL 17

OPERATION NEPTUNE, *MINES*

The Royal Navy begins laying mines off the German-held Channel coast, as part of the preparations for Operation Neptune. Between now and early June over 6800 sea mines will be dropped

off the Channel ports between Ijmuiden in Holland and Brest in France. This is an offensive operation, employing mine-laying warships as well as flotillas of smaller vessels, including motor torpedo boats and motor launches for use inshore. The aim is to keep German surface vessels, particularly E-boats, in their bases.

SECURITY, *COMMUNICATIONS*

Stringent new security measures come into force throughout Great Britain. From today, all foreign diplomats, except those from the United States, Soviet Union and the British Dominions, are forbidden to leave the country. All mail to the Irish Republic will be censored and all telephone conversations monitored.

These moves put particular strain on relations with the French and Polish governments in exile. The Free Poles have forces fighting in Italy and units preparing for Overlord. Their leader,

DECISIVE WEAPONS

THE LANDING SHIP, TANK (LST)

The importance of the LST to the invasion was due to its size and adaptability. This allowed large numbers of tanks and vehicles to be shipped across wide stretches of sea and unloaded without the need for docks and cranes. The LST had first been developed by the British in 1940, when two shallow-draft oil tankers were converted by having their bows cut away and replaced with hinged bow doors and long, folding ramps. The idea was that if the vessel had a shallow enough draft it could be beached, so that vehicles could be driven on and off. American engineers standardized the design in 1942, creating a vessel that could be mass-produced from welded prefabricated steel sections, powered by two locomotive-sized diesel engines. Ingeniously, they also built into the vessels ballast tanks, which could be emptied and filled with sea water, allowing a deep draft for ocean voyages and shallow draft for beaching. Thus was created a vessel that could sail anywhere in the world and deliver armour and troops across any stretch of coast as long as it was flat and large enough. These were two criteria that drew Allied planners to the choice of the Normandy coast in 1943.

The LST was 100m (327ft) long and 165m (540ft) wide, and it could carry up to 40 Sherman tanks, or 26 vehicles and 200 troops, and had a cruising speed of about 9 knots. Its role in the invasion was not limited to shipping the armies. Some LSTs were used as hospital ships, while others were employed to tow elements of the Mulberry harbours.

▲ *Some 235 ocean-going Landing Ship, Tank (LST) vessels were built during World War II. They were capable of landing up to 40 Sherman tanks onto a beachhead.*

General Kazimierz Sosnkowski, wants to visit his men in Italy but is refused permission. Far more serious for the United States and Britain are the worsening relations with de Gaulle's Free French. Since the beginning of the month, his Committee of National Liberation has been denied access to invasion plans. The new movement ban proves the final straw. From his headquarters in Algiers, de Gaulle signals his military delegate in London, General Pierre Koenig, to break off contact with the Allies. Churchill tries to mend diplomatic fences and makes arrangements for his personal plane to fly de Gaulle to England in time for the landings.

TUESDAY, APRIL 18

PLANNING, *INTELLIGENCE*
British Chiefs of Staff meet with the Joint Intelligence Committee in London to discuss the latest assessments of German force levels in western Europe.
SECURITY, *COMMUNICATIONS*
Further steps are taken to prevent any

◄ *As well as new recruits, the 1st Polish Brigade also had veterans serving in the ranks. They brought with them useful experience and were a steadying hand.*

security leaks out of Great Britain, and foreign diplomats are again the targets. In moves denying them their historic privileges, from today all transmission or receipt of coded telegrams is forbidden and diplomatic bags are to be opened and the contents censored. Once again, diplomats from the United States, Soviet Union and British Dominions are excluded. In another measure to ensure that the invasion runs smoothly the British government issues a Defence Regulation laying down severe penalties for anyone found inciting industrial strikes.

Despite all attempts to pull a veil of secrecy over Overlord, a senior US officer compromises security very publicly, in the dining room of a London hotel. Major-General Henry J. Miller, commander of the US Ninth Air Force Service Command, exclaims how difficult it is getting personal goods from the US, but says all will change by 15 June, when the invasion "would have taken place." He is reported

WEDNESDAY, APRIL 19

immediately and Eisenhower's reaction is swift. The next day Miller is stripped of his command, demoted to colonel and flown back to the United States.

WEDNESDAY, APRIL 19

SECURITY, *COMMUNICATIONS*
The diplomatic movement ban is extended to include military personnel of the governments-in-exile in Great Britain. The ban will run until June 19.

SUNDAY, APRIL 23

GERMAN DEFENCES, *FRANCE*
Rommel makes another bid to win control of some of the armoured divisions in the OB West sector. At the moment, 2nd, 21st and 116th Panzer Divisions are under the effective command of General Geyr von Schweppenburg's Panzer Group West,

▶ *A German Air Force Heinkel He-111 medium bomber. Despite overall Allied aerial superiority, these aircraft still posed a threat to Allied plans in 1944.*

while 1st SS Panzer, 12th SS Panzer, Panzer Lehr and the 17th SS Panzergrenadier Divisions form an OKW (German Army High Command) reserve under Hitler's control. Rommel wants his Army Group B HQ to have control of von Schweppenburg's divisions, but von Schweppenburg insists he keep them, arguing that his panzer group forms a

powerful mobile reserve to counter the expected Allied airborne landings in the French interior. Rommel writes to General Jodl, chief of operations for the OKW, explaining his strategy for beating the invasion, stating why he needs a powerful armoured reserve behind the fixed defences along the coast, and why those defences need strengthening:

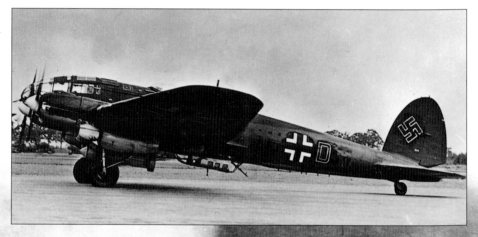

◀ *General Alfred Jodl, Chief of Operations for the German Army High Command. (OKW). Despite his position, by 1944 Hitler was taking all the decisions in OKW.*

MONDAY, APRIL 24

SECURITY, *COMMUNICATIONS*
The Home Office bans all civilian travel overseas. Great Britain is now effectively sealed off from the world.

AIR CAMPAIGN, *FIGHTER-BOMBERS*
Allied fighter-bombers join the campaign against France's road and rail networks. Eight RAF Typhoons of 438 Squadron, carrying two 1000lb bombs apiece, demolish a bridge at St Saveur in northern France. This is the first use of such heavy ordnance on these single-engine aircraft, and the raid's success will lead to similar actions before and after the invasion.

TUESDAY, APRIL 25

GERMAN AIR FORCE, *PORT RAID*
A recent Allied air assessment has estimated that the German Air Force

"If in spite of the enemy's air superiority, we succeed in getting a large part of our mobile force into action in the threatened coast defence sectors in the first few hours, I am convinced that the enemy attack on the coast will collapse completely on its first day. Very little damage has so far been done by the heavy enemy bombing to our reinforced concrete installations, although our field positions, dugouts and communication trenches have in many places been completely obliterated. This shows how important it is to get concrete over all our positions, even those, such as artillery, anti-aircraft and reserve positions, which are located behind the front."

◀ *A French railway marshalling yard is attacked by Allied bombers. The pressure to deny German forces freedom to move was incessant before D-Day.*

WEDNESDAY, APRIL 26

still has at least 450 bombers in the West capable of attacking Great Britain. Tonight, some of them show their effectiveness, when about 40 aircraft raid Portsmouth, stepping up German efforts to disrupt invasion preparations. The recent decision by the British Chiefs of Staff to concentrate anti-aircraft defences on embarkation ports is proved to have come at just the right time.

WEDNESDAY, APRIL 26

OPERATION NEPTUNE, *REHEARSAL*
A full-scale rehearsal of Operation Neptune begins, known as Exercise Tiger. It involves Force U, commanded by Rear-Admiral Don P. Moon, US Navy. During the day the US 4th Infantry Division, VII Corps, under Major-General Raymond O. Barton, embarks from ports on the south Devon coast. Force U then sails into Lyme Bay proceeded by minesweepers.
GERMAN AIR FORCE, *PORT RAID*
Tonight there is another German air raid on Portsmouth. At least 80 bombers make the attack and sortie farther north towards Basingstoke.

▼ *German submariners are rescued by a British warship following an Allied attack on their U-boat.*

THURSDAY, APRIL 27

OPERATION NEPTUNE, *REHEARSAL*
By this second day of Exercise Tiger, Admiral Moon's Force U has doubled back towards the Devon coast during the night and, by morning, has anchored in Start Bay, off Slapton Sands. Watching proceedings are Admiral Ramsay and General Montgomery. After an initial naval bombardment, the 4th Infantry Division attempts to land. Ramsay is unimpressed. He describes the exercise privately as a "flop". Communications break down between the navy and the assault units, with the result that only two infantry companies get ashore in the first wave. However, the exercise continues and throughout the day the 4th Infantry is landed. A follow-up

▲ *A Royal Navy Abdiel class cruiser, possibly HMS Abdiel. The Abdiel class consisted of six vessels, each armed with six 4in guns, and capable of laying mines.*

convoy of nine LSTs are expected off Slapton Sands early Friday morning.

FRIDAY, APRIL 28

OPERATION NEPTUNE, *REHEARSAL*
Disaster strikes Exercise Tiger. At about 01:30 hours nine torpedo-armed E-boats, out of Cherbourg, attack the follow-up convoy of eight Landing Ships, Tank (LSTs) in Lyme Bay. The German boats have avoided a patrol of Royal Navy destroyers and motor torpedo boats, and only one small warship, the British Corvette *HMS Azalea*, is in close escort. The E-boats attack the rear of the convoy and the

▲ *British motor torpedo boats on patrol in the English Channel. Leading up to D-Day, these small craft were vital in protecting the fleet.*

first LST to be torpedoed is 507, which withstands the explosion but catches fire. Soldiers and sailors abandon ship only to find themselves in a burning sea, as fuel oil ignites. The chaos is made far worse because the men have not been told how to use life belts.

Then LST 531 is hit amidships by two torpedoes, and in 10 minutes has capsized and is sinking. There is now panic and wild firing from the remaining transports in the convoy. At about 02:30 hours the E-boats strike again, and LST 289 has her stern blown off. The crew contain the fire and she remains afloat and under power. The five remaining landing ships exchange fire with the E-boats, which disengage at 03:30 hours, at about the same time as the Royal Navy destroyer *HMS Saladin* arrives. A search for survivors does not begin in earnest until 05:30 hours, by which time some men have been in the freezing Channel waters for over two hours, causing even more deaths.

▶ *One of the lucky ones. A Royal Navy sailor is about to be hauled aboard a rescue vessel following an attack by German E-boats on his convoy.*

SATURDAY, APRIL 29

This attack has dealt a serious blow to invasion preparations. Nearly 200 sailors and 500 soldiers are dead. Most of the soldiers are from one unit, the 1st Engineer Special Brigade, and they are specialists in the job of building and maintaining the invasion beachhead. They are men that the Allies can ill-afford to lose. Two of the LSTs have been sunk and one seriously damaged. This loss wipes out the operational reserve of LSTs for Operation Overlord, and will mean that three replacement landing ships will have to be ordered to sail from the Mediterranean immediately.

COMMANDERS, *MONTGOMERY*

The advanced headquarters of Montgomery's 21st Army Group assembles in the grounds of the Southwick House, north of Portsmouth. This will be the home of Montgomery's personal staff until about D+1, when the headquarters is due to pack up and sail to Normandy. The general himself will have temporary quarters in nearby Broomfield House.

GERMAN DEFENCES, *FRANCE*

Field Marshal Rommel calls a meeting at his headquarters, based at the castle of La Roche-Guyon, on the Seine, west of Paris. It is an attempt to settle the argument between him and General

▲ *A German Air Force Junkers Ju-88. This aircraft was the backbone of the German air fleet, with over 15,000 produced from 1939 to 1945.*

von Schweppenburg about control of the panzer divisions that are currently in von Schweppenburg's Panzer Group West. No compromise is reached, however, and the problem of who exactly commands the panzer divisions in northern France is referred up, to OB West, for Field Marshal von Rundstedt to resolve.

▼ *Pilots of the 351st Fighter Squadron gather their equipment onto jeeps, ready to board their aircraft.*

SATURDAY, APRIL 29

SECURITY, *SAFEGUARDING PLANS*
The German E-boat attack on the LST convoy yesterday has created another serious problem for the invasion, and this time it has come from an unexpected quarter. Checking through the lists of the missing it is discovered that on board the two destroyed LSTs, 507 and 531, were 10 officers with the

KEY PERSONALITIES

FIELD MARSHAL ERWIN ROMMEL

Erwin Rommel (1891–1944) was a decorated World War I officer who slipped into relative obscurity until Hitler rose to power. During the 1940 invasion of France, his speedy advance into France and to the English Channel earned him a reputation as a daring tank commander.

As commander of the Afrika Korps from 1941, Rommel became a master of desert warfare tactics. The "Desert Fox" was promoted to field marshal, having led the Afrika Korps to a string of victories.

He left North Africa in 1943, tasked with establishing the anti-invasion plans, and he commanded Army Group B after the Allied landings in June 1944. Rommel was badly wounded during an air attack and returned to Germany. Implicated in the failed July 1944 assassination attempt on Adolf Hitler, Rommel took poison to avoid a trial and his family being harmed.

high-level BIGOT security clearance. These men had knowledge of Overlord's plans and some of its most closely guarded secrets. The fear is that one or more of them has been rescued from the sea by an E-boat and captured. A search now begins to check the hundreds of dead and to confirm the fate of the officers.

GERMAN AIR FORCE, *PORT RAID*
Plymouth suffers an air raid tonight. This is another in a series of attacks the German Air Force is making on the embarkation ports. Despite the inflicting of damage, the invasion

preparations continue. The momentum on the Allied side is now too powerful to be stopped by enemy raids and piecemeal interventions.

PLANNING, *AIRBORNE TROOPS*
Leigh-Mallory and SHAEF's air staff raise doubts with Eisenhower about the viability of the American airborne plan for the Cotentin Peninsula. There are now enough transport aircraft and crews to drop two divisions as planned, but Leigh-Mallory now insists that the glider-borne troops be dropped at dusk on D-Day, and not during the morning as part of the main

airborne assault. The American glider-borne force consists of two reinforced infantry regiments, plus four battalions of field artillery, with headquarters and support units. Leigh-Mallory fears that flying these units in during daylight would lead to catastrophic losses from anti-aircraft fire. This latest proposed change in plan would mean that the paratroopers making the initial

▼ *RAF ground crew work on a "Horsa" transport glider. First deployed during the 1943 invasion of Sicily, the Horsa was to be crucial in the early stages of D-Day.*

SATURDAY, APRIL 29

▶ *A Royal Navy Fighter Direction Tender, FDT 13. Early examples of command and control radar ships, they were responsible for early warning and communications.*

landings would be fighting without artillery support or reinforcements for the best part of a day.

OPERATION NEPTUNE, *SEA MINES*
German surface vessels operating off the French coast are becoming increasingly aggressive as they attempt to stop the Allied navies from laying mines close inshore. This morning, off the coast of Brittany, the *Athabaskan* and the *Haida,* of the Royal Canadian Navy, engage two German torpedo boats about to close in to attack a flotilla of mine-layers. One torpedo boat is driven ashore and destroyed, but the *Athabaskan* is hit by gunfire in the stern, and it explodes and sinks.

COMMANDERS, *HEADQUARTERS*
Admiral Ramsay, the Allied naval commander, moves his headquarters and staff out of Norfolk House in central London and relocates to Southwick House, north of Portsmouth, completing a move that has been in progress since the end of February.

Ramsay has timed his arrival to coincide with the beginning of Exercise Fabius, the final training exercises for the task forces O, J, G and S, which are starting next week. Elsewhere in the grounds of Southwick

▼ *Winston Churchill (centre), with Field Marshal Sir Alan Brooke to his right, observes a training exercise in southern England.*

House, SHAEF begins to establish a forward HQ in a number of trailers in the surrounding woodland. General Eisenhower, the Supreme Commander, is due to relocate here from London's Bushy Park in the days prior to D-Day. Southwick House, a former stately home, was the Royal Navy School of Navigation and is being used as the operational base for the invasion because it is only about 1.5km (1

▲ *Destruction of the French rail network, while controversial, was seen by Allied military commanders as essential to the success of the invasion plans.*

mile) away from the Royal Navy's Portsmouth HQ at Fort Southwick, the most important Home Command headquarters involved in Neptune. This well-established HQ, with its extensive communications facilities, has also been the base of Combined Operations, which has been organizing cross-Channel raids since 1942.

AIR CAMPAIGN, *RAIL TARGETS*
Winston Churchill persuades General Eisenhower to reduce the number of rail targets in France intended for destruction under the Transportation Plan. Although air raids on the rail network have been going on since Eisenhower gave his approval to the

plan on February 9, Churchill is still concerned about French civilian casualties and the political problems these will cause. He is particularly worried now, since relations with General de Gaulle's Liberation Committee have all but collapsed, while in occupied France the leader of the collaborationist Vichy regime, Marshal Pétain, made a broadcast only yesterday warning of civil war after an Allied invasion. Eisenhower is as aware of these developments as Churchilll and orders the removal of 27 target locations from the current list of 80.

▶ *Field Marshal Henri-Philippe Pétain, leader of Vichy France. A World War I hero, Pétain fled after D-Day, only to return and be tried as a traitor.*

May 1944

The Allies staged a final invasion rehearsal at Slapton Sands, Devon, England and the Overlord plan received final VIP approval. Rommel substantially reinforced the coastal defences in France as invasion targets were bombed continually. In Great Britain tension rose as D-Day got closer and troops made their way to the embarkation areas. And a *Daily Telegraph* crossword gave security chiefs the chills.

MONDAY, MAY 1

PLANNING, *INVASION TIMING*
At SHAEF's current HQ, the former air force base in Bushy Park, London, a meeting begins between the Supreme Commander, Tedder, Montgomery, Leigh-Mallory and Ramsay to decide on the final timing of H-Hour, the code-name for the landing times of the first assault wave on D-Day.

Recent photo-reconnaissance has shown an enormous increase in beach obstacles constructed by the Germans along the low water line of the landing beaches. To allow enough time for these to be destroyed on a rising tide, which will also be needed to bring the assault units ashore, and to have enough dawn light to allow the pre-invasion bombard-ment to begin, is a tricky

◄ *Aided by British SOE and US OSS agents, French Resistance fighters plan to make sabotage attacks during the invasion.*

KEY WEAPONS

BEACH OBSTACLES

Leading up to the Allied invasion of northern France, considerable effort was made by the Germans to prepare effective defences against an amphibious assault along potential landing areas. In addition to the Atlantic Wall fortifications, Rommel ordered the construction of all manner of beach obstacles to prevent and hinder landing Allied attempts. These included iron girder constructions designed to rip the bottoms off landing craft, wooden stakes, cross-shaped obstacles known as "Czech hedgehogs", as well as other devious designs. Many of these obstacles were made more deadly with the addition of mines and explosives. The obstacles were quite successful, causing significant casualties and gave Allied commanders another problem to solve.

▲ *Resistance fighters, or Maquis, from the Haute-Loire region of France, are given a lesson in stripping a Sten gun.*

calculation. It will also have take into account the need for sufficient moonlight the previous night to help the airborne assault. These considerations will, by necessity, result in a change in the invasion date, currently May 31. The chance of catching a period of full moon this month has now been missed, so the date will have to move back to June.

INTELLIGENCE, *U-BOATS*

An assessment of U-boat numbers in the Channel by the Royal Navy's Operational Intelligence Centre in Whitehall makes for sombre reading. Analysts estimate that as many as 44 Type VIII boats are currently stationed within reach of the Channel and that

▶ *The Free French fighters were to play a crucial role in attacking railway lines and German supply routes.*

they will all sail "on or before D-Day or at least D+1". This estimate is far lower than that of early February, which put the numbers at about 175; but it is still a warning against complacency.

DECEPTION, *ACTION IN EUROPE*

To draw the enemy's attention away from the final invasion preparations, SHAEF's deception directorate, the Committee of Special Means, issues the

◄ A Junkers Ju-88, fitted with radar for night-fighting capabilities. This variant was the German equivalent of the Mosquito.

▲ *An RAF Mosquito fighter-bomber pulls up after a rocket attack on a German cargo ship below.*

▲ *The Avro Lancaster heavy bomber. Lancaster squadrons carried out 156,308 operational sorties during the war.*

radio message "Word is Vendettta" to agents and resistance groups throughout occupied Europe. This sparks off a wave of sabotage, assassination and deception operations from Norway to the Balkans.

SABOTAGE, *FRANCE*

The sabotage operations in France run by the British Special Operations Executive (SOE) and US Office of Strategic Services (OSS) today come under the formal direction of SHAEF, with the incorporation of a new Special Forces Headquarters into Eisenhower's command. SOE and OSS will now tailor their French operations to assist Overlord. Prior to D-Day, sabotage will be directed at rail and canal networks and factories producing German war *matériel*. Where possible, blackmail will be used to persuade factory owners to sabotage their own plants. Also targeted will be power supplies, electricity generating plants and petrol and oil depots. After the invasion, priority will be given to obstructing the movement of German reinforcements towards the bridgehead and coordinating the activities of French guerrilla units (and assisting them with technical advice and arms).

Special Forces HQ will also organize and coordinate operations behind the lines undertaken by the SAS Brigade, the Operational Groups of the OSS, and the Jedburgh Teams. The "Jedburgh" organization consists of 90 three-man teams, hand-picked from British, US and French personnel. From D-1 they will be dropped into France to locate, arm and coordinate attacks by Resistance groups and bands of the Maquis.

TUESDAY, MAY 2

PLANNING, *INVASION TIMING*

At Bushy Park, the Supreme Commander's conference to decide H-Hour concludes. It is agreed that H-Hour for all beaches will be made on a rising tide three hours before high water and between 12 minutes before and 90 minutes after sunrise – which will be at 05:58 hours, British double Summer Time. As the tide moves from west to east this will mean a different H-Hour for each beach, beginning at Utah, at 06:30 hours, and ending at Sword, at 07:55 hours. The choice of day would depend on the moon. Planning staff scour the lunar almanacs and come up with two sets of dates next month when the maximum amount of moonlight is available: June 5–7 and 18–20. Some provision will have to be made for a possible postponement for bad weather, but General Eisenhower's decision, as of today, is to make D-Day June 5, the earliest possible date. Admiral Ramsay is to advise him whether this date fits in with his own movement schedules for Operation Neptune.

TRAINING, *FULL-SCALE ASSAULT*

Exercise Fabius gets under way, with Admiral Ramsay in operational control, in liaison with 21st Army Group. It is by far the biggest invasion rehearsal to be undertaken and is designed to cover all aspects of Operation Neptune and the beach landings short of actually crossing the Channel. Orders state that the exercise should resemble the invasion landings "as closely as limitations of equipment and facilities will permit". About 25,000 troops are involved.

Fabius is scheduled to continue for the next seven days and will test four of the five assault forces, O, G, J, and S. Force U is not included as it completed Exercise Tiger last week. The exercise is divided into six parts:

Fabius I: Force O, under Rear-Admiral John L. Hall, US Navy. Embarking the assault units of the US 1st Infantry Division (commanded by Major-General Clarence Huebner) and the 29th Infantry Division (commanded by Major General Charles H. Gerhardt), and the Provisional Engineer Special

WEDNESDAY, MAY 3

Brigade Group from Portland and Weymouth, Dorset, and landing them at Slapton Sands, Devon.

Fabius II: Force G, under Commodore Douglas-Pennant, RN. Embarking assault units of the British 50th (Northumbrian) Division (commanded by Major-General D.A.H. Graham) from Southampton and

▼ *French civilians survey the damage done to a housing block. There was genuine concern among British politicians about French civilian casualties.*

Lymington, and landing them on Hayling Island, Hampshire.

Fabius III: Force J, under Commodore Geoffrey Oliver, RN, embarking assault units of the Canadian 3rd Division (commanded by Major-General R.F.L. Keller) from Southampton and Gosport and landing them at Bracklesham Bay.

Fabius IV: Force S, under Rear-Admiral Arthur G. Talbot, RN. Embarking assault units of British 3rd Division (commanded by Lieutenant-General J.T. Crocker) from Portsmouth and landing them at Littlehampton.

Fabius V: Marshalling exercise around the Thames estuary and east

coast ports for follow-up Force L, destined for the British/Canadian beaches. Units will be assembled but not embarked.

Fabius VI: Marshalling exercise around Portland, Weymouth and Southampton for follow-up Force B, scheduled to reinforce the American beaches. Included will be troops and vehicles of the 2nd Armored Division, the first US armoured scheduled to enter France.

SECURITY, *CODENAMES*

In today's *Daily Telegraph*, one of the most widely read newspapers in Great Britain, there is an interesting clue in crossword 5775. Clue 17 Across, with four letters, is: "One of the US". The answer is Utah – surely a coincidence, but to those in the know any public reference to an Overlord codeword might mean a possible security leak.

WEDNESDAY, MAY 3

AIR CAMPAIGN, *MILITARY TARGETS*

RAF Bomber Command increases its raids on German military targets in France. Tonight 346 Lancasters attack a German tank depot at Mailly-le-Camp, east of Paris. Over 1900 tonnes (1930 tons) of bombs are dropped. They destroy barrack blocks and vehicle maintenance buildings. However, German night fighters respond aggressively and shoot down 42 aircraft. Farther south, eight Mosquito light bombers raid an ammunition depot at Chateaudun, northwest of

▶ *General Johannes von Blaskowitz, seen here in Paris, 1944. He was commander of German Army Group G.*

Orléans. The bombs cause secondary detonations, and up to 90 buildings are destroyed.

THURSDAY, MAY 4

SECURITY, *COMMUNICATIONS*

The communications ban imposed on diplomats in Great Britain last month is eased slightly, after it is realized that it was too severe and imposed too early. From now on, diplomatic messages can be transmitted overseas, but British authorities must be given plain language copies to review first, as well as copies of the ciphers in which the messages are to be sent.

Neutral and allied diplomatic missions accept these restrictions with continued understanding, except the Free French, who still regard them as gross impositions, bordering on insult.

GERMAN DEFENCES, *FRANCE*

In a deployment aimed at countering a possible airborne attack by the Allies into Brittany, the German 5th Parachute Division moves into the area of Rennes.

It joins the 3rd Parachute Division as part of the II Parachute Corps.

There is also a reorganization at army level. Field Marshal von Rundstedt at OB West orders the formation of a new army group HQ. This will be known as Army Group G and will take command of the First Army guarding the Biscay coast, headquartered in Bordeaux, and the Nineteenth Army on the Mediterranean coast, headquartered

▼ *Three of Germany's highest-ranking officers in the West. From left to right, von Blaskowitz, Rommel and von Rundstedt.*

in Avignon. The new army group will be commanded by General Johannes von Blaskowitz and will be based in Toulouse. von Blaskowitz is also given command of three Panzer divisions, the 9th, 11th and 2nd SS Panzer.

SATURDAY, MAY 6

GERMAN DEFENCES, *FRANCE*
Following a conference on the situation in the West, Hitler's attention is suddenly drawn to Normandy, and this results in an unexpected phone call to OB West in Paris from General Alfred Jodl, the chief of operations of OKW in Berlin. Jodl tells von Rundstedt's chief of staff, General Blumentritt, that "the Führer attaches particular importance to Normandy and the defence of Normandy". Orders are issued immediately for more fortifications to be built along the Calvados coast. Also, OKW orders Panzer Lehr back to France from Hungary, while 21st Panzer Division is moved from Brittany to Caen. The transfer of these armoured divisions, together with the reinforcement of II Parachute Corps in Brittany, could not have come at a worst time for the Allies. The only comfort is that Hitler still

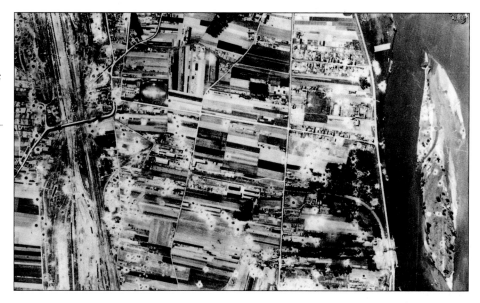

▲ *The railway marshalling yards at Tours, France. The terrain is pock-marked with hundreds of craters from many bombs.*

seems to believe that the invasion will come through the Pas de Calais, since no German units have been transferred from east of the River Seine.

SUNDAY MAY 7

AIR CAMPAIGN, *BRIDGE TARGETS*
So far the Allied bombing campaign has not targeted bridges over the Seine, because the road and rail routes across them lead into Normandy. Despite the danger of bringing Normandy to the Germans' attention, today bombers of the US Ninth Air Force prove bridge attacks are practical by destroying four of them in a single trial raid. Allied signals intelligence then picks up a report from Luftflotte (Air Fleet) 3, which concludes that the raids point to an Allied attack somewhere between the ports of Le Havre and Cherbourg. For the Allies, this is too near the truth; attacks are halted until at least D-15.

◄ *A German train-mounted radar station. These pieces of equipment were difficult to find and even harder to hit.*

As Allied bombing of French targets intensifies, concern grows among some senior British politicians about the civilian casualties. Although these are fewer than first estimated in February, nevertheless there is a growing opinion that the raids are damaging the Allied war effort and undermining its moral authority. Churchill is forced to write to Roosevelt to seek reassurance that the Allies are following the correct policy: "I ought to let you know that the War Cabinet is unanimous in its anxiety about these French slaughters, even reduced as they have been, and also in its doubts as to whether almost as good military results could not be produced by other methods."

MONDAY, MAY 8

GERMAN DEFENCES, *FRANCE*
Field Marshal von Rundstedt calls a tri-service meeting in Paris with the six

▲ A US fighter strafes a stricken aircraft on the runway at a German airfield near Chartres, France.

senior officers commanding in the West. Present are General Blaskowitz (Army Group G), Field Marshal Rommel (Army Group B), General Geyr von Schweppenburg (Panzer Group West), Field Marshal Hugo Speerle (Air Fleet 3), and Admiral Theodore Kranke (Navy Group West). It is called partly to settle the Rommel/von Schweppenburg dispute over command of the armoured reserve and also to make a show of activity after Hitler's call on Saturday for greater effort in the West. At the end of it, Rommel still has not won control of the panzer reserve and must content himself with the infantry

divisions on the coast and construction of the fixed defences.

TRAINING, *FULL-SCALE ASSAULT*

Exercise Fabius comes to an end. For the assault divisions this has been the last full-scale rehearsal before D-Day. For Admiral Ramsay, it has been the final opportunity to check whether the mass of loading schedules and navigation instructions for Operation Neptune actually work in practice. Ramsay and his staff return to Southwick House to check through the after-exercise reports, but already the Allied naval commander is confident enough in his men and the plan to signal the Supreme Commander that June 5 is "go" for D-Day.

TUESDAY, MAY 9

PLANNING, *NEPTUNE FINALIZED*

Admiral Ramsay informs Eisenhower that as of 09:00 hours, May 12, Neptune will be frozen and all planning will stop. Following the assessments of Exercise Fabius, no other revisions or last-minute alterations will be made.

AIR CAMPAIGN, *AIRFIELDS*

The US Eighth Army Air Force fighter-bombers begin attacks on German air-fields, hitting targets in Laon, Orleans, Florennes, Bourges and Thionville.

GERMAN DEFENCES, *FRANCE*

Rommel begins a tour of inspection of army units and fixed defences

▼ RAF Typhoons, freshly painted with the distinctive D-Day black-and-white stripes, line up on a landing strip. These particular aircraft are equipped with rockets.

along the Normandy coast. He has become increasingly concerned that this stretch of coast is too thinly defended, particularly as he still has no direct call on the panzer reserve.

WEDNESDAY, MAY 10

FRENCH RESISTANCE, *SABOTAGE*

Proof of the growing confidence of the Resistance comes from an intelligence assessment made to OB West, the German theatre command in Paris: "military formations alone reported the loss and sabotage of 129 locomotives from March 1–10." Everywhere in the north of France Allied activity is on the increase, but there is still no evidence of where or when invasion will come.

▶ *Admiral Ramsay (centre), commander of the Allied Naval Expeditionary Force, inspects sailors on parade.*

AIR CAMPAIGN, *RADAR TARGETS*

Air raids begin to destroy the German radar chain along the north coast of France. The Allies estimate that there are about 66 enemy radar stations between Brest, in Brittany, and Dunkirk. Some of these are already being jammed by the electronic techniques of Bomber Command's Radio Counter Measures units; but the decision has been made to destroy some sites and wreck the German radar network permanently. The attacks will blind the Germans, disrupt their fighter control and knock out the targeting systems of the biggest coastal-defence batteries.

THURSDAY, MAY 11

AIR CAMPAIGN, *AIRFIELD TARGETS*

The German Air Force in France comes under increased Allied air attack. The objective of these raids is to deny the German Air Force use of airfields and aircraft maintenance facilities within a distance of 240km (150 miles) of the Normandy beachhead, and maintain those attacks so that the enemy is forced to rebuild bases away from the assault area. Targeted for destruction are approximately 40 German fighter airfields and 59 bomber bases.

President Roosevelt replies to Churchill's message of May 7, about Allied air raids on France, and ends any further moral debate: "I share fully with you your distress at the loss of life among the French population .... However regrettable the attendant loss is, I am not prepared to impose from this distance any restriction on military action by the responsible commanders that in their opinion might militate against the success of Overlord or cause additional loss of life to our Allied forces of invasion." Attacks will continue until the commanders of Overlord decide otherwise.

TRAINING, *AIRBORNE ASSAULT*
The US 82nd and 101st Airborne Divisions take part in Exercise Eagle, which is held around the 101st's base at Newbury, Berkshire. The US 28th Infantry Division assumes the enemy role. Paratroopers from both divisions make a night drop, while glider-borne units fly in tomorrow. Airlift for the two divisions is supplied by US IX Troop Carrier Command.

FRIDAY, MAY 12

PLANNING, *NEPTUNE CONCLUDED*
As of 09:00 hours all work on the plans for Operation Neptune stop. There will no further alterations or revisions.

ORDER OF BATTLE, *US FORCES*
The US 35th Infantry Division departs from New York harbour for England. It is earmarked for Patton's Third Army.

MONDAY, MAY 15

AIR CAMPAIGN, *RADAR TARGETS*
Allied air operations against the enemy radar chain are given formal direction from today, as Radio Counter Measures Advisory staff from Bomber Command joins SHAEF, under the direction of an air vice marshal. Their role will be to allocate targets and assess progress.

PLANNING, *FREE FRENCH*
With the invasion imminent, de Gaulle's National Committee positions

▼ *The planned Allied assault routes for D-Day. Before the assault, the sea-going elements would meet up in the Channel.*

itself for a political takeover of France after the liberation. The National Committee renames itself the Provisional Government of the French Republic. As evidence of legitimacy, its Minister of the Interior has proclaimed that its Resistance movement, known as the French Forces of the Interior, now numbers 175,000 fighters. This overwhelming confidence in de Gaulle's ability to take power is not shared by the British and American

▲ *Before the assault, all personal weapons had to be waterproofed and prepared, as with the PIAT shown above.*

governments, which have still not shared any information about Overlord with the Free French leader.

PLANNING, *FINAL STAGES*
As the plans for Operation Neptune are now complete, General Montgomery makes his final presentation of the Overlord battle plan at St Paul's School,

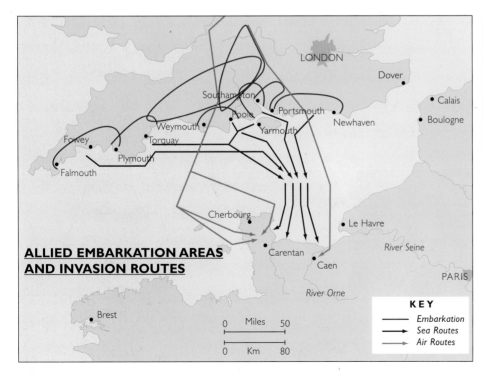

ALLIED EMBARKATION AREAS AND INVASION ROUTES

LONDON

Dover

Southampton

Calais

Poole Portsmouth

Boulogne

Weymouth Yarmouth Newhaven

Fowey Torquay

Plymouth

Falmouth

Cherbourg

Le Havre

River Seine

Carentan

Caen PARIS

River Orne

Brest

KEY
—— Embarkation
→ Sea Routes
→ Air Routes

0 Miles 50

0 Km 80

THE FINAL OVERLORD BRIEFING, LONDON, MAY 15

In notes on Montgomery's final presentation made later by Allied air chief Leigh-Mallory, he recalled how Eisenhower concluded the meeting. The Supreme Commander stood up in front of the collected Anglo-American high command, and, despite the enormous gravity of the occasion, began with a joke: "A few minutes from now, Hitler will have missed his last chance to wipe out the entire leadership of this operation with a single, well-placed bomb." Levity aside, he continued, "I want everyone here to see himself as being part of a staff college of the future ... in which there is neither Army or Navy or Air Force; not British or American; but a college consisting of nothing but fighting men who are there to learn, and to teach others, the art of future wars."

the 21st Army Group HQ. Listening to his briefing, which describes in detail the opening 90 days of the liberation, is one of the largest collections of senior Allied figures ever assembled. From the Supreme Commander down, there are generals, air marshals and admirals, as well as the British Chiefs of Staff, the War Cabinet, Prime Minister Winston Churchill, and King George VI.

As the meeting breaks up, Churchill asks Admiral Ramsay privately to come up with a plan for him to sail with the assault force on D-Day, so that he can witness the opening bombardment and land briefly on one of the beaches. The admiral has to accede to the prime minister's wish, but reports the conversation to Eisenhower, who objects strongly to Churchill's idea.

WEDNESDAY, MAY 17

PLANNING, *INVASION TIMING*

General Eisenhower confirms in a signal to senior officers that D-Day will be June 5, and that Y-Day, the date on which all preparations must be complete, will be June 1. His decision comes after Montgomery's final briefing on Monday, and after studying the latest photo-reconnaissance of the landing area.

▼ *A Mosquito fighter-bomber, just before take-off on a dangerous night mission over enemy-occupied Norway.*

THURSDAY, MAY 18

EMBARKATION, *ASSEMBLY*

All preliminaries are now over. SHAEF and 21st Army Group issues an order to all assault and follow-up units to leave their training grounds and travel south to assemble at their marshalling areas ready for embarkation. This begins the simultaneous movement of over 175,000 personnel and thousands of vehicles.

The marshalling areas lie up to 16km (10 miles) inland from the embarkation ports, and are mostly located along paved secondary roads near woodland. The roads provide secure parking areas for the vehicles, while the woodland

◄ *A Lancaster bomber is "bombed-up" by its ground crew. It could carry up to 28 of the 500lb bombs shown, but would usually carry a mixture of different bombs.*

provides camouflage for the tented camps of the troops. The areas, known to the troops as "sausages" after their appearance on maps, have been rigorously planned, with entry and exit routes marked and supply dumps located. Once the troops are inside them, the camps are sealed and patrolled by military police.

For the troops, the marshalling areas are the final stops before the invasion. Now the work begins to prepare vehicles and men for the Channel crossing. From rifles to tanks, everything must be waterproofed. Radio equipment is sealed into rubber bags, drivers layer grease over every working part of their vehicles, and artillerymen protect gun breeches with rubber sheeting. Once all this work is done and their equipment prepared, the soldiers can only wait for the order to move to their ships and embark.

SUNDAY, MAY 21

AIR CAMPAIGN, *RAIL TARGETS*

The decision is made to extend attacks on the French rail network and make moving trains legitimate targets. Until now these have been forbidden, because the trains may be civilian ones. But this policy has changed. By now

the bomb damage to the French rail system has been so extensive that the only movement on the network is expected to be German military. RAF 2nd Tactical Air Force and US Eighth and Ninth Army Air Forces all send sorties out today with orders to destroy locomotives and rolling stock. Thunder-bolts, Typhoons, Spitfires, Tempests and Marauders fly as far as Germany. By the end of the day Eighth Army Air Force alone claims 91 locomotives destroyed out of 225 attacked.

▶ *Row upon row of 40mm Bofors light anti-aircraft guns await transportation to the front. In the wake of the landings, these guns would be deployed in the field.*

MONDAY, MAY 22

SECURITY, *CODENAMES*

In today's *Daily Telegraph*, another invasion codeword appears in a crossword clue: 3 Down, with five letters, is: "Red Indian on the Missouri". The answer is Omaha. Two codewords appearing within three weeks in the same series of crosswords is, for some, surely stretching coincidence.

EYEWITNESS

A MASS OF SHIPPING

This extract is from a report by the Royal Navy Commander-in-Chief, Portsmouth:

"It is a commonplace expression to say that an anchorage is 'full of ships', but in the case of the East and West Solent, with an available area of approximately 22 square miles in which to anchor ships, it was literally true. On 18 May, the Admiralty offered the C-in-C Portsmouth the services of HMS *Tyne*, but it was only possible to accept her because HMS *Warspite* was not being sent to Portsmouth till D-Day, which gave us one berth in hand."

TUESDAY, MAY 23

INTELLIGENCE, *MINEFIELDS*

Station X at Bletchley Park decrypts a German naval signal revealing the start of new minelaying in the assault area of the Bay of Seine. Aircraft and Royal Navy motor torpedo boats are then dispatched to intercept the minelayers, effectively stopping any extension of enemy minefields into the Channel.

WEDNESDAY, MAY 24

EMBARKATION, *ASSEMBLY*

All units taking part in the D-Day assault are now in their assembly areas, which have now been sealed off. The marshalling of the invasion army has taken just one week to complete.

AIR CAMPAIGN, *BRIDGE TARGETS*

The Allied air forces renew their raids on the road and rail bridges leading into Normandy. Bridges in three areas will be attacked. Priority is given to the 24 bridges over the River Seine, from Rouen to Mantes-la-Jolie. To confuse the Germans over Allied intentions another series of bridges will be attacked

▼ *German armour, including fearsome Tiger II tanks, hide under the canopy of a tree-lined French avenue. This cover prevented detection from the air.*

beyond Paris, from Etaples in the north to Clamency in the south. To the south of the invasion area, bridges crossing the River Loire east of Nantes are scheduled for attack after D-Day.

OPERATION NEPTUNE, *ORDERS*

A signal is sent out from Admiral Ramsay's headquarters to all holders of the Operation Neptune orders. So far the orders have remained sealed in burlap bags, but they are to be opened and read by all recipients tomorrow night at 23:30 hours. To prevent the shock that the sheer size and complexity of the orders might create among some more inexperienced vessel commanders, Ramsay also sends a message of reassurance. The orders are large, but only part will relate directly to individual vessels,

▲ *Small Royal Navy Motor Gun Boats patrol the Channel. These vessels were tasked with attacking German MTB's, destroying flak boats and clearing mines.*

and all queries will be dealt with at pre-operation briefings.

THURSDAY, MAY 25

SECURITY, *COMMUNICATIONS*

All mail of personnel taking part in Operation Neptune is impounded until further notice. Press correspondents accredited to vessels of the invasion fleet are quietly taken from London to the embarkation ports and secretly briefed. To avoid their sudden disappearance, and the signal that might indicate that the invasion is imminent, they are all sent back to London with a warning to be prepared to return to the fleet at a moment's notice.

OPERATION NEPTUNE, *ORDERS*

At 23:30 hours all recipients of the Neptune naval orders open and read them for the first time.

INTELLIGENCE, *GERMAN DEFENCES*

The British Joint Intelligence Committee makes its final assessment of possible U-boat numbers in the Channel during the invasion. As has been the case for months the committee's estimate is pessimistic. The JIC now guesses that there could be at least 70 Type VIII boats at the Biscay ports and another 10 available in the eastern Atlantic. Submarine numbers in the Channel after D-Day might be as high as 45 at D+2 and 60 by D+5.

There is also sobering news about the growing strength of the German Army in Normandy. Intelligence sources report the arrival of the 21st Panzer Division near Caen, although its exact whereabouts is unknown, while the Ultra decrypts from Bletchley Park indicate increased German activity in the Cotentin Peninsula. The D-Day landings in the British sector are expected to be opposed by the whole of the 21st Panzer Division, which could be reinforced by three more panzer divisions, including 12th SS Panzer on D+1. From these assessments the JIC comes to the uncomfortable conclusion that the Germans might have guessed that the invasion is coming between Cherbourg and Le Havre.

GERMAN DEFENCES, *FRANCE*

Rommel's drive to speed up construction of coastal defences draws a complaint from General Dollman's Seventh Army headquarters in Le Mans to the Army High Command in Berlin. Seventh Army reports that every one of its units is now employed building defences and that its troops are given no time for training. This is hardly surprising. Since January Rommel has embarked on a building project that requires most of the Seventh Army to complete it. Training has suffered,

but the past four months have seen over four million land mines laid and six different types of beach obstacle improvised, built and emplaced along the coast. Meanwhile, inland, open fields have sprouted "Rommel's Asparagus", an anti-glider defence consisting of poles 30m (98ft) apart, topped with mines or artillery shells linked with detonation wires.

In fact, the only units in the Seventh Army area exempt from construction work are the élite 3rd and 5th Parachute Divisions, in Brittany. Typical of the German chain of command, the paratroopers are German Air Force troops, and the head of the air force, Hermann

▲ *Allied soldiers queue up to provide administrative information in a marshalling area shortly before D-Day. Note the barbed wire in the foreground.*

Goering, has forbidden them to take part in Rommel's work.

FRIDAY, MAY 26

ORDER OF BATTLE, *US FORCES*

As US divisions are preparing to cross the English Channel, so others are arriving across the Atlantic. The 35th Infantry Division begins to arrive from New York and the build-up of American forces goes on, turning England into one huge staging post for the liberation of Europe. The

▶ *A Panzer IV of the Hitlerjugend (Hitler Youth) Division in France.*

SATURDAY, MAY 27

35th Division will cross into France in July as part of XIX Corps, Third Army.

SATURDAY, MAY 27

SECURITY, *CODENAMES*
The *Daily Telegraph* crossword comes up with yet another invasion codename: in puzzle no. 5797, clue 11 Across, with eight letters, is: "But some big-wig like this has stolen some of it at times". Answer: Overlord. Security officers now make enquiries to find out who sets the *Telegraph* crossword. Coincidence can go only so far.

OPERATION NEPTUNE, *PREPARING*
The first steps are taken to clear the way for the Channel crossing. To avoid accidental attack by Allied aircraft on the invasion fleet, air attacks on German surface ships west of Dunkirk are stopped. The only aircraft permitted over the Channel now are to be patrol aircraft of Coastal Command.

GERMAN AIR FORCE, *PORT RAID*
Despite the huge concentration of Allied air power and the raids on enemy airfields, the German Air Force tonight manages a show of defiance. About 15 bombers raid Portland harbour, but manage to inflict only minor damage on two Landing Craft, Tank (LCT) and an American warship, the *Thomas Jefferson*.

SUNDAY, MAY 28

OPERATION NEPTUNE, *START*
On the French side of the Channel, Allied minelaying operations off German Navy bases are completed ahead of schedule. From Southwick House,

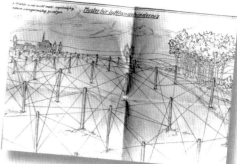

▲ A copy of Rommel's hand-drawn plans to guard against airborne attack. Dubbed "Rommel's Asparagus", the stakes and wire were designed to prevent glider landings.

▲ Allied aircraft, painted with black-and-white stripes to distinguish them from German aircraft, await the order to go.

Admiral Ramsay sends the signal "Carry out Operation Neptune". Naval assault forces are informed that D-Day will be 5 June and each of them is given the H-Hour of their landing beach. For security reasons all crews are now restricted to their warships and landing vessels, and contact with the outside is forbidden.

Despite all the months of concern over the possible shortage of landing craft, Admiral Ramsay now has sufficient numbers of them to be able to complete the lift to the Far Shore. Vessels at his disposal include 229 LSTs (Landing Ships, Tanks), 169 of which are US Navy, 245 LCI (Landing Craft, Infantry), and over 900 LCTs (Landing Craft, Tanks).

As Ramsay's order is received, so the initial moves of the fleet begin. The first vessels to sail are the old, slow merchantmen, codenamed "corncob" ships, which will be scuttled off the Normandy coast to form the outer breakwaters of the Mulberry harbours.

◄ DUKW landing craft line up ready for action. In the sealed-off marshalling areas on the south coast of England, May was a period of intense activity and final invasion preparations.

▶ The disposition of German armies and Army Groups across France before the Allied landings in June 1944.

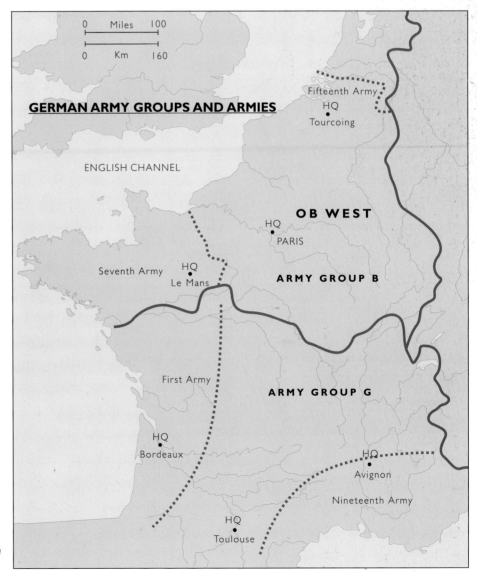

GERMAN ARMY GROUPS AND ARMIES

0   Miles   100

0   Km   160

ENGLISH CHANNEL

Fifteenth Army
HQ
Tourcoing

OB WEST

HQ
PARIS

Seventh Army
HQ
Le Mans

ARMY GROUP B

First Army

ARMY GROUP G

HQ
Bordeaux

HQ
Avignon

Nineteenth Army

HQ
Toulouse

▲ *General von Blaskowitz (far right) commander of Army Group G, discusses battle plans with his subordinate commanders in France.*

OPERATION NEPTUNE, *WEATHER*
The invasion fleet and the troops are prepared and ready; now all they need is a spell of good weather to see them safely across the English Channel. SHAEF has been receiving five-day forecasts from a syndicate of British and American meteorologists since February. But now Group Captain John Stagg, head of the Allied Meteorological Committee, sets up his headquarters in the grounds of Southwick House to supply daily weather reports. Stagg and his deputy, Colonel Yates of the US Army Air Forces, are linked by phone to meteorologists serving US forces, the Royal Navy and Royal Air Force. The group captain's job is to collate their forecasts and present to Eisenhower and the invasion commanders a summary of conditions over the next two or three days. It is on Stagg's recommendation that the Supreme Commander will issue the final order for the invasion force to sail for France.

PLANNING, *AIRBORNE ASSAULT*
At this very late stage in invasion preparations, with the ground troops in their marshalling areas preparing to board their transports vessels, there are doubts about the feasibility of the American airborne plan. Latest intelligence indicates that the German 91st Infantry Division is moving into the Cotentin Peninsula, and Air Chief Marshal Leigh-Mallory is having last-minute fears that the air drop behind Utah will be a catastrophe. The Allied air commander writes to Eisenhower expressing fears that his transport aircraft will be at serious risk and that the airborne troops, landing over a wide area in totally unsuitable flooded country, are likely to suffer casualties of over 50 per cent. Such doubts should have been aired at Montgomery's briefing on May 15, but nevertheless Leigh-Mallory is too senior an officer for his concerns to be dismissed. Eisenhower consults General Bradley. Bradley states bluntly that without an airborne operation Utah is a non-starter. The commander of the 82nd Airborne, General Ridgeway, agrees and says his division is equal to the job.

COMMANDERS, *CHIEFS OF STAFF*
Eisenhower is informed that the US Chiefs of Staff will fly to London a few

▶ *A column of German Tiger tanks moves into a new position. By keeping on the move, German armour was able to keep the Allies guessing where they were going.*

days after D-Day. They will be on hand to confer with the British should major decisions be necessary, including any decision to retreat from the beachhead in the event of imminent failure.

PLANNING, *FRIENDLY FIRE*

SHAEF orders all ground force units to carry a white star on the sides and tops of vehicles. The aim is to aid Allied identification, and avoid friendly fire.

TUESDAY, MAY 30

PLANNING, *AIRBORNE ASSAULT*

Leigh-Mallory goes to see General Eisenhower to press his objections to the Utah Beach air drop. It will be, he tells the Supreme Commander, a "futile slaughter" of two divisions. Eisenhower considers the problem and phones Leigh-Mallory later that night. The air chief is told that the attack on Utah must go ahead and the airborne drop must go in to support it, though the risks, Eisenhower admits, are great.

Following Leigh-Mallory's objections, and the evidence of a German build-up in the Cotentin, the landing zones for the 82nd Airborne are revised, to about 9km (6 miles) closer to Utah Beach. Instead of landing around St Sauveur-le-

▼ *A German tank commander emerges from his Panzer IV, which is coated with Zimmerite, an anti-magnetic paste to prevent the attachment of mines.*

▲ *British commandos prime Mills fragmentary hand grenades, ready for the invasion of occupied Europe.*

Vicomte and the River Douve, it will concentrate its effort astride the River Merderet and the road junction through the village of Ste Mère Eglise. Once these objectives are secure the division is to move west towards the Douve.

AIR CAMPAIGN, *RADAR TARGETS*

Photo-reconnaissance shows that only 14 out of 120 German radar sites have been destroyed. Sorties against radar stations are stepped up, with heavy bombers now brought in to attack the 12 most important sites. In all, 42 sites are scheduled for destruction from now until D-Day.

OPERATION BOLERO, *US BUILD-UP*

The number of US military personnel to arrive in Great Britain reaches 1,526, 965, an increase of 589,657 since January. Of these 620,504 are US Army ground troops, 426,819 are members of the US Army Air Forces and 459, 511 are service and supply troops. There are also 124,000 US Navy personnel. The tonnage of supplies and equipment shipped across the Atlantic now stands at 5,297,306 tonnes (5,382,063 tons), up 3,770, 341 tonnes (3,830,666 tons) since January.

▶ *A German oil refinery explodes in flames after a heavy bombing raid by the US Eighth Army Air Force. The fires burned for many weeks after the attack.*

◄ *French Resistance fighters gather to plan sabotage. They will act as soon as they receive word by coded Allied signals. These signals were broadcast by the BBC.*

continues to cause security officials concern. For the fourth time this month an Overlord codeword appears, in puzzle no. 5799: clue 11 Across, with eight letters, is: "This bush is a centre of nursery revolutions". Answer: Mulberry.

WEDNESDAY, MAY 31

OPERATION NEPTUNE, *LOADING*
Loading begins of troops, vehicles and equipment onto the invasion fleet.

Tonight, three Royal Navy motor launches lay 10 sonic buoys 40km (25 miles) south of Portsmouth, at the edge of the German mine barrier. The buoys will become active on D-1 to guide in motor launches fitted with a radio navigation system. These launches will act as markers for the minesweepers tasked with clearing 10 approach channels to the Normandy coast.

AIR CAMPAIGN, *BOMBING RUNS*
RAF Bomber Command has been active on 27 nights this month, flying 11,000 sorties, dropping 37,590 tonnes (37,000 tons) of bombs on Germany and the occupied countries.

FRENCH RESISTANCE, *SUPPLIES*
Over 6000 containers of equipment have now been dropped to French Resistance groups, fulfilling Churchill's promise to SOE earlier in the year to increase supplies and the numbers of delivery aircraft. SOE is confident that the Resistance now has enough equipment to fulfil its role on D-Day.

GERMAN DEFENCES, *FRANCE*
Field Marshall von Rundstedt, of OB West, reports to Hitler today that there is no indication that the Allied invasion is "immediately imminent".

INTELLIGENCE, *DISINFORMATION*
Station X, at Bletchley, picks up a message from the Japanese ambassador in Berlin to Tokyo, which seems to indicate that the Fortitude operations are meeting with success. Following a meeting with Hitler at Berchtesgaden, the ambassador reports that Hitler is convinced that the invasion will come through the Pas de Calais, between the rivers Seine and Somme, and that any Allied attack on Normandy or Brittany will only be a feint.

SECURITY, *CODENAMES*
The *Daily Telegraph* crossword

▼ *Hitler greets the Japanese Ambassador to Berlin, Hiroshi Oshima. Allied intercepts of his messages back to Tokyo provided very useful intelligence for the Allies.*

June 1-5 1944

The embarkation of troops continued unabated as Allied commanders attended daily weather briefings, hoping and praying for good conditions. The BBC broadcast coded messages to Resistance fighters in France, warning them to prepare for sabotage missions. Intelligence reports suggested German forces were not expecting an attack in the near future, due to forecasts of poor weather.

THURSDAY, JUNE 1

OPERATION NEPTUNE, *Y-DAY*
Embarkation of invasion troops goes on. Meanwhile, at Southwick House, Admiral Ramsay assumes operational command of the invasion fleet and the sea area of the English Channel. One of

▼ *The American battleship USS Nevada. She was tasked with bombarding the German positions off Utah Beach.*

◄ *US troops packed into an infantry landing ship. The next few days aboard the transports would be uncomfortable.*

his first acts in charge is to persuade Winston Churchill and King George VI not to sail with the fleet. Both of them had expressed a wish to be with the Allied forces on D-Day.

COMMANDERS, *EISENHOWER*

So far Eisenhower has divided his time between Admiral Ramsay's HQ at Southwick House, SHAEF HQ at Bushy Park, and the Allied air force HQ at Stanmore, north of London. From today, Y-Day – the date set for the end of all invasion preparations – Eisenhower will be based at Southwick House, at SHAEF's forward HQ, to be present for D-Day and beginning of Overlord.

PLANNING, *WEATHER*

Eisenhower, together with SHAEF staff and the three commanders-in-chief, Montgomery, Ramsay and Leigh-

▼ *US troops load a halftrack vehicle on a landing craft. As the order to embark transports was given, frantic activity ensued.*

Mallory, will now meet morning and evening in Southwick House to hear the latest weather forecasts from Group Captain Stagg. The commanders hope for settled weather from June 3 to June 5, the planned date for D-Day.

▲ *An English coastal port pulsates with activity, as two Landing Craft, Tank vessels are loaded in the distance.*

FRIDAY, JUNE 2

FRENCH RESISTANCE, *SABOTAGE*
From Bush House in central London, the BBC begins to broadcast a message to Resistance groups warning them that the invasion is imminent. The message, which is not in code, comes from the Baker Street headquarters of SOE and consists of the first three lines of the opening verse of Paul Verlaine's poem "Chanson d'Automne": "Les sanglots longs/Des violons/De l'automne." This alerts the Resistance to prepare their acts of sabotage. It will be followed on D-1 by the next three lines ("Blessent mon coeur/D'une langeur/Monotone"), which will be the order for sabotage to begin. SOE has over 1000 acts of sabotage planned for D-Day, mostly targeting French railways.

The BBC broadcast is picked up by Fifteenth Army's intercept station near Lille in northern France, but the Germans misinterpret the meaning of the message. They know from a captured SOE wireless operator that it refers to general action against trains, but they don't make a connection between the call to sabotage and imminent invasion.

SECURITY, *CODENAMES*
Another Overlord codeword is revealed in the *Daily Telegraph* crossword. In the last month, "Utah", "Omaha", "Overlord", and

◀ A British mini-submarine sets sail for the French coast in early June. It will linger offshore and send back intelligence on the invasion beaches.

"Mulberry" all appeared as answers to clues, and today's crossword includes, as clue 15 Down, "Brittannia and he hold to the same thing" Seven letters. Answer: Neptune. M15, the British counter-intelligence organization, has now found the man responsible for setting the puzzles. He turns out to be Leonard Dawe, headmaster of a school in Surrey, who is interviewed and cleared of any deliberate intent to breach security. It transpires that he compiled the crosswords months ago

and his use of the codewords in his answers is just a rather strange but inopportune coincidence.

FRIDAY, JUNE 2

AIR CAMPAIGN, *ROAD TARGETS*
Leigh-Mallory presents Eisenhower with his pre-invasion bombing plan. This is designed to destroy major road routes into the assault area, with the objective of slowing down German reinforcements. It will, by necessity, target villages and towns, endangering civilians. But the need to protect Allied forces during the critical build-up phase of Overlord is paramount, and Eisenhower approves the plan.

OPERATION NEPTUNE, *EMBARKING*
The embarkation of troops continues, while in Scotland warships of the bombardment groups begin to sail south from the River Clyde. Tonight, at 21:30 hours, two Royal Navy midget submarines – *X-20*, commanded by Lieutenant Ken Hudspeth, and *X-23*, commanded by Lieutenant George Honour – leave Portsmouth harbour.

▼ An American landing craft is unloaded during a training exercise. The Allies had been practising loading and unloading for weeks before the final embarkation date.

They are to proceed to the Normandy coast and lie offshore Juno and Sword beaches. Their task, when the invasion fleet arrives, is to surface and act as markers for Assault Forces J and S, because Juno and Sword are flat, with few identifying landmarks. Confusion

among the assault craft as to which beach is which could be disastrous.

PLANNING, *WEATHER*
At Southwick House, Group Captain Stagg forecasts an end of the present quiet weather in the Channel with a marked deterioration by Tuesday the 6th, with winds of up to Force 5 and heavy cloud cover. This means a treacherous seaborne landing and no airborne assault. Admiral Ramsay reports in his diary that the news is "unpromising". General Eisenhower asks, in the final briefing of the day, whether an improvement is likely by Wednesday June 7. Stagg replies negatively.

GERMAN DEFENCES, *FRANCE*
Despite all the indications that the Allied invasion is to begin in a matter of weeks, again Hitler strips OB West of mechanized units to support defences elsewhere. In Italy, the US VI Corps has broken out of the Anzio bridgehead and Rome is under threat from the south. Hitler orders the transfer of 19 air force divisions and several tank battalions from the West to reinforce a new defence line north of the city.

SATURDAY, JUNE 3

AIR CAMPAIGN, *RADAR TARGETS*
Continuing the raids on the German radar network, 95 aircraft of Bomber

▶ *German military commanders pore over plans of the French coast. While they know an attack is coming, they do not know exactly when, nor, crucially, where.*

▲ *US GIs aboard their landing craft. Crammed in with them is all manner of equipment, including jeeps.*

Command, guided by Mosquitoes, destroy the Signal Intelligence Service headquarters, near Cherbourg.

PLANNING, *WEATHER*
At his briefing at 08:30 hours, Stagg reports no change from his forecast of the previous evening. By 21:30 hours Stagg has to inform the Allied commanders that conditions in the Channel are getting worse. There are

now winds of Force 4 along the French coast, which are driving in depressions from the eastern Atlantic. By tomorrow, cloud cover is likely to be as low as 150m (500ft), with a risk of fog. D-Day is now in danger of being delayed until the weather clears. Eisenhower, in fact, provisionally postpones the invasion for 24 hours, but orders another briefing at 04:15 hours tomorrow morning to confirm the decision.

INTELLIGENCE, *ENEMY READINESS*

The Joint Intelligence Committee makes its final report on enemy assessments of Allied invasion plans: "There has been no intelligence during the last week to suggest that the enemy has accurately assessed the area in which our main assault is to be made. He appears to expect several landings between the Pas de Calais and Cherbourg." However, it goes on: "The enemy considers Allied preparations sufficiently advanced to permit operations at any time now."

Sunday, June 4

PLANNING, *WEATHER*

At the 04:15 hours briefing at Southwick House, Group Captain Stagg reports that there is no sign that the weather is improving. Eisenhower therefore confirms the postponement of D-Day by 24

▶ *General Eisenhower in serious mood. The Allied meteorologists' reports of poor weather gave him cause for concern.*

hours, and 21st Army Group HQ sends out the signal "Bowsprit" to all commands, informing them of the delay. The invasion is now scheduled for Tuesday June 6, but this depends on a rapid improvement in conditions in the next 12 hours. The Supreme Commander schedules the next weather briefing for 17:45 hours.

OPERATION NEPTUNE, *CONFUSION*

At 04:00 hours the two miniature submarines, *X-20* and *X-23*, arrive off Juno and Sword beaches. They remain submerged all day, and only come up to periscope depth at 08:00 hours to check their positions. Having been out of radio contact, they are unaware that the invasion has been postponed and that they have arrived on station a day early. The submariners surface at 21:30 hours ready to pick up the signal from Allied naval command confirming that the invasion is going ahead – a signal that does come.

One convoy of Assault Force U, including over 120 LCTs (Landing Craft, Tanks), also fails to receive the order to postpone the invasion, and sets sail. By 09:00 hours it is 40km (25 miles) south of the Isle of Wight and heading for France before it is turned back by two destroyers, which have raced from Portsmouth.

PLANNING, *WEATHER*

At his next briefing Stagg reports better news. A period of settled weather is

◀ *German air defence troops on the French coast train their 88mm anti-aircraft gun at the skies.*

forecast from Monday evening until about dawn on Tuesday. It is not the lengthy spell of good weather the invasion commanders have been hoping for, but it is the best forecast they have heard in three days.

Stagg reports again at 21:00 hours, and confirms that better weather is expected in the Channel tomorrow. The north Atlantic depression, which was expected to move east, is now moving further south, and he forecasts wind speeds down to Force 2–3 and a cloud ceiling up to 915m (3000ft).

These conditions, though an improvement, are still far from ideal. The fleet will find keeping station offshore difficult, but the sea will not be rough enough to disrupt the passage of the shallow-draft landing vessels, while the cloud ceiling will permit the airborne assault and the aerial bombardment to go ahead.

There is a discussion in the briefing room as the invasion commanders offer their advice to the Supreme Commander. Admiral Ramsay reminds everyone present that for all elements of the invasion fleet to be on station off the French coast, by first light on June 6, he must issue the order to sail within the next 30 minutes. Montgomery recommends giving the order to go, but Tedder and Leigh-Mallory have doubts that the cloud cover might impede operations of medium and heavy bombers. Eisenhower decides that he must give the order for the invasion to start. He is later reported to say: "Well, boys, there it is, I don't see how we can possibly do anything else." Admiral Ramsay sends the order for the invasion fleet to sail on the morning tide. The time is 21:45 hours. A final meeting with Stagg is scheduled tomorrow morning at 04:15 hours to confirm his forecast and Eisenhower's order.

KEY PERSONALITIES

GENERAL DE GAULLE

Charles de Gaulle was born in Lille 1890, and saw action as a young officer during World War I, being injured twice and captured. Following the war, he continued in the French Army, right up until June 1940 and the German seizure of France. Escaping to England, he called on the people of France to fight against the German occupiers and renounced the collaborationist Vichy Regime headed by his one-time friend, Marshal Pétain. In exile, de Gaulle became the figurehead of the French Resistance, and became militarily and politically involved in the conduct of the war. Other Allied leaders often found him difficult. He was incensed at being left in the dark about the plans for D-Day, only being told shortly before the actual invasion. Following the Allied victory, de Gaulle went on to become the president of France, and was heavily involved in French politics until his death on November 9, 1970.

GERMAN DEFENCES, *FRANCE*

A German Air Force meteorologist in Paris advises that because of the bad weather in the Channel the Allied

▼ *German halftrack vehicles mounting quad 20mm anti-aircraft cannons move into position in northern France.*

invasion should not be expected for at least another two weeks,

HOME FRONT, *GREAT BRITAIN*

Winston Churchill travels to Portsmouth for the day. He visits embarkation areas and takes a motor launch down the Solent to see the invasion fleet. At 13:00 hours he meets General de Gaulle, who flew into Great Britain from Algiers earlier in the morning. It is a difficult meeting, at which the prime minister explains that it is "a bad thing" that the liberation of France is about to be begin without the French being informed. He also regrets the French civilian casualties caused by the air campaign. The prime minister then explains the scale of the invasion operation and how it is to be carried out. Both men then drive to SHAEF's Southwick House HQ, where de Gaulle is briefed by General Eisenhower.

The visit is, however, a political disaster. The French leader is furious at what he is told. Not only are the invasion forces taking their own money with them (over two billion francs in special US-printed "invasion currency"), but Eisenhower's address, to be broadcast to the French people on D-Day, makes no mention of de Gaulle or his provisional government. Instead, it asks the people to obey instructions from SHAEF and to accept, for the time being, the existing pro-German civil authorities. De Gaulle asks by what authority Eisenhower does this. Is France to be occupied by SHAEF? The meeting breaks up. De Gaulle will not publicly endorse Eisenhower's message and instead will make his own D-Day broadcast to the French people.

AIR CAMPAIGN, *RAIL*

Photo-reconnaissance shows that the Transportation Plan has not been a total success. There are still 13 rail lines running uncut into the assault area and they are capable of carrying up to 250 trains per day. This news is something of a

◀ *US and British troops receive a final briefing on board their landing craft. It was only now that their missions were revealed.*

▲ *An A-20 Havoc, on its way to destroy enemy positions in northern France, passes over ships of the Allied invasion fleet.*

vindication for the Special Operations Executive (SOE); it has always argued that a saboteur with explosives can do more damage to a railway than a bomber. There is better news for the air forces regarding enemy gun batteries. Reconnaissance reveals 21 out of the 49 of them in the assault area damaged.

AIR CAMPAIGN, *ENEMY DEFENCES*

Bomber raids on German coastal defences are stepped up for a last push before D-Day. In the last four days the US Eighth Army Air Force alone has made 2200 bomber sorties.

MONDAY, JUNE 5

OPERATION NEPTUNE, *SUBMARINES*

At 00:55 hours, the Royal Navy submarines *X-20* and *X-23*, lying off

Juno and Sword beaches, surface and finally receive the postponement signal. They submerge again and will remain out of sight until late tonight.

PLANNING, *INVASION GO-AHEAD*

At 04:15 hours, Group Captain Stagg briefs Eisenhower and the invasion commanders and confirms the weather reports of the previous evening. The interval of fair weather he forecast has now begun and will last until late on Tuesday. The Supreme Commander confirms his decision that the invasion is to proceed. From this moment there is no turning back from D-Day.

OPERATION NEPTUNE, *SETTING SAIL*

The invasion fleet begins to sail. At 09:00 hours the commander of Force S, Rear-Admiral Arthur G. Talbot, signals from his flagship *HMS Largs*, "Good Luck – drive on", as the first LST (Landing Ship, Tank) and escort ships move out of the Solent. At about

▲ *The journey across the Channel was no pleasure cruise. The seas were choppy, and many troops were seasick.*

the same time Forces J and S set sail. They constitute the Eastern Task Force, under the command of Rear-Admiral Philip Vian in his flagship *HMS Scylla*. Also on board is the British 2nd Army commander, General Miles Dempsey.

The remaining two assault forces, U and O, do not begin to sail until about 16:00 hours. Coming from ports in Dorset, Devon and Cornwall, west of the Solent, they have less congested waters to navigate. Forces U and O comprise the Western Task Force, commanded by Rear-Admiral Alan G. Kirk in the heavy cruiser *USS Augusta*.

Also on board is the commander of the US First Army, General Omar N. Bradley.

All assault forces make their way into the Channel, converging through four routes towards a rendezvous known as Point Z, 13km (8 miles) southeast of the Isle of Wight. This becomes an assembly area, called "Piccadilly Circus", 8km (5 miles) in radius from where the convoys move south through 10 channels cleared through the German minefield.

▼ *Ready for the off! A few of the thousands of Allied landing craft near the English coast in early June 1944.*

MONDAY, JUNE 5

Although the weather is improving, it remains rough in mid-Channel, with winds gusting up to Force 5 and waves up to 1.8m (6ft) high. It makes the crossing extremely uncomfortable for many of the soldiers in the landing craft, and sea-sickness is rife.

To protect the fleet from German Navy vessels operating in the English

▲ *Men of the 2nd Battalion, 503rd Parachute Infantry Regiment, board aircraft of the 60th Troop Carrying Group.*

Channel, Royal Navy warships begin to take up station between Brittany and Cornwall. They include a force of 8 destroyers and 36 motor torpedo boats. These are supported, 210km (130 miles) west of Land's End, by three escort carriers. Meanwhile, closer to the French coast, two patrol lines of destroyers establish an anti-submarine screen 80km (50 miles) northwest of Ushant island.

▼ *US paratroopers board their C-47 transport. They knew that for some there would be no return journey.*

AIR CAMPAIGN, *FIGHTER COVER*
SHAEF orders all Allied air forces to paint a distinctive invasion insignia on their fighters, tactical bombers, transport aircraft and assault gliders. This takes the form of four stripes in alternate white and black on the body and wings, which will, it is hoped, distinguish aircraft from enemy planes over the assault area.

As the invasion fleet begins to assemble south of the Isle of Wight, it is given fighter cover from 16:00 hours by patrols of American P-38s. This is kept light at this stage of the operation, to avoid drawing attention to the vast offensive task force assembling in mid-Channel. In fact, air operations throughout southern Britain are kept about 50 percent lower than normal, in order to rest and prepare crews for the huge air offensive that is about to begin in the early hours of June 6.
COMMANDERS, EISENHOWER
From London, Winston Churchill sends a telegram to Stalin in Moscow, informing the Soviet leader that the Allies are about to open the long-awaited Second Front. "Tonight we go", it says.

At SHAEF forward HQ, at Southwick House, General Eisenhower holds a press

◄ *An aerial view of the massive invasion fleet forming up in the Channel, before the journey to the beaches takes place.*

Southwick House and is driven up to the area of Newbury, Berkshire, where he visits the men of the 101st Airborne, who are preparing to board the planes and gliders that will take them into battle. This is a private and unofficial visit by the Supreme Commander, who wants to meet and talk personally with the soldiers who will be among the first Americans to fight on the continent of Europe.

After meeting them, Eisenhower returns to Southwick House, where, as the time approaches midnight, the focus of everyone's attention is drawn to the operations room on the ground floor, which is filled with plot tables, charts and telephones, and is dominated by a huge plywood map of the Channel and assault area. It covers the whole of one wall. It is in this room that, in the next 24 hours, the invasion commanders will follow the progress of the fleet and the beach assaults.

GERMAN DEFENCES, *FRANCE*

The bad weather in the Channel has also caused problems for the Germans. Heavy seas during the day result in a cancellation of E-boat patrols, while reconnaissance flights by the German Air Force are also cancelled. Not having the precise weather information that is available to the Allies, the German meteorological office in Paris fails to see the band of settled weather into which the Allied invasion fleet has sailed. It lends an air of false security to the German Army in France.

Field Marshal Rommel draws up a situation report for von Rundstedt at

conference to brief the journalists who will cover the invasion. He then prepares, in private, a personal statement to be given to the press in the event that the invasion fails. He writes in pencil on a small piece of notepaper:

"Our landings in the Cherbourg–Le Havre area have failed to gain a satisfactory foothold and I have with-drawn the troops. My decision to attack at this time and place was based on the best information available. The troops, the air and the navy did all that bravery and devotion to duty could do. If any blame or fault attaches to the attempt, it is mine alone."

At about 18:00 hours Eisenhower leaves

▼ *Paratroopers of the US 101st Airborne Division before boarding. Their unit insignia has been scribbled out by censors.*

P
315087

MONDAY, JUNE 5

▲ *Troops of the 1st Polish Armoured Division on their way to face the German Army, joining the battle in August.*

OB West, stating that because of bad seas there is no imminent danger of invasion. Von Rundstedt promptly copies this to Berlin. The Seventh Army commander, General Dollman, orders a relaxation of the standing alert along the coast, and summons senior officers to a war-game exercise in Rennes, 200km (125 miles) from Normandy.

With everything quiet, Rommel sets off by car for his home in Heelingen, Germany, to spend a night with his family before going on to Berchtesgaden for a conference with Hitler.

Things begin to change at about 21:15 hours. A Fifteenth Army intercept station picks up the BBC broadcast of the second part of the Resistance action message, the second three lines of the Verlaine poem, "Chanson d'Automne": "Blessent mon coeur/D'une langeur/Monotone". Some Allied action is imminent, but what, and where will it come? The German Secret Service believes the signal heralds the Allied invasion within 48 hours. Fifteenth Army Intelligence reports the signal to Rommel's HQ. His chief-of-staff, General Hans Speidel, contacts the Fifteenth Army commander, General Hans von Salmuth, who puts his army on a pre-alert status, at 22:30 hours. But the Seventh Army in Normandy is not informed.

AIR CAMPAIGN, *FIGHTER ACTION*
Six squadrons of Mosquito night fighters provide cover for the fleet. The only combat reported is the probable downing of a German Junkers Ju-188 reconnaissance aircraft.

Pre-invasion sorties over France begin at about 22:00 hours, when 98 Mosquito night fighters patrol an area

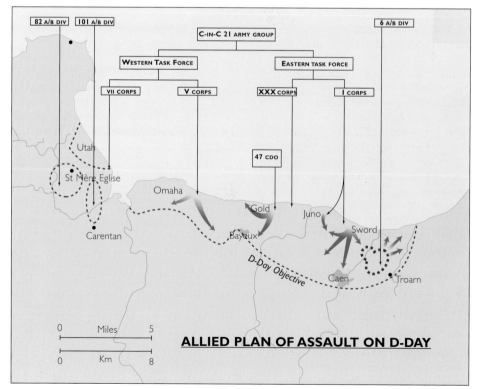

ALLIED PLAN OF ASSAULT ON D-DAY

▲ *A group of seemingly relaxed US paratroopers poses for a photo. Despite the smiles, they would have been nervous.*

▲ *A B-25 Mitchell bomber flies over a steel works in Caen, France. Note the bombs detonating on the ground below.*

south of the invasion area, from Rennes to Le Mans to Lisieux, with instructions to attack road and rail junctions. To the north, 36 Mitchell bombers attack Caen, hoping to disrupt the 21st Panzer Division, known to be near there. Only 19 aircraft locate the target. From 23:30 hours, Bomber Command attacks two targets on the Cotentin Peninsula, on the main road north of what will soon become known as Utah Beach: 92 Lancasters drop 508 tonnes (500 tons) of bombs on Crisbecq, while other Lancasters attack St Martin-de-Varreville.

AIRBORNE ASSAULT, *TAKE-OFF*

The first US airborne troops take off at about 21:50 hours. Loaded into C-47 transports, they are the pathfinder

▶ *British glider-borne soldiers laugh at the messages scrawled on the side of their aircraft. Revenge was clearly on their minds.*

teams of the 101st Airborne, flying out of Berkshire. They are to land 30 minutes ahead of the main paratroopers, to identify and mark drop zones (DZ) with flares and radio direction sets.

At 22:30 hours they are followed by the 82nd Airborne pathfinders, flying out of Lincolnshire airfields. At 23:15 the 82nd's assault force of over 6390 paratroopers takes off, followed, 15 minutes later, by the 6600 paratroopers of 101st Airborne. The journey is scheduled to take about one hour, with the C-47s taking a long loop over the Channel, approaching the Cotentin Peninsula from the west.

At 22:49 hours, the lead elements of the British 6th Airborne Division begin taking off, by towed glider, from airfields in Gloucestershire. They are tasked with Operation Tonga, to secure the British left flank, east of the Orne. First to leave are support units for the assault on the Merville battery by the 9th Para-chute Brigade.

At 22:56 hours the assault force

for capturing the River Orne bridges (Operation Coup de Main) takes off from a Dorset airfield in six Horsa gliders. The 171 men of B and D Company, Oxfordshire and Buckinghamshire Light Infantry, with 30 Royal Engineer sappers, are commanded by Major John Howard.

FRENCH RESISTANCE, *CONTACT*

Between 22:33 and 23:07 hours, three RAF bombers take off, to parachute French and British soldiers of the 1st SAS Brigade, an SOE guide and a three-man Jedburgh team into the Brittany area, so that they can make contact with Resistance groups.

June 6 1944

D-Day began in earnest as the invasion fleet in the Channel headed for the invasion beaches. Overhead, Allied airborne assault forces began their operations to seize key bridges and road junctions behind enemy lines. Fortunately for the Allies, German forces were taken completely by surprise.

▲ Troops of a German mortar platoon. Wehrmacht infantry had to rely on mortars because of a field gun shortage.

▼ A Panzer IV of the SS "Hitler Youth" Panzer Division in northern France. Note how young the crew are.

00:00 HOURS

GERMAN DEFENCES, *NORMANDY*

The first German units to face the Allied invasion will be the six infantry and three panzer divisions posted in Normandy. They are concentrated in the Cotentin Peninsula, protecting the port of Cherbourg, and along the Calvados Coast, from the River Vire, in the west, to the River Dives, 16km (10 miles) east of Caen. The divisions vary widely in their equipment, personnel and fighting effectiveness.

The Cotentin is held by the 243rd, 709th and 91st Divisions. The 243rd is spread out along the west coast of the peninsula. Officially, the division is supposed to be motorized, but by June 6 only six infantry companies have been issued with trucks, and the division artillery is drawn by teams of horses. The 709th is posted along the east coast of the Cotentin, from Cherbourg to Carentan, and is a static unit, having no transport at all. Its main role is to garrison Cherbourg. The 709th consists of poorly trained, over-age soldiers and a large number of Osttruppen (Eastern troops) from the conquered lands of Eastern Europe and the Soviet Union.

▲ *A German machine-gun position in Normandy. The weapon is a 7.92mm MG42, an excellent piece of equipment.*

The 91st Division defends the southern part of peninsula from the River Merderet west to the coast. It arrived in the Cotentin in late May with the specific task of countering airborne landings. Despite its training, the 91st is not a frontline division, being barely six months old and made up of conscripts.

▼ *German infantry move into position close to the Orne sector, prior to the Allied parachute drop.*

It is, however, well stocked with artillery, having three battalions of 105mm and 155mm guns.

Supporting these divisions around Carentan is the 6th Parachute Infantry Regiment, part of the 2nd Parachute Division, which in May began to be transferred from Brittany. The 6th is an

élite unit of volunteers, commanded by veteran paratrooper, Colonel Frederick von der Heydte.

The 352nd Division defends the coast from the Vire estuary east about 38km (24 miles) to Asnelles-sur-Mer, including the areas around Isigny-sur-Mer and Bayeux. The 352nd has been in this sector since March and has spent the time strengthening the coastal defences. It consists of over 12,000 combat veterans, organized into four grenadier regiments, and supported by five battalions of field, anti-tank and anti-aircraft artillery based inland.

The area north of Caen, from Asnelles across the estuary of the River Orne to the River Dives, is the responsibility of the 716th Division. This is another static division organized for defence only. It consists of many veterans invalided out of the Eastern Front, as well as two battalions of Eastern European troops. The division is supported by a regiment of artillery, but it has too few soldiers to defend a sector covering over 34km (21 miles). The division commander has therefore had to concentrate his men around 50 fortified positions: strong along the coast but providing for very little defence inland. The 716th Division forms the right flank of Seventh Army's LXXXIV Corps.

The River Dives forms the boundary between the Seventh and Fifteenth Armies. The most westerly formation of Fifteenth Army is the 711th Division, holding the sector from the Dives to Honfleur. This static division also has a high percentage of former invalids from the Eastern Front, as well as a battalion of Eastern troops. As with all the conscripted units from the East, their loyalty is questionable, but they fulfil a need in manning fortifications.

Supporting these infantry divisions are three panzer divisions, held inland as a mobile reserve. Closest to the

LADDER STOWAGE HERE

▲ Paratroopers jump from their transport during training. The parachute jump as a method of massed deployment rose and fell with World War II, since high attrition rates from injury and scattering of forces made it a liability.

▼ Under the cover of darkness, Allied gliders like these swooped down, landing behind enemy lines. The journey was perilous, and many overladen gliders crashed, killing both passengers and pilots.

▶ *Strategically important bridges in Normandy, such as this one over the Orne, were key objectives for airborne forces.*

coast is the 21st Panzer Division, located east of Caen astride the River Orne, in support of the static 716th Division. The original 21st Panzer was destroyed in Tunisia in 1943, but it was re-constituted with personnel from many different units. Looked on as rather second-rate, the new division is equipped with largely obsolete weapons and captured French vehicles. A far more impressive armoured unit is located southeast of Normandy, between Le Mans and Orléans. The Panzer Lehr Division includes an armoured regiment, an armoured artillery regiment, two armoured infantry regiments, an anti-tank battalion and an armoured reconnaissance battalion. It has a total strength of over 14,500 officers and men and 183 tanks, including Panther and Tiger tanks and Jagdpanzer IV and StuG assault

▼ *The assault area, showing the various sectors of the beaches. This was the grand plan, though sea and weather conditions in the Channel meant many troops landed away from their designated sectors.*

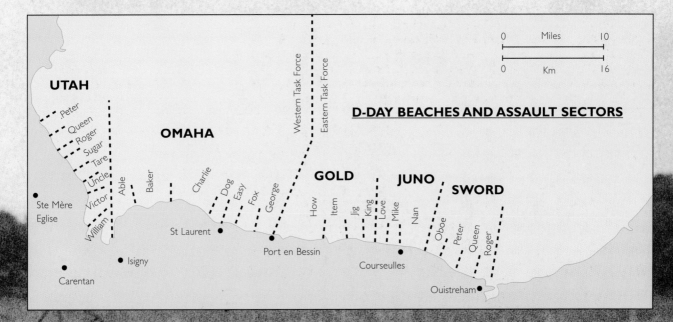

D-DAY BEACHES AND ASSAULT SECTORS

UTAH

Peter
Queen
Roger
Sugar
Tare
Uncle
Victor
William

Ste Mère Eglise

OMAHA

Able
Baker
Charlie
Dog
Easy
Fox
George

St Laurent

Isigny

Carentan

Port en Bessin

Western Task Force
Eastern Task Force

GOLD

How
Item
Jig
King
Love
Mike
Nan

Courseulles

JUNO

SWORD

Oboe
Peter
Queen
Roger

Ouistreham

0   Miles   10
0   Km   16

guns. The third panzer division near Normandy is the most powerful. On 6 June the 12th SS Panzer Division *Hitlerjugend* (Hitler Youth) is spread over an area about 65km (40 miles) southeast of Caen. It is a new élite division and is made up of 20,000 volunteers, most of whom have come from the Hitler Youth movement. They are committed Nazis, sworn to defend the Reich. The division's order of battle includes a panzer regiment, two panzer-grenadier regiments and an artillery regiment. It is equipped with Panther tanks, Jagdpanzer IVs and halftracks carrying multiple 20mm flak guns.

The German divisions settle in for another quiet night in Normandy. The Allies are mounting a few air raids, but nothing to be too concerned over. The rough weather in the English Channel gives the region a sense of security. The Allies won't be putting to sea tonight, and in any case the tide is going out and it is a widely held belief that the

▼ *Panzergrenadiers continue their push towards the Allied paratroopers. The paratroopers have been spread across the French countryside, and are scrambling to organize before German forces get to them in strength.*

▲ *German Panzergrenadiers move along the Bocage in Normandy to counter-attack the Allied airdrop. They are supported by a Panther tank.*

Allies will only attack at high tide and in daylight, as they did in the Mediterranean theatre.

AIRBORNE ASSAULT, *BRITISH SECTOR*

The six Horsa gliders carrying Major Howard's troops heading for the Orne River bridges cross the Normandy coast. Separating from their towing aircraft at 1830m (6000ft) the plywood gliders, each laden with over 7000kg (15,400lb) of men and equipment,

sweep over Cabourg, northeast of Caen, at 145km/h (90mph). One glider becomes separated and veers off towards the River Dives to land about 13km (8 miles) from target; but the rest make a turn west for a glide of 8km (5 miles) to the objective. With no navigational aids other than a stop-watch and a map, the army pilots pick up the Orne Canal at about 365m (1200ft). No.

1 glider crash-lands on the east bank of the canal at about 00:16 hours and ploughs straight through a belt of barbed wire before coming to a halt at a road embankment just 43m (140ft) from the canal bridge. It is followed at one-minute intervals by gliders 2 and 3, which land directly behind.

The platoon from No.1 glider, led by Lieutenant Brotheridge, is the first out, and its men make it up the embankment to the bridge and then split up. Three men grenade a pillbox on the right while Brotheridge leads the rest of his men in a charge across the bridge to attack the German slit trenches on the far bank. Meanwhile, sappers are already climbing over the underside of the bridge to cut the wires of any demolition explosives. The two platoons from gliders 2 and 3 are also now in action along the east bank while Brotheridge and his men engage a machine-gun nest to their right. In the face of the sudden onslaught, the garrison, all foreign conscripts, are retreating fast, but their German NCOs are making some show of a fight, and Brotheridge is mortally wounded, before grenades and Bren gun fire silence the machine gun. Men from the two other platoons are now over the bridge and securing the far bank. By

00:22 hours, the canal bridge is almost secure and the sappers have found no explosives. It seems the Germans were wiring the bridge for demolition but had not yet put the charges in place.

Major Howard moves his command post into the pillbox to await news from the platoons in gliders 4, 5 and 6 attacking the river bridge 365m (400yds) east. The first of these, glider 5, lands at about 00:20 hours. With no sign of the other gliders, Lieutenant Fox leads his platoon straight to the bridge. There is German machine-gun fire from the east bank, which is

promptly silenced by a bomb from the platoon's mortar. The defenders run off into the night and Fox crosses the bridge at about 00:21 hours, by which time glider 6, carrying Lieutenant Sweeney and his platoon, has landed. By the time Sweeney's platoon joins Fox and his men, the river bridge is secure. By 00:30 hours, Major Howard is having the radio message "Ham and

▼ The Allied deception strategies on D-Day, involving both radar jamming and creating false radar images (red areas) and dummy paratroop drops.

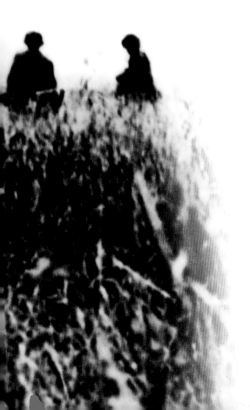

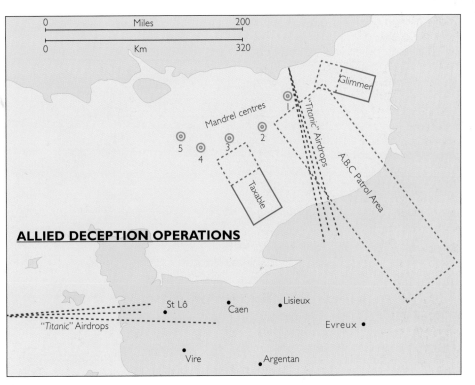

ALLIED DECEPTION OPERATIONS

Jam" sent back to England. It is the call sign that Operation Coup de Main has been a complete success.

With both bridges secure, Howard's priority is defence. News of the attack will have reached the villages of Bénouville and Le Port by now, and Howard's men take their places in the trenches on the west bank of the canal to await the expected German counter-attack. Relief by parachute companies of the 7th Battalion, 5th Parachute Brigade, 6th Airborne, is expected from about 01:00 hours. But until they arrive over the bridge, from their drop zones (DZs) around the villages of Ranville and Bréville, Howard and his men of the "Ox and Bucks" are on their own.

00:30 HOURS

AIRBORNE ASSAULT, *PATHFINDERS*
Transports are now flying in over the Cotentin Peninsula and the area between the Orne and Dives rivers to drop those paratroopers who will act as pathfinders for the three Allied airborne divisions. The pathfinders are meant to land, identify and mark the DZ for the first airborne troops, now just 30 minutes behind them; but as soon as they fly in, their mission starts to go wrong.

▶ An M-22 Locust light tank emerges from a giant Hamilcar glider. The M-22 was designed to give airborne troops much-needed firepower.

Over the American sector of the Cotentin, pilots fly straight into a cloud bank, which, they discover, covers most of the peninsula. Those aircraft that climb to clear it have to drop the pathfinders without sight of the ground, while those that dive below it are targeted by German flak and forced to scatter. Of the 18 US pathfinder teams, only one lands in the correct place, leaving five DZs unidentified. The British pathfinders of the 22nd Independent Parachute Company are more fortunate. Their drop is also scattered by low cloud and flak, but about half the company finds its way to the three DZs for the lead elements of the 6th Airborne's 5th Parachute Brigade.

AIR CAMPAIGN, *BRITISH SECTOR*

A force of 100 Lancasters and Halifax bombers attack the four concrete casemates of the Merville battery, east of Caen. The raid is meant to support the attack by men of the 9th Parachute Brigade, led by Colonel Terence Otway, scheduled to begin at 02:35 hours. In fact, a reconnaissance party of paratroopers is already on the ground and hears the aircraft release their bombs. It is terrifying spectacle to watch, but it does the paratroopers little good: the bombs have missed the German battery completely.

00:50 HOURS

AIRBORNE ASSAULT, *BRITISH SECTOR*

The lead aircraft carrying the 5th Parachute Brigade and forward units of Otway's Merville attack force fly in at a height of little more than 120m (400ft). The pathfinders begin to mark the DZ with flares as the Germans in the surrounding villages begin to realize that something serious is about to start. From his command post at the Orne Canal bridge, Major Howard sees their arrival, and recalls later, "We had a first-class view of the division coming in. Searchlights were lighting up the 'chutes and there was a bit of firing going on and you could see tracer bullets going up into the air as they floated down to the ground. It really was the most awe-inspiring sight."

01:00 HOURS

DECEPTION, *FORTITUDE SOUTH*

As part of Fortitude South, a large number of deception schemes and

▲ *A German soldier inspects the wreckage of a crashed Allied Horsa glider. If not killed in the landing, the Allied troops would have long gone.*

electronic warfare operations are in operation over the English Channel and Normandy coast to mask the invasion fleet and draw the Germans away from the airborne DZs.

For the past 24 hours Operation Mandrel has been underway. Bombers filled with anti-radar equipment have been flying circuits over the Channel, jamming enemy ground radar, while over the Pas de Calais what are known as ABC patrols are being flown by specially equipped Lancasters to jam and interrupt the radio frequencies used by the German fighter control network. While German radar is being jammed over the real invasion fleet, Operations Taxable and Glimmer are providing German radar with images of two phantom fleets off the coast, at Le Havre and Boulogne: at sea, motor launches tow radar-reflecting balloons, while overhead bombers scatter huge amounts of "Window" – aluminium strips that create a radar shadow over 22km (14 miles) long.

▼ *Troops of the 12th SS Panzer Division "Hitler Youth", supported by armour, move through a French village to counter Allied action.*

Inland, the SAS's Operation Titanic aims to divert German reserve forces from the airborne DZ by dropping over 500 dummy paratroopers: man-shaped sandbags, about one-third life size, fitted with small parachutes and explosive gunfire simulators. They are crude, but in the dark, and in big numbers, they have German reserve regiments chasing around the country-side looking for Allied "troops". Titanic targets four separate locations: north of the River Seine, east of the River Dives, southwest of Caen and west of St Lô.

◀ *A typical Allied Limpet mine. These were placed on railway lines by French Resistance members to disrupt German military movements.*

01:00 HOURS

AIRBORNE ASSAULT, *US SECTOR*
The first of over 900 C-47 transport aircraft appears over the Cotentin Peninsula to drop the 101st and 82nd Airborne Divisions into France. But from the moment the planes cross the west coast of the peninsula, the operation begins to descend into chaos. Not only are most of the DZs unmarked, but the transport pilots get lost in the cloud cover, and heavy flak from the German divisions below breaks up their formations. The pilots – not combat-trained – climb, dive and accelerate away from the gunfire and order their paratroopers to jump at the best opportunity. Transports are shot down, order is lost, and as a result the two divisions are scattered all over the southeast of the peninsula, from the River Merderet to the coast. Some

▲ *Royal Navy minesweepers, such as these seen in harbour, had been busily clearing a channel for invasion craft to surge towards the beaches.*

paratroopers drop into the English Channel, while two unfortunate plane-loads of men drop right in the middle of the village of Ste Mère Eglise, to be shot dead with their parachutes still entangled in trees and telegraph wires. Elsewhere, men drown in areas flooded by the Germans to prevent such airborne assaults. Companies, even platoons, are split up, with no idea where they are. But amid the failure of the drop, the paratroopers hold to their tasks. They start to assemble in small groups, get their bearings and begin to move north towards the four exits from Utah beach, west to the Merderet and Ste Mère Eglise, and south towards the crossings over the River Douve.

GERMAN DEFENCES, *RESPONSES*
Allied airborne troops have been landing for nearly an hour before the enemy begins to try and organize a response. At about 01:00 hours, the 711th Division goes on alert when British paratroopers mistakenly land close to its headquarters at Pont l'Evêques on the River

Dives. The 716th Division, around Caen, follows suit a few minutes afterwards on news of Allied paratroopers in action east of the Orne. The news is passed up to LXXXIV Corps HQ at St Lô and the LXXXI Corps HQ at Rouen, which both go on alert; but it is not until 01:35 hours that the Seventh Army HQ, at Le Mans, informs Army Group B HQ, near Paris. Rommel's chief of staff, General Speidel, is woken by the call, but does not forward the news to either OB West or Rommel because he refuses to accept that the Allied attack is anything more than a raid or diversionary feint. Meanwhile, the commander of the German 6th Parachute Regiment in Périers is getting reports of Allied landings around Ste Mère Eglise; but his

attempts to contact LXXXIV Corps HQ all fail because the US paratroopers are now busy destroying the German communications network.

The German Navy reacts with a little more efficiency. At 01:30 hours, Vice-Admiral Rieve, commander of the

▼ *A German 88mm flak battery attempts to drive off the Allied bombers pounding the Normandy coast, hours before the first vessels land.*

Channel coast, informs Admiral Kranke's HQ in Paris of the American landings. Kranke puts Navy Group West on alert in preparation for action.

01:40 HOURS

AIRBORNE ASSAULT, *REINFORCING*

Fifty-two gliders carrying the first reinforcements and heavy equipment for the 101st Airborne Division are towed into the air from Aldermaston airfield. Their loads are vital to support the lightly armed paratroops. They include 16 six-pounder guns, 13 tonnes (13.2 tons) of ammunition and equipment, 24 vehicles and a small bulldozer. Gliders also carry companies of engineers and medics and the division's HQ staff. There is no communication between the paratroopers scattered across the Cotentin and England, so these men have no idea of what they flying into.

01:30 HOURS

AIRBORNE ASSAULT, BRITISH SECTOR, *GERMAN ATTACK*

As the German Army chain of command attempts to sort out what is going on in Normandy, units of the 716th Division begin the first counter-attack on Major Howard's men at the Orne Canal. Two Panzer IV tanks advance slowly out of Bénouville, heading for the canal bridge, followed by infantry. The lead tank gets to within 45m (50yds) of the bridge when it is

▼ *British paratroopers from the 6th Airborne Division unload their equipment from a Horsa glider near Ranville. The soldiers here were lucky enough to have experienced a successful landing.*

hit by a round from a PIAT and explodes. The burning tank blocks the road and the attack peters out. Shortly afterwards the first companies of the 5th Parachute Brigade arrive and take position on the west bank of the canal in preparation for an advance into Bénouville and Le Port.

FRENCH RESISTANCE, *SABOTAGE*

By 01:37 hours the first three SAS and Jedburgh liaison teams have been dropped into Brittany. The first to land is ambushed at the DZ: one French SAS soldier is killed and the rest of the team are captured. The other teams land safely. Throughout northern France the Resistance goes into action

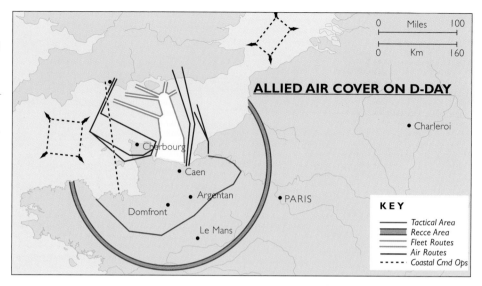

ALLIED AIR COVER ON D-DAY

KEY
— Tactical Area
— Recce Area
— Fleet Routes
— Air Routes
- - - Coastal Cmd Ops

▲ *Fighters covered the fleet routes (yellow), while tactical and reconnaissance missions were flown far inland. The invasion area was well protected.*

against 1050 designated targets, 950 of which will be attacked in the next 24 hours. Cutting rail lines is the priority, especially those needed to reach Normandy by German divisions posted elsewhere in France. The likely routes of two divisions, in particular, have been targeted: the 275th, currently in Redon, 200km (125 miles) to the south-west, and the 2nd SS Panzer Division *Das Reich*, in Toulouse, 720km (450 miles) to the south.

AIRBORNE ASSAULT, *BRITISH FORCES*

Around 01:40 hours, 72 gliders are towed into the air carrying the British 6th Airborne Division headquarters, its commander Major-General Gale, reinforcements and heavy equipment, including anti-tank guns and jeeps. Meanwhile, in France, engineers of the 5th Parachute Brigade are busy clearing DZs of anti-glider poles and preparing eight landings strips ready for their arrival.

01:59 HOURS

AIRBORNE ASSAULT, *REINFORCING*

The lift begins of 52 gliders carrying the first reinforcements and heavy equipment for the US 82nd Airborne Division. They carry 16 57mm anti-aircraft guns, 22 jeeps, 10 tonnes (10.1 tons) of ammunition, as well as the head-quarters staff and signallers.

OPERATION NEPTUNE, *MINES*

From 02:00 hours flotillas of minesweepers and their destroyer escorts begin to arrive off the

▶ *Flat-bottomed British landing craft like these gave their occupants an uncomfortable ride in choppy waters.*

Normandy coast, exactly on schedule. The passage across has, so far, suffered the loss of only one vessel, the US Navy minesweeper *Osprey*, which hit a mine and sank yesterday evening. The minesweepers now begin the task of clearing areas offshore prior to the arrival of the five Assault Forces U, O, G, J and S. This work must be finished in the next three hours, before low water and the turning of the tide at 05:00 hours that will help carry the landing craft and the troops ashore.

▲ *American landing craft, including DUKW amphibious vehicles carrying supplies, stream towards the shore within hours of the first assault wave.*

Daybreak begins 15 minutes later, with sunrise at 06:00 hours. Thirty minutes after that, the first of the assault troops will hit Utah and Omaha beaches at their scheduled H-Hour of 06:30. H-Hours for beaches in the British and Canadian sectors will begin 65 minutes later to catch the tide as it rises, west to east.

TUESDAY, JUNE 6

▶ *US troops leave England for France. The ambulances in the background must have been a sobering reminder of the fighting and mayhem that awaited them.*

As the assault forces exit the cleared channels from England they reassemble in Transport Areas 10km (just over 6 miles) offshore. The warships tasked with the pre-landing bombardment take station in Fire Support Areas in front, and to the side, of the Transport Areas, with the smaller vessels such as destroyers ahead. From each Transport Area to the coast are cleared boat lanes, which will take the assault craft and landing ships to shore.

At 02:30 hours, off Utah Beach, the HQ ship of Task Force U, USS *Bayfield,* drops anchor. Its commander, Admiral Moon, issues the order "Lower all landing craft", and within minutes unloading has begun. There is no sign of a reaction from the enemy, but there is real fear that they will launch an E-boat sortie out of Cherbourg.

GERMAN DEFENCES, *RESPONSES*

At 02:15 hours, General Speidel, at Army Group B HQ, receives another phone call. Major-General Pemsel, chief of staff of Seventh Army in Le Mans, tells him that a large-scale Allied airborne operation is in progress, and that this may be the first moves in the Allied invasion. While some German soldiers have been in action since just after midnight, it seems that the higher up the German chain of command the news travels, the less it is believed. Seventh Army cannot go on full-scale alert without permission from OB West, and Speidel is unwilling to pass

the information on at this hour of the morning. Personally, he does not believe it is the start of the invasion, but finally agrees to contact OB West HQ. He receives a reply to his message at about 02:40 hours. Von Rundstedt's staff informs Rommel's chief of staff that the field marshal "does not consider this to be a major operation".

Meanwhile, General Marcks, commander of LXXXIV Corps, is taking action in the face of a rapidly

deteriorating situation. The 709th and 91st Divisions and the 915th Infantry Regiment near Bayeux are ordered to move against the airborne troops in the Cotentin. But Marcks's efforts are hindered because many regimental officers are away from their posts at

▼ *American LCI (Landing Craft, Infantry) on their way across the Channel. Some 245 LCIs took part in the D-Day landings, half of which were supplied by the US Navy.*

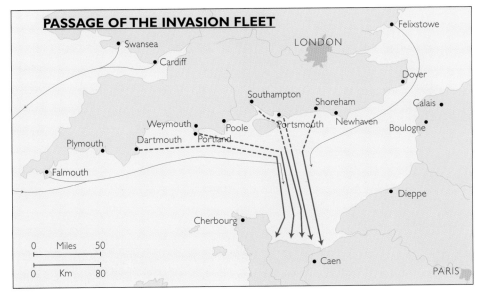

PASSAGE OF THE INVASION FLEET

Swansea • Cardiff • LONDON • Felixstowe • Dover • Southampton • Shoreham • Calais • Weymouth • Poole • Portsmouth • Newhaven • Boulogne • Dartmouth • Portland • Plymouth • Falmouth • Dieppe • Cherbourg • Caen • PARIS

```
0      Miles      50
0      Km      80
```

◄ *The route to victory. The red lines denote the passage of the invasion fleet as it made its way from the many English harbours to the Normandy coast.*

Seventh Army war games in Rennes, and he cannot ask for help from the panzer divisions: they are held as an army group reserve, controlled from Berlin. The situation is particularly exasperating for General Feuchtinger, the commander of the 21st Panzer Division. He is sitting with his tanks west of the Orne, watching British airborne troops land in their thousands on the other side of the river, but is unable to move against them because he has no orders.

Out at sea it is at about 03:00 hours when German radar stations along the coast finally discover the Allied invasion fleet. Admiral Kranke orders the coastal batteries under his command to engage and sends out a flotilla of three E-boats and two armed trawlers to sortie from Le Havre. News of the arrival of the Allied fleet is sent

to the U-boat headquarters at Wilhelmshaven, Germany, which puts the boats of Group Landwirt, based on the Brittany and Biscay coasts, on alert.

02:50 HOURS

AIRBORNE ASSAULT, *BRITISH SECTOR*
Colonel Otway and men of the 9th Parachute Battalion set off from their DZ towards the Merville battery. The drops and glider landings for this operation have nearly all gone astray, leaving Otway with only 150 men out of the 600 he was planning to use in the attack. To make matters worse, none of the expected heavy equipment has arrived. The battery's defences were meant to be tackled with mortars, flamethrowers, mine detectors and scaling ladders; but all the battalion now has are its small arms plus one

machine gun and 20 lengths of Bangalore torpedo. Otway is undeterred, and, like so many airborne soldiers this morning, decides to get on with the job anyway. The operation to destroy the guns must be completed by 05:50 hours, when a naval bombardment by cruiser HMS *Arethusa* is to begin.

Farther south, all except 13 of the gliders carrying the 6th Airborne HQ and reinforcements arrive, although 34 glider pilots are killed in the landings. Major-General Gale sets up a divisional HQ in Ranville. From the Orne Canal bridge, companies of the 7th Battalion, 5th Parachute Brigade, begin to attack German positions in Bénouville.

AIR CAMPAIGN, COASTAL TARGETS
As part of the pre-assault bombardment, aircraft of RAF Bomber Command attack enemy concentrations along the invasion coast from 03:14 hours. Over the next 75 minutes the villages of La Pernelle, Maisy, Longues, Mont-Fleury and Houlgate are all attacked. The raids are heavy, with as many as 100 aircraft taking part in each, which leave the villages in ruin. Maisy is hit with over 500 tonnes (508 tons) of high explosive in 14 minutes.

03:54–04:10 HOURS

AIRBORNE ASSAULT, *US SECTOR*
Gliders carrying the reinforcements and heavy equipment for the 101st and 82nd Airborne divisions begin to land. The DZ for the 101st is around the

TUESDAY, JUNE 6

▶ *To prevent the Allies from landing and moving easily, the Germans flooded vast areas of rural France. In some places the water was waist deep.*

village of Hiesville, almost 10km (6 miles) from Utah Beach and 5km (3 miles) from the second of the four beach exits. The DZ for the 82nd is northwest of Ste Mère Eglise, between the road and rail line running north from Carentan. Out of the 52 gliders of the 82nd that left England, five actually land on the DZ and 15 others land within a couple of miles. But 22 are destroyed and 12 are badly damaged, many through collision with the sturdy Normandy hedgerows, which prove thicker and higher than intelligence reports had estimated. There are three deaths. Most of the jeeps they were carrying are destroyed, but 11 still work, as do eight of the anti-aircraft guns. Of the gliders of the 101st, six land on the DZ with the majority of the others coming in within 3km (2 miles) of it. Five men are killed, including the assistant division commander, Brigadier-General Pratt, and the unfortunate pilots of the glider carrying the bulldozer, which breaks

free on landing and smashes through the front of the aircraft, crushing them. Nevertheless, this proves one of the more successful glider drops of the morning, and soon over 100 troops, with six of the surviving anti-tank guns, are establishing themselves around the drop zones.

The paratroopers by this time are beginning to assemble and organize, usually in groups of no more than a dozen men, often from different outfits. To identify friend from foe in the dark, each paratrooper has been issued a "cricket", a metal toy that makes a clicking sound: one click being met with a two-click answer. The trouble is that men have lost their crickets in the drop and the toy sounds similar to the drawing of a rifle bolt. And the huge numbers of paratroopers wandering around Normandy in the dark is itself a problem. As one paratrooper recalled, "There were so many clicks and counterclicks that night that nobody could tell who was clicking at whom."

OPERATION NEPTUNE, *UTAH*

It is still dark as the transport ships of Task Force U begin to embark the first troops into their assault craft, the flat-bottomed, square-bowed LCA (Landing Craft, Assault), known as "Higgins" boats. These are ideal for landing on a beach, but in the 1.2m (4ft) swell now rising in the channel they make for a less than comfortable ride for soldiers who still have two and half hours to go until H-Hour. The troops embarking are from Companies B, C, F and E, 2nd Battalion, 8th Infantry Regiment, 4th Division. They will be among the first men ashore on D-Day. Now that

▼ *As dawn broke in northern France, Allied paratroopers skirmished with German forces, trying to take key strategic junctions and positions.*

embarkation of the LCA is underway, eight LCTs (Landing Craft, Tanks), each carrying four DD (Duplex-Drive) amphibious tanks, form up at the line of departure, 3660m (4000yds) from the two assault beaches designated as Tare Green and Uncle Red. They will be the first wave of vessels to sail towards Utah, the idea being to have tanks on the beach before the troops arrive. There are planned to be 26 waves of boats in the assault, which will be organized and guided by six control craft. For each beach, there will be one Patrol Craft acting as a primary control vessel, assisted by two LCC (Landing Craft, Control) fitted with radio and radar.

04:15 HOURS

AIRBORNE ASSAULT, *BRITISH SECTOR*

Colonel Otway launches his attack on the Merville battery, despite the fact that three gliders scheduled to land inside the battery perimeter with a company of paratroopers and sappers fail to arrive. However, in one of the few elements of the operation to go as planned, a reconnaissance party has been at work on the outer perimeter for the last couple of hours, cutting gaps in the wire and clearing four paths through the minefield. The enemy garrison is on alert, but unaware that its outer defences have been breached. Otway decides on a surprise

assault, attacking the main gate and the four artillery casemates simultaneously. He is banking on speed, surprise and aggression to compensate for his lack of manpower and equipment. At 04:15 hours, a squad of seven men create a diversion with a rush on the main gate as Bangalore torpedoes tear two gaps in the inner wire. With a cry of "Everybody in", Otway leads the charge. Two teams of paratroopers break into the casemates with grenades, while a third destroys the machine-gun posts outside. The fighting inside the case-mates quickly becomes the type of close-quarter battle the paratroopers are trained to win. Within 25 minutes of the start of the attack, Otway's men have captured the battery. Over 100 of the German garrison are dead, and 22 are prisoners. The paratroopers have taken 70 dead and wounded, reducing the colonel's battalion to 80 out of the 600 who left England last night.

Improvised charges are laid, the demolition explosives having been lost, and the guns – old French 75mm pieces, not the big German artillery guns that were expected – are blown up. With the job done, Otway leads his men on a march south towards the area where the 6th Airborne Division is concentrating its battalions along a ridge of high ground, east of Ranville.

To the southeast of Merville, from 04:00 hours, paratroopers attack six road and rail crossings over the River

Tuesday, June 6

Dives. At Bures and Troarn, bridges are demolished by Royal Engineers attached to the 3rd Parachute Squadron, while bridges at Varaville and Robehomme are targeted by men of the squadron's No.3 Troop, attached to the 1st Canadian Parachute Battalion. In one remarkable exploit, at Troarn, nine sappers, in a commandeered medical corps jeep, race through the main street under enemy fire to reach the bridge, which they demolish with explosives before making their get-away. By 09:30 hours, all crossings of the Dives have been cut. Because the Germans have flooded a huge area east of the river, their 711th Division is now isolated from the invasion bridgehead, making the Allied left flank now more secure.

05:00 HOURS

AIRBORNE ASSAULT, *US SECTOR*

After a chaotic drop and several hours wandering in the dark, US paratroopers are beginning to get into the fight, which at first involves them in a series of small actions: ambushing German patrols, clearing villages and hamlets and establishing roadblocks.

As dawn approaches, men of the 101st Airborne are moving to hold the road exits from Utah Beach. Exit 3, around the village of Audouville-la-Hubert, is secured by Lieutenant-Colonel Robert Cole of the 502nd Regiment and a mixed unit of 75 men who have marched in from the area of Ste Mère Eglise. To the south, men of

▼ *Young German troops manning an anti-aircraft position pose for a photograph before D-Day. Like many of their comrades, they are barely adults.*

▶ *Allied bombers dropped many tons of bombs onto German positions along the coast and the beaches. However, much of it was poorly targeted.*

the 506th Regiment are advancing to secure Exit 2 at Houdenienville and Exit 1 at Pouppeville. Meanwhile, farther south along the River Douve, near Brévands, about 100 men of the 501st Regiment, led by Captain Charles G. Shettle, are dug in and holding the northwest bank, denying the enemy a road crossing and therefore access to the left flank of Utah Beach.

Inland, in the 82nd Airborne area east of the River Merderet, men of the 3rd Battalion, 505th Regiment, led by Lieutenant-Colonel Krause, capture Ste Mère Eglise. Amazingly, they find the German garrison in bed, despite the earlier fighting when US paratroopers landed in the middle of the village! Krause has his men attack the billets with knives and grenades: 30 of the enemy surrender immediately, and 10 are killed when they offer resistance. In support of Krause, the 505th's 2nd Battalion, under Lieutenant Colonel Vandervoort, advances about 3km (2 miles) north of the village to establish a defence line at Neuville-au-Plain, across the main road to Cherbourg.

AIR CAMPAIGN, *COASTAL TARGETS*

Bomber Command begins the last of its pre-dawn attacks, with a raid by 110 Lancasters on Ouistreham, the port north of Caen. As day begins to break, at 05:15 hours, the RAF bombers depart, but the assault is resumed at first light 45 minutes later by the heavy bombers of the US Eighth Army Air Force. They attack targets behind Omaha Beach and the British sector, west of Caen. The area around Utah is tasked to medium bombers of the Ninth Army Air Force,

because the lighter bomb loads, to be dropped at lower levels, are likely to be safer for the Allied airborne troops now operating there. This wave of attacks is part of the Joint Fire Plan, designed to suppress coastal defences as the assault craft come ashore. They will continue until about 08:00 hours, when fighters and fighter-bombers take

▶ *German troops lay out barbed wire before D-Day. By dawn of June 6, all such preparations to hinder the Allied invasion were about to be tested.*

over to provide close-air support for the ground troops and fighter cover for the fleet and bridgehead.

OPERATION NEPTUNE, *JUNO AND SWORD*

Around 05:00 hours, the two Royal Navy midget submarines, *X-20* and *X-23*, having arrived 24 hours early for D-Day, finally surface after having spent the best part of the last 72 hours submerged. *X-20* takes up station off Juno, while *X-23* lies off Sword. Their green flashing lights mark the positions of the two beaches. Their presence is important, because the beaches here are flat and almost featureless. There are also several miles of offshore reef and rocky coast on the east side of Juno, to be marked out, for safety.

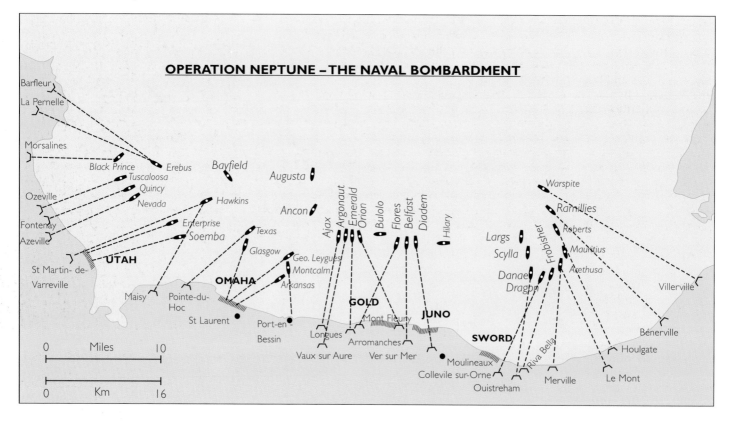

OPERATION NEPTUNE – THE NAVAL BOMBARDMENT

Barfleur
La Pernelle
Morsalines
Black Prince *Erebus* *Bayfield*
Tuscaloosa *Augusta*
Quincy
Ozeville *Nevada*
Hawkins *Ancon*
Fonteney *Enterprise*
Azeville *Soemba* *Texas*
UTAH *Glasgow*
Warspite
Ramillies
Roberts
Largs *Mauritius*
Scylla *Arethusa*
Danae
Dragon
Frobisher
St Martin- de-
Varreville
Geo. Leygues
Montcalm
Maisy Pointe-du- *Arkansas*
Hoc **OMAHA**
St Laurent
Port-en-
Bessin
Longues
Vaux sur Aure
Arromanches
Ver sur Mer
Ajax Argonaut Orion Bulolo Flores Diadem Hilary
Emerald Belfast
GOLD
Mont Fleury
JUNO
Moulineaux
Colleville sur-Orne
Ouistreham
SWORD
Riva Bella
Merville
Le Mont
Houlgate
Bénerville
Villerville

0 Miles 10
0 Km 16

GERMAN DEFENCES, *U-BOATS*
Also at around 05:00 hours, with a
major Allied landing now clearly
underway, the U-boats of Group
"Landwirt" (Farmer) are ordered into
the Channel. A total of 36 boats
prepare to set out from Brest, St
Nazaire, La Pallice and Lorient, and they
include all available snorkel boats:
these are submarines fitted with the

latest technology, and they are able to
remain submerged for long periods.

05:30 HOURS

OPERATION NEPTUNE, *UTAH*
In the middle of Task Force U's assault
area are the two tiny islands of St
Marcouf, about 6km (4 miles) offshore.
They are suspected of holding a
German observation post. To clear and

▲ *The positions of the Allied warships
in the bombardment groups. The lines
indicate the direction of their
bombardment of coastal defences.*

▼ *Allied ships in the Channel heading for
France. Note how each vessel has a
barrage balloon above. The balloons were
designed to discourage dive-bombing.*

secure them, men of the 4th and 24th Cavalry Squadrons are landed. They do not find any enemy German personnel there, but the soldiers take casualties from the mines and booby traps previously laid by the enemy.

OPERATION NEPTUNE, *SWORD*

German Navy E-boats launch a torpedo attack on Task Force S. Under orders from Navy Group West, three E-boats and two armed trawlers had sortied from Le Havre at 03:48 hours, and by 05:15 hours the E-boats were closing in on the fleet. Taking advantage of a smokescreen laid by the Allies to shield their own ships from the gun batteries at Le Havre, the E-boats begin their attack at 05:30 hours. Torpedoes narrowly miss the battleships *Ramillies* and *Warspite* and the headquarters ship HMS *Largs*; but the Norwegian destroyer *Svenner* is hit amidships. She breaks in two and goes to the bottom, although most of her crew are saved. The E-boats attempt to make their escape, but they are tracked by the radar on HMS *Warspite*, and the warship opens fire, sinking one of the E-boats. Other Allied warships also begin firing, and the cruiser *Arethusa* claims one trawler sunk. This attack is to be the only surface action the German Navy will fight today.

05:36 HOURS

OPERATION NEPTUNE, *UTAH*

The naval bombardment of the Normandy coast begins ahead of

▶ *The German Goliath was a miniature radio-controlled, motorized vehicle, designed as a remote tank-killer. A number were found near the landing beaches.*

schedule to counter German gunfire. For nearly two hours German coastal batteries have been under orders to open fire on the fleet, but, because their targeting radar has been hit by air attack, only as first light approaches can they find targets. Off Utah Beach the US destroyers *Fitch* and *Corry* are shelled at about 05:05 hours, followed soon after by the minesweepers working inshore. The cruiser HMS *Black Prince* returns fire and quickly finds herself targeted. With a battle escalating by the minute, the commander of the Western Task Force Bombardment Group, Admiral Deyo, decides to order all his ships to open fire, 20 minutes ahead of the planned time. By 05:36 hours, Utah and Omaha are under naval bombardment. Off Gold Beach, the bombardment ships are in action even earlier: the cruiser *Orion* opens fire on a battery at Arromanches at 05:10 hours.

At his command post near the Orne Canal bridge, 8km (5 miles) from the coast, Major Howard, whose D-Day was already nearly six hours old, could feel the effects of the naval guns:

"The barrage coming in was quite terrific. It was as though you could feel the whole ground shaking toward the coast, and this was going on like hell.

Soon afterward it seemed to get nearer. Well, they were obviously lifting the barrage farther inland as our boats and craft came in, and it was very easy, standing there and hearing all this going on and seeing all the smoke over in that direction, to realize what exactly was happening and keeping our fingers crossed for those poor buggers coming in by sea."

▼ *The American battleship USS Nevada providing naval gunfire support for the US troops about to assault Utah Beach on D-Day.*

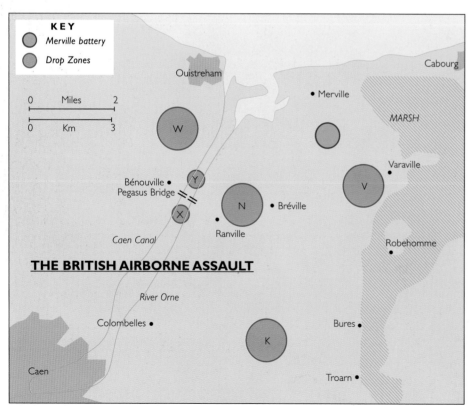

▲ *A French house in ruins. After the landings, the effects of Allied naval and aerial bombardment on the areas near the beachheads could clearly be seen.*

06:30–07:45 HOURS

THE BEACH ASSAULTS,
US, BRITISH & CANADIAN SECTORS
This short period of time, of one and a quarter hours, marks the H-Hours for the beach assaults themselves. Against the vicissitudes of sea currents and geography, facing unpredictable enemy opposition, and in a situation where the neatly drawn plans so often have to be cast aside in favour of on-the-spot improvisation, Allied seaborne forces attempt to gain a toehold on Nazi-occupied northern Europe. It is fragile hold, to be sure, and by midnight many units will be well short of their D-Day objectives. But it will be enough. (The momentous events of the seaborne assaults on Utah, Omaha, Gold, Juno and Sword beaches are described in their own separate chapters, below.)

The landings will test how successfully the airborne forces have prepared the ground in the early morning, while those now vulnerable and scattered airborne troops are eagerly awaiting the arrival of reinforcements and armour from the beaches. The beach landings will also make quite it clear to Hitler's commanders that this is, indeed, the Allied invasion.

07:30–24:00 HOURS

AIRBORNE ASSAULT,
BRITISH SECTOR
As the British 3rd Division begins to land on Sword, the 6th Airborne Division is holding the Allied left flank, east of Caen, with five battalions centred on the canal and river bridges of the Orne. The 6th has no artillery, the naval guns offshore can reach only as far south as Le Plein, and its tactical reserve is down to just 60 men.

According to the schedule, units of the 3rd Division are due to be at the Orne two hours after H-Hour; but by 09:00 hours there is no sign of them, and German activity everywhere is increasing. There is street fighting in Bénouville and the bridges are under

◀ *The British drop zones were spread out northeast of Caen, on both sides of the River Orne and its canal. The famous Pegasus Bridge lay between zones X and Y.*

THE BRITISH AIRBORNE ASSAULT

KEY
● Merville battery
● Drop Zones

Ouistreham
Cabourg
Merville
MARSH
W
Bénouville •
Pegasus Bridge
Y
V
Varaville
N • Bréville
X
Ranville
Caen Canal
Robehomme •
River Orne
Colombelles •
Bures •
K
Caen
Troarn •

0 Miles 2
0 Km 3

▶ *Dozens of Allied gliders lie abandoned by the troops they were carrying. The three gliders in the centre illustrate how close each landing came to disaster.*

constant sniper fire. At about 10:00 hours, the Germans make a sortie in two small gunboats down the canal from Ouistreham and a lone fighter-bomber makes a bomb run, though both actions are ineffective.

The situation east of the river stays relatively quiet until about 11:00 hours, when 21st Panzer's Battle Group Von Luck attempts to take Ranville from the south. The two-hour fight ends when the Germans withdraw to regroup.

At 13:30 hours, Lord Lovat's commandos, of the 1st Special Service Brigade (1st SSB), reach the canal, and are deployed in the frontlines. A link has been made with the beachhead, but 6th Airborne's hold remains tenuous throughout the afternoon and evening, as it fights off renewed attacks from Battle Group Von Luck and has to reinforce Bénouville. The division's area is finally secured at about 20:50 hours, with the arrival of 246 gliders bringing in the 6th Air Landing Brigade. It includes three battalions of infantry, together with engineers, light artillery and a regiment of light tanks.

AIRBORNE ASSAULT, *US SECTOR*
In two separate operations, about 128 gliders land in the Cotentin between 20:50 and 23:00 hours, with ammunition and supplies for the 101st and 82nd Airborne. Among the heavy equipment and reinforcements also brought in are a field artillery regiment with 16 105mm howitzers, medical and signals troops, and nearly 100 jeeps.

OPERATION NEPTUNE, *FOLLOW-UP*
At about 16:00, the lead convoys of the follow-up Task Forces B and L begin to arrive off the Normandy coast to catch the afternoon high tide. Force B arrives off Omaha Beach, carrying regiments of the 1st and 29th Divisions, engineers and headquarters troops. Force L, off Gold and Juno beaches, brings units of the 3rd (Canadian) Division, the 51st (Highland) Division and the tactical HQ of Montgomery's 21st Army Group.

▼ *The 6th Airborne Division positions east of the Orne were to be reinforced by 12:00 hours by lightly armed commandos such as these.*

TUESDAY, JUNE 6

On D-Day evening, Montgomery and his staff leave Southwick House to join the HQ. They embark on the destroyer HMS *Faulknor* and sail by 22:00 hours.

GERMAN AIR FORCE, *RESPONSES*
Despite being heavily outnumbered, some units and aircraft of Air Fleet 3 manage to break through the Allied fighter screen in an attempt to disrupt Allied landings. At about 09:00 hours, two FW 190 fighters fly a low-level sortie along the invasion coast from Sword to Omaha. Later in the day, 50 FW 190s of Ground Attack Wing 4 are ordered from eastern France to bases around Tours, south of Normandy. Allied fighters shoot down five aircraft, but enough land to launch three sorties against Sword Beach in the afternoon. They are all driven off with losses. From 22:30 hours, German aircraft, in ones and twos, begin uncoordinated raids on the invasion fleet.

▼ *British infantry from Sword look on as gliders of the 6th Airborne Division make their main assault at 21:00 hours.*

▶ *General "Sepp" Dietrich, commander of I SS Panzer Corps (left, wearing peaked cap). He was caught unawares on D-Day, visiting a unit in Belgium.*

GERMAN DEFENCES, *MOBILIZING*
The landings of US paratroopers in the Cotentin have LXXXIV Corps in St Lô on a state of alert before dawn, and by 08:30 hours its commander, General Marcks, has realized this is an invasion. Along the coast both the 352nd and 716th divisions are being pushed inland and there is news of British tanks active north of Bayeux and Caen.

At the Paris HQ of OB West, Field Marshal von Rundstedt can get no orders from OKW – because Hitler is asleep – and finally acts on his own initiative. He hands control of the 21st Panzer Division to the Seventh Army and Marcks's corps, finally freeing division commander General Feuchtinger from his eight-hour wait for orders to move against the British. Meanwhile, at the chateau at La Roche-Guyon, HQ of Army Group B, chief of staff General Speidel phones Rommel at his home in Germany with the news. The field marshal sets off immediately, but does not reach his headquarters until 21:30 hours.

During the afternoon, OKW finally rises from its stupor: 12th SS Panzer and Panzer Lehr are taken out of reserve and placed under the control of Seventh Army, with orders to advance west towards Caen for an attack on 7 June. Command of the panzers is taken away from LXXXIV Corps, with the arrival near Normandy of I SS Panzer Corps

HQ under Lieutenant-General Josef "Sepp" Dietrich.

At 16:53 hours, with nine Allied divisions now ashore, Hitler sends his first message of the day to von Rundstedt. It emphasizes "the desire of the Supreme Commander [Hitler] to have

▲ *The smashed remains of a British Horsa glider that landed on D-Day.*

the enemy in the bridgehead annihilated by the evening of June 6", and concludes: "The beachhead must be cleaned up not later than tonight."

DECISIVE MOMENTS

HOW THE WORLD LEARNED OF D-DAY

The Nazi regime itself first told the world about D-Day; and US newspapers first published that news. Nazi Propaganda minister Josef Goebbels, spotting an opportunity if the landings were defeated on the beaches, had the news transmitted from Berlin via his TransOcean News Agency at 07:00 hours. The Associated Press, working seven hours behind Berlin, picked this up, and the *New York Times* had a special edition on the city's streets only 90 minutes after the Omaha landing began.

In Britain, with news tightly controlled by SHAEF, the public learned of D-Day only at 09:30 hours, when the BBC broadcast SHAEF's terse "Communiqué No.1": "Allied naval forces, supported by strong air forces, began landing Allied armies this morning on the coast of northern France." Meanwhile, journalists from the free world were locked in a Ministry of Information building. They were given four press conferences during the day, but could not leave the building without escort, and had to submit their stories for censoring before publication.

June 6
UTAH BEACH

▲ An Allied rocket ship, essentially a converted LCT, fires high-explosive ordnance onto German positions. These craft were top-secret before D-Day.

American troops made good progress on Utah, meeting light resistance from poorly armed German soldiers. Engineers had cleared the beach by noon. Company strength attacks took out enemy strongpoints, and troops waded neck-deep through fields flooded by the Germans. By midnight on June 6, 23,000 men had landed at Utah, plus 1700 tanks, guns and trucks, with only 197 casualties suffered.

H-HOUR: 06:30 HOURS

At 05:30 hours the first waves of landing craft from Task Force U are on their way towards beaches Uncle Red and Tare Green, which form a front of about 2010m (2200yds). In the lead are eight LCTs (Landing Craft, Tanks), which carry 32 DD (Duplex-Drive) tanks of the 70th Tank Battalion, scheduled for launch 4575m (5000yds) offshore. Behind them are assault craft carrying companies of the 1st and 2nd Battalion, 8th Infantry Regiment, and a detachment of engineers. These specialists, organized into eight-man Underwater Demolition Teams (UDTs), are tasked with blowing up beach

▶ A US battleship pounds enemy positions on the shore, as an LCT, carrying reinforcements of US troops, heads for Utah Beach.

▲ *Wading through the surf, US troops make their way onto Utah Beach to support the advance parties that had landed before them.*

obstacles ahead of the rising tide, clearing safe areas for the succeeding waves of invasion craft to beach.

As the assault troops close in on the beaches, the Joint Fire Plan moves into its next phase. The naval bombardment lifts, and soon afterwards 270 Marauder medium bombers of the Ninth Army Air Force make a bomb run on enemy positions. At sea, close fire support for the troops will be given by LCGs (Landing Craft, Guns), armed with 4.7in guns, which take position on the flanks of the first boat wave. Also on station, about 640m (700yds) offshore, are specially converted tank landing craft fitted with rocket launchers, which can blanket 155m (170yds) of beach with 790 5in rockets launched in salvo.

The boat waves are still several thousand metres from the beach when their landing schedule starts to break down. A strong tidal current is pushing the landing craft off course, and at about 05:45 hours the Patrol Craft acting as the

primary control vessel for Tare Red hits a mine and sinks. The LCC (Landing Craft, Control), which are to set up the line of departure, cannot take a bearing on the beach because it is hidden by the dust and smoke of the shore bombardment. They identify the wrong stretch of coast, and the assault craft carrying troops set off to land 1370m (1500yds) south of the intended beach area.

Meanwhile, the launch plan for the DD tanks has also gone wrong. Having lost their control vessel, the LCT are now behind the first assault wave when they should be in front. The disorganization is made worse when an LCT hits a mine and sinks, taking four DD tanks with it. The commander of the remaining control vessel decides at this point to abandon the schedule and take the remaining LCT inshore and have them launch their tanks about a

mile from the beach, to land 15 minutes behind the first assault wave.

At 06:30 hours, exactly on schedule, the 8th Infantry hits Utah Beach. The tide has pushed them even farther south, and they are now 1830m (2000yds) from where they should be. It means companies have lost their assault objectives; but this area proves to be a far better proposition. It is less heavily defended, and the companies make it ashore almost unopposed.

▼ *Captured German prisoners are marched, hands on heads, to a holding pen by troops of the US 4th Infantry.*

JUNE 6, UTAH BEACH

▶ *US soldiers make their way inland from Utah Beach through the fields, which were flooded by German forces in an attempt to prevent glider landings.*

In the first wave is the assistant commander of the 4th Infantry Division, Brigadier-General Theodore Roosevelt. The general has volunteered to be among the first men ashore, and it is his command decision on the beach that sets the US Army's campaign in Europe in motion. Realizing that his men have landed in the wrong place, Roosevelt calls an impromptu conference with 8th Infantry's three senior officers. The choice is whether to transport the regiment to where it should be or move inland from where it is, which, Roosevelt discovers, is opposite the causeway to Exit 2: in the plan, Victor Green and Victor Red. With DD tanks now landing, UDT engineers blowing up obstacles and troops beginning to advance inland, the decision is effectively made already. In later reports, Roosevelt is reported as giving the order with the words: "We'll start the invasion from right here."

By 08:00 hours units of the next infantry regiment, the 22nd, have begun to arrive, while along the shoreline UDT engineers have cleared

▼ *A US mobile signalling battery sets up its equipment on the shore of Utah Beach. The equipment was used to signal to shipping out at sea in the Channel.*

640m (700yds) of beach, and are preparing to blow gaps in the concrete sea wall, to allow vehicles access inland. German resistance along the beachhead has all but collapsed. It is found that the sector has been held by a regiment of Osttruppen (Eastern troops), mainly from Soviet Georgia, who surrender at the first opportunity.

There is still some shelling by 88mm artillery, mainly at the landing craft, but save for random mortar fire the build-up of troops and supplies on the beach goes on without hindrance. The third infantry regiment, the 12th, begins to land at 10:30 hours. At 10:45 hours, Admiral Moon, commander of Task Force U, receives a signal from the beachhead: "Landings can be made anywhere on Red Beach ... obstacles no longer obstacles." Six waves of landing craft set off immediately.

The assault battalions begin to move inland to secure the roads from the beachhead, in order to link up with the paratroopers they hope have secured the exits. They are faced with two obstacles. The dunes behind the beach are seeded with tens of thousands of anti-personnel and anti-tank mines, while farther inland an area up to 1.6km (1 mile) wide has been flooded. The 2nd Battalion, 8th Infantry, moves south along the beach road to pick up Exit 1 causeway, which leads to Pouppeville. With support from tanks, German strongpoints are easily overrun, but the battalion takes

▶ *Carrying with them all the necessary equipment to take the fight to the Germans, GIs of the US 4th Infantry Division move inland from Utah Beach.*

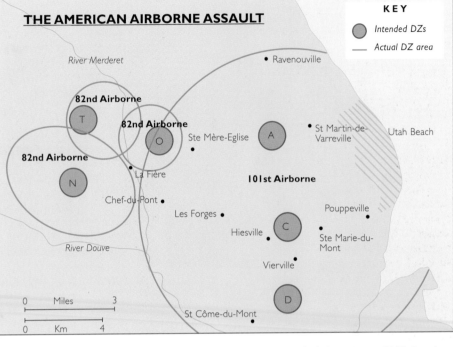

THE AMERICAN AIRBORNE ASSAULT

KEY

⬤ Intended DZs

— Actual DZ area

River Merderet

• Ravenouville

82nd Airborne

T

82nd Airborne

O

Ste Mère-Eglise

A

• St Martin-de-Varreville

Utah Beach

82nd Airborne

N

• La Fière

Chef-du-Pont

101st Airborne

Les Forges •

Hiesville

C

Pouppeville

Ste Marie-du-Mont

River Douve

Vierville •

D

St Côme-du-Mont

0 Miles 3

0 Km 4

▲ **The intended drop zones (DZ) for the US airborne forces. However, the area that the parachute and glider forces actually landed in was very wide.**

casualties from the anti-personnel mines. At 11:10 hours, the first contact is made between US seaborne forces and the paratroopers when the battalion crosses the causeway and links up with men of the 501st Regiment, 101st Airborne Division, east of Pouppeville. The village has been under attack from a small mixed force of paratroopers since about 08:00 hours, and by now is largely in US hands. The 8th Infantry move in to secure it, while the paratroopers advance east to their next divisional objective, the village of Ste Marie-du-Mont. To the north, the 8th Infantry's 3rd and 1st battalions are moving inland to secure the causeways to Exits 2 and 3.

By late-morning there is

A US paratrooper, armed with an M1 Thompson submachine gun, boards his transport the night before the Allied airborne assault.

serious congestion on the beachhead. None of the exits has been entirely secured, and vehicles are beginning to back up along the beach roads. This causes difficulties for the beach controllers, the specialist battalions tasked with organizing the movement of assault forces off the beaches. For the colonels commanding the 12th and 22nd Infantry regiments, it means their men cannot use the roads to get inland, making a bad situation worse. They are already a long way south of where they should be, and with time moving on, reaching their D-Day objectives will mean immediate action. The commanders decide to take the difficult option and march their battalions across the flooded country towards the higher ground around the village of St Martin-de-Varreville, due to be in the hands of the 101st Airborne. From there, the 12th will continue on to the area northeast of Ste Mère Eglise, held, according to the plan, by the 82nd Airborne, while the 22nd Infantry will move north to hold the right flank of the bridgehead, between St Germain-de-Varreville and the coast.

The march takes nearly four hours to cover just over 1.6km (1 mile). One sergeant in the 12th Infantry later recalls the journey: "Aerial reconnaissance had estimated that the flooded area was maybe ankle deep, except in irrigation ditches, which they estimated to be about eighteen inches deep. Well, they made a big mistake. That flooded area was in some places up to your waist and the irrigation ditches were over your head. Some brave souls would swim across the irrigation ditches and throw toggle ropes back and haul the rest of us across."

Despite the difficulties of the march, both regiments make it across the inundated plain without encountering any Germans, save an occasional sniper. Clear of the floods, the 12th Infantry makes a rapid advance through St Martin-de-Varreville, and by dusk, about 22:30 hours, is over 8km (5 miles) inland at Beuzeville-au-Plain northeast of Ste Mère Eglise, and preparing to move north. The 12th Infantry has a battalion of the 502nd Parachute Infantry (of the 101st) on its right. The 22nd Infantry, meanwhile, holds St Germain de Varreville with two battalions, while a third has moved up the beach road to hold a position 6km (4 miles) north of the assault beaches. By nightfall on D-Day, the right flank of the Allied invasion front is being held by seven battalions of infantry.

By midnight on 6 June, the 8th Infantry, having access to the roads leading from Exits 1, 2 and 3, and supported by tanks, are over 9km (6 miles) inland. The 2nd Battalion has moved through St Marie-du-Mont and made contact with the 3rd Battalion from Exit 2 to the north. They have seized the crossroads of the main Carentan–Cherbourg road at Les Forges and are 3km (2 miles) south of Ste Mère Eglise; but they now face a large pocket of German resistance before they can relieve the paratroopers holding the village. Facing the Germans to the east is the 1st Battalion, which has advanced up the road from Exit 3 through the hamlet of Audouville la Hubert.

The D-Day landings on Utah Beach can be reckoned a qualified success. Over 20,000 troops have been landed, with 1700 vehicles, while the casualty figure for the 4th Division is only 197, of whom 60 have been lost at sea. The Utah bridgehead, however, remains very small and the division's advance is nearly 11km (7 miles) short of the D-Day objective set by 21st Army Group.

AIRBORNE ASSAULT, *UTAH AREA*

At 09:30 hours, three hours after the landings on Utah Beach began, the Germans launch a counterattack south of Ste Mère Eglise, in a bid to retake the village captured at dawn by the 82nd Airborne's 505th Regiment. The 2nd Battalion, under Lieutenant-Colonel Vandervoort, holding a position 3km (2 miles) north of the village at Neuville-au-Plain, is pulled back to strengthen defences, leaving only a platoon of 42 men to hold Neuville, now under attack from units of the German 1058th Regiment. Outnumbered five to one, the paratroopers hold them off for the next eight hours. But just 16 out of the 42 paratroopers survive the fight. South of the town, the German assault is held, and a company sized counterattack by the paratroopers on a German convoy on the Carentan road secures Ste Mère Eglise for the rest of D-Day.

▼ *As US forces create a bridgehead, hundreds of extra troops, as well as vehicles and equipment, flood ashore to support the thrust inland. It was a scene of organized chaos.*

▲ *A knocked-out US Sherman tank, surrounded by the wreckage of other pieces of equipment, lies stricken on Utah Beach.*

To the west of the village, along the Merderet, fighting continues throughout the day. Elements of the 82nd are trying to secure two bridges at La Fière and Chef-du-Pont, and make contact with isolated groups of paratroopers holding positions west of the river, around Amfreville, and under threat from the German 1057th Regiment.

Along the River Douve to the south, units of the 101st are also having difficulty seizing their objectives. One of the most important of these, for the invasion's planners, is the lock gates at la Barquette. By mid-morning, a force led by Captain Shettle holds the north bank of the river, near le Port; but farther upstream paratroopers have met strong opposition from a battalion of the German 1058th Regiment in the town of St Côme-du-Mont. To the south, units of the élite German 6th Parachute Regiment, based in Carentan, are defending the road and rail bridges over the Douve that the 101st is meant to destroy. However, by nightfall a mixed force of 150 paratroopers has succeeded in taking the lock gates and has dug-in on the south bank.

After a chaotic series of drops and landings, the American airborne divisions hold some of their D-Day objectives – but tenuously; and all around they face superior numbers of German forces. Fortunately, the disorganized assault has confused the Germans, who are staying in their fixed positions and not counterattacking: they do not know how many paratroopers they face and what their objectives are. Aggression in the face of the enemy has hidden the fact that the two airborne divisions are dangerously understrength. Of over 12,000 paratroopers that boarded in England barely 5000 are organized and facing the enemy at the end of D-Day. The rest are scattered, lost, or dead.

June 6 OMAHA BEACH

On Omaha US troops struggled to make headway on the beach as intense German machine-gun and mortar fire inflicted enormous losses on the invaders. The amphibious DD tanks designated to take out fortified positions sank like stones, leaving the infantry exposed. Only acts of heroism and supreme bravery forced the Germans back.

▼ *The view of Omaha Beach as seen from the deck of USS* Ancon, *the flagship of the landing forces in that sector.*

06:30 Hours, H-Hour

The first minesweepers arrived off Omaha just after midnight, and by 00:55 hours had completed sweeping and identifying the Transport Area with marker buoys. By 02:20 hours, the bombardment warships were arriving, and 30 minutes later the first 16 transport ships of Task Force O, commanded by Rear-Admiral John L. Hall, began dropping anchor 17.5km (11 miles) offshore. The Task Force is anchoring this far from the coast to be out of range of German 155mm guns, believed to be in concrete emplacements on the cliffs of the Pointe-du-Hoc, about 8km (5 miles) west of Vierville-sur-Mer. The guns are reckoned to impose such a threat that a Ranger Group, made up of the 2nd and 5th battalions, are to make an assault to capture and destroy them.

▶ *The US battleship USS* Nevada *fires a salvo with her heavy guns at enemy shore batteries on the Cherbourg Peninsula on D-Day.*

For the assault on Omaha to work, V Corps is relying on overwhelming firepower to break the coastal defences, allowing the first wave of infantry to land largely unopposed. The bombardment will be provided by air force bombers, naval warships and DD (Duplex-Drive) tanks, which are due to land five minutes ahead of H-hour. The first assault wave to land will consist of

▲ American landing craft carrying troops stream towards Omaha Beach. In the background sits USS Augusta, the Western Task Force invasion flagship.

▼ The massive guns of USS Nevada fire yet another salvo at German positions along the French coastline.

STRATEGY & TACTICS

THE CHOICE OF OMAHA

A seaborne assault on Omaha beach was always part of the Allied invasion plan. Even the operation proposed by COSSAC in December 1943, using a limited front of three divisions, envisaged a landing west of Port-en-Bessin, between the villages of Vierville-sur-Mer, St Laurent and Colleville.

The reason was geography. Between the estuary of the River Douve and the village of Arromanches to the east, a distance of 40km (25 miles), this area has the only firm sandy beach suitable for a landing. The beach itself is about 9.5km (6 miles) long and lies in a crescent shape, between cliffs which rise to 30m (100ft). At low tide the beach is about 275m (300yds) wide, and in 1944 was backed by a wide stretch of shingle about 2m (6ft) high. Behind this was a sea wall of wood and stone, a beach road and area of marshy ground up to 180m (200yds) wide. Rising up from this is a huge escarpment– a series of steep, scrub-covered bluffs over 50m (160ft)

high, which dominate the whole beach. For the invasion troops with their vehicles and artillery, the only way off the beach and up to the plateau above was through four small ravines, or draws. Only the most westerly of these had a paved surface and led from the beach road to Vierville, about 1km (half a mile) away; the next, near a group of deserted beach houses at Les Moulin, was a dirt road leading to St Laurent; the third was no more than a dirt track, while the fourth led to Colleville.

To assault this type of ground from the sea posed one of the greatest challenges of D-Day; but it was essential it succeed. It held the key to the Allied right flank. With the invasion front extended to Utah Beach, US divisions fighting in the Cotentin Peninsula would be cut off and in danger of being overwhelmed by German units from Brittany – unless the men from Omaha could make it inland and link up with the British sector beginning at Gold Beach, near Arromanches.

eight infantry companies, each assaulting one beach sector. On the right are four companies of the 116th Regiment, and on the right four companies of the 16th Regiment. Each has been trained to tackle a specific draw (ravine exit). The plan is not to become involved in a fight on the beach but to move inland immediately to control the beach exits and secure perimeters around assembly areas near the villages Vierville-sur-Mer, St Laurent and Colleville. For this reason they are heavily laden with over 132kg (60lb) of equipment, including mortars, flame-throwers and demolition equipment. There will be no charge up the beach.

Once the draws are secure, engineering equipment will land to clear the shingle bank and anti-tank ditch – tracked vehicles cannot move on the stones of the shingle. This will allow tanks and vehicles to move up the bluffs and advance inland.

The plan goes wrong from the very first. The naval bombardment begins on schedule at 05:50 hours, but the air bombardment, due to strike at 06:00 hours, does not materialize. Five hundred heavy bombers of the Eighth Army Air Force miss the coast completely because of low cloud, and drop 1220 tonnes (1200 tons) of bombs 5km (3 miles) inland. At sea, meanwhile, the DD tanks are sinking. Launched

▶ *Approaching Omaha Beach, under heavy German machine-gun fire, US troops jump from the ramp of a Coast Guard landing craft and head for shore.*

▼ *Seen from another landing craft, hundreds of US soldiers struggle to get ashore. On entering the water, many had to abandon their heavy kit to avoid drowning, and arrived on land unarmed.*

STRATEGY & TACTICS

GERMAN DEFENCES AT OMAHA

German commanders had also identified the beach between Vierville and Colleville as a potential landing site, and from April 1944 had been making preparations to defend it. This work turned the already difficult terrain along Omaha Beach into an almost impregnable defensive position.

Along the beach there were three belts of anti-landing obstacles, located between the high and low tidal marks. At the high water line, beyond the shingle embankment, there was a triple belt of barbed wire and mines along the sea wall. Beyond the beach road, the Germans dug an anti-tank ditch 1.8m (6ft) deep. The first bunkers were located on either side of the entrances to four draws

(ravines). The draw codenamed D1, which carried the beach road to Vierville, was blocked by a concrete barrier over 3.6m (12ft) thick. The bluffs above were defended with mines, barbed wire and trip-wired explosive charges. The flat marshy land adjoining the bluffs was also mined.

It was above the beach that German forces concentrated their most powerful defences. On the crest of the plateau, overlooking the four draws, were eight concrete strongpoints, manned by up to 30 men. They were each equipped with about 10 machine guns and heavier weapons, including 50mm cannon and artillery pieces of 75mm or 88mm calibre. To support these positions, mortars, rocket launchers and light artillery pieces were located in emplacements inland, while

anti-tank guns covered the exits from the draws. These weapons were pre-sighted on positions along the beach and had overlapping fields of fire. The crescent shape of the beach also allowed the positioning of emplacements on the cliffs at either end to provide enfilading fire by artillery and machine guns along the length of the beach. Manning these defences were about 800 men of the 916th Grenadier Regiment, 352nd Division, who had had three months to prepare their positions. The regiment had a large number of "Osttruppen" conscripts, controlled by a cadre of veteran German NCOs from the Eastern Front. The failure to recognize the presence of the 352nd Division behind Omaha was one of the most serious intelligence deficiencies of the Allied invasion.

▲ *US assault troops huddle behind the protective front of a landing craft as it nears the beachhead at Omaha. Nerves would have been shredded at the sight of the carnage ahead.*

4575m (5000yds) offshore at 05:40 hours, no consideration has been made for the rough seas. A strong tidal current and westerly wind whip up a swell that swamps all but 5 of the 32 first-wave tanks. The rough seas are also pulling the assault craft out of position, and as they approach the beach at 06:30 hours, most of them are over 900m (1000yds) east of where they should be. Meanwhile, the naval bombardment comes to an end after just 40 minutes – not enough time to destroy the German defences. As the landing craft approach the beach at H-hour, the German defenders hold their fire: but the moment the craft beach and their ramps go down, every German gun on Omaha opens up on the US troops.

It is a slaughter. The infantry land to find not one tank on the beach and all the German defences intact. Boat-loads of men are killed before they even leave their landing craft. As enemy fire increases, the crews of many assault craft stop too far from shore or hit submerged sandbars, and the troops jump into deep water and drown. Those that do make it ashore, waterlogged and carrying heavy gear, struggle under fire across the 275m (300yds) of beach towards the shingle bank, where they try to take shelter behind the beach obstacles. Within minutes of the start of the invasion, the command structure of the assault companies has begun to collapse. Company A of the 116th, the only company in the first wave to land in the right place, loses all its sergeants and all but one of its officers in the space of the first 10 minutes. Elsewhere, men get ashore only to find themselves lost and out of sight of the beach exits. While survivors, many

▶ *Seen here in training, these US troops would not have been prepared for the sights and sounds of Omaha Beach. While they knew the drill, they could not have anticipated the dire situation to come.*

without weapons, huddle against the shingle bank trying to dig-in, the enemy begins to target them with mortars.

As the first assault wave dies on the beach, the follow-on waves of troops and equipment keep coming. Radio contact with the lead companies has been lost – all the radios have been destroyed – so without news that the first wave has failed the invasion schedule carries on as planned. Soon, landing craft carrying tanks, vehicles, supplies, even admininstrative and maintenance troops, are coming into land only to hit beach obstacles that remain intact because the engineers sent to destroy them have been killed. Those vehicles that do manage to land either sink in the rising tide or are destroyed within minutes, adding to the chaos. By 08:30 hours, not a man or vehicle has moved off the beach. The plan to take Omaha has collapsed and the invasion is in danger of failing.

A signal has finally gone out from the navy beach controllers suspending the landing of all vehicles, but follow-up units are still coming in, and many of those troops that make it ashore alive later describe the beach as a vision of Hell. Hundreds of dead and wounded men litter the beach, vehicles and landing craft are burning, as are the bluffs above, set alight by constant explosions. Everywhere there is enemy fire. One captain of the 16th,

▼ *Crossed rifles in the sand are a comrade's tribute to this American soldier, who was hit while trying to take cover behind a wooden beach obstacle.*

Fred Hall, remembers particularly "the noise – always the noise, naval gunfire, small arms, artillery, and mortar fire, aircraft overhead, engine noises, the shouting and the cries of the wounded, no wonder some people couldn't handle it".

Offshore, word is finally getting back to the generals in the Task Force that the landings are in deep trouble. First Army commander, General Bradley, begins to consider abandoning Omaha altogether and ordering Task Force O east to land with the British on Gold.

2ND RANGERS, *POINTE-DU-HOC*

As the fighting on Omaha begins, three companies of the 2nd Rangers, led by Colonel James E. Rudder, scale the cliffs of the Pointe-du-Hoc and attack the six huge concrete emplacements there. Intelligence reports say they hold 155mm guns. The Rangers arrive off the Pointe about 40 minutes late, because of the heavy seas, and begin their attack at 07:10 hours. Their LCA

▼ *Surrounded by ammunition boxes, three US soldiers provide covering fire for their comrades up ahead with a .30in M1919 machine gun.*

(Landing Craft, Assault) land them within 27m (30yds) of the cliff. Each LCA is mounted with three pairs of rocket-propelled grapnels, which project ropes and rope ladders onto the cliff edge. The Rangers also carry light 34m (112ft) tubular steel ladders,

▲ *With order gradually emerging from chaos, US troops organize their German prisoners of war on Omaha.*

which they quickly assemble. Using this equipment, the Rangers scale the cliff and within 15 minutes have

146

increasing sniper fire from German troops, who are beginning to move back in towards the Pointe-du-Hoc. Rudder's command of about 200 is scheduled to be reinforced by 500 men of the 5th Ranger Battalion together with two more companies of the 2nd Rangers from Omaha. But Rudder's men are unaware of the chaos on the beach and that there are no reinforcements on the way. Rudder discovers this only when a message from the 1st Division gets through in the afternoon, by which time the Rangers are under attack from a full German battalion and are being pushed back towards the Pointe-du-Hoc.

08:30 HOURS

As the Omaha plan disintegrates, the infantry, pinned down under enemy fire, begin to advance off the beach. To begin with, this is simply a matter of survival. In the words of Colonel George Taylor, commander of the 16th Infantry: "There are two kinds of people on this beach: the dead and those about to die. So let's get the hell out of here!"

Organization begins to reassert itself among the shattered survivors of the first boat waves, huddled at the sea wall. In small groups, often led by an NCO or junior officer, they blow gaps in the wire and begin to climb up the bluffs. They are helped by the naval destroyers, who come close inshore to deliver fire support.

established themselves on the top in company strength. There is no German resistance. By 07:45 hours, all three companies are on the cliff top and Colonel Rudder has established his command post in a bomb crater.

Assault parties now set off to take the gun emplacements. There is some fighting as they run into small groups of Germans inside, but the action is short-lived. Once inside the emplacements, the Rangers discover that the guns have been removed and replaced with wooden dummies to save them from Allied bombing. Five of them are later discovered by a patrol about 1.6km (1 mile) away, in an orchard, and camouflaged. They are mounted and being prepared to fire. Rangers destroy their breaches with thermal grenades.

▶ Wounded of the US 3rd Battalion, 16th Infantry Regiment, take shelter from enemy fire under the cliffs at Omaha.

With their mission completed, at about 08:30 hours the Rangers move south about 1.6km (1 mile). Here they begin to dig in, as they come under

JUNE 6, OMAHA BEACH

▶ *The positions of the German and US forces around Omaha at 23:00 hours on June 6, 1944. Note how little ground had been taken in the east compared to the area around Les Forges.*

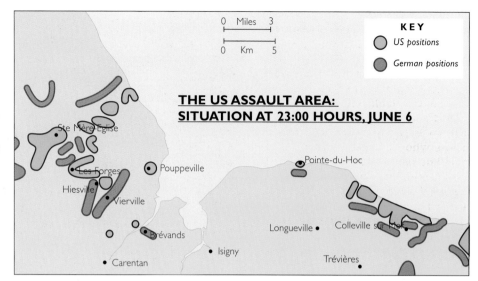

THE US ASSAULT AREA:
SITUATION AT 23:00 HOURS, JUNE 6

KEY
US positions
German positions

0 Miles 3
0 Km 5

Ste Mère Eglise
Les Forges
Hiesville
Vierville
Pouppeville
Brévands
Carentan
Isigny
Pointe-du-Hoc
Longueville
Colleville sur Mer
Trévières

By 08:30 hours, men of Company C of the 116th, with General Norman Cota, assistant commander of the 29th Division, have made it to the top of the Les Moulins draw towards St Laurent. They are reinforced by the 5th Ranger Battalion, under Colonel Max Schneider: he has managed to land his entire command almost without loss. Farther east, men of the 16th Infantry are on the plateau between the St Laurent and Colleville draws.

To the senior officers on the command ships stationed several miles out, with almost no communication with the shore, the situation is still confused and the outcome looks in doubt. But the men on the beach are making slow, but steady, progress. At 09:50 hours, General Clarence Huebner, commander of the 1st Division, receives a message: "There are too many vehicles on the beach; send combat troops." This is the first optimistic sign of the morning, and Huebner orders the 18th and 115th Infantry Regiments to land on Easy Red, the central beach sector.

At 11:00 hours, forward observers at sea report "men advancing up slope behind Easy Red, men believed ours on

skyline". By midday, the US forces have four lodgement areas established on the plateau above the beach, and are beginning to move inland. Although the landing beach is still under heavy fire, and will be for the rest of the day, the draw to St Laurent, codenamed E1, is open to vehicles at 13:00 hours. The afternoon sees attacks on the villages, with the Rangers and sections of the 116th moving west towards Vierville, the 115th approaching St Laurent and the 16th on the outskirts of Colleville. The

▶ *One of the most famous images of D-Day. Men of the US 2nd Infantry Division – one of V Corps's follow-up divisions – make their way inland from Omaha Beach.*

last draw in German hands (D1), carrying the beach road to Vierville, falls into US hands at 17:00 hours, when engineers blow up the concrete roadblock.

▼ *Stepping over wounded comrades and equipment, US GIs move supplies up onto the cliff to re-equip those fighting farther inland.*

▶ *American soldiers round up German prisoners. From here they would have been passed back into special holding areas.*

The commanders of the 1st and 29th Divisions and V Corps feel confident enough to establish their HQs ashore.

At the end of D-Day, the 1st and 29th Divisions have lost over 4000 men. Those who have made it ashore hold a frontline only 1.6km (1 mile) from the beach, with little more than their personal weapons to defend it. Fifty tanks have been lost, and five battalions of artillery destroyed or lost at sea. Only about five percent of the scheduled supplies have landed safely. In spite of all this, the fight for Omaha has broken the frontline strength of the German 352nd Division, while the British attack from Gold Beach has divided its reserve. As night falls, a feared German counterattack fails to materialize.

June 6 GOLD BEACH

▲ *British forces assaulting the beach, as seen from a landing craft coming in to drop off more troops.*

On Gold Beach Allied naval gunfire successfully destroyed many German positions, and the DD tanks made it onto the beach by 07:25 hours to support the infantry. Some casualties were suffered, but by Omaha standards they were light. French civilians greeted the British troops with cheers and cascades of flowers. By the evening, the 50th Division had reached the Bayeux–Caen road.

▼ *The British warship HMS Ajax, which took part in the bombardment of German shore batteries on Gold.*

07:25 HOURS, H-HOUR

Task Force G, carrying the British 50th (Northumbrian) Division, arrives off the Gold area 16km (10 miles) east of Omaha at 05:30 hours. It assembles 11km (7 miles) from the coast, 6km (4 miles) closer inshore than the US Task Forces. It is hoped this will give the DD (Duplex-Drive) tanks a better chance of landing safely. Underwater reefs

▶ *A Royal Marine commando in action at a roadside. He is firing the Bren light machine gun.*

offshore will delay H-Hour until 07:25, hours which allows the naval bombardment to begin early. At 05:10 hours, the cruiser HMS *Orion* begins it.

Just before 06:00 hours, a German battery of 155mm guns near Longues fires on the HQ ship, *Bulolo*. Cruisers *Ajax* and *Argonaut* reply. By 08:45 hours, the battery has been silenced with two direct hits on its guns.

The assault sectors of Gold are over 5km (3 miles) wide, and large enough to land four battalions in two brigade groups, side by side: on the left, the 231st Brigade at the village of Le Hamel (Jig Green), and on the right the 69th Brigade at La Rivière (King Green). Both villages are defended with strongpoints and gun emplacements, which enfilade the beach; but the coast in between is defended only at certain points, and it is flat, making it ideal for an assault landing.

To break the German beach defences, manned by the 726th Infantry Regiment, the British are relying on the specialist AVREs (Armoured Vehicles, Royal Engineers)

of the 79th Armoured Division. The first assault wave will consist of LCTs (Landing Craft, Tanks) carrying six teams of such vehicles, three for each landing sector. The landing craft will motor straight through the beach obstacles and land the armour, which will then cut six paths through the minefields and low dunes to the beach road.

The AVREs are meant to be followed by the DD tanks. But the current and strong winds causing so much havoc on Omaha are also affecting Gold. It is decided to land the DD tanks directly

from beached LCTs, thus bringing them in five minutes behind the infantry.

The infantry assault waves come in on time, but the current pulls the 231st Brigade hundreds of metres to the east, and it lands on Jig Red. The left-hand battalion, the 1st Hampshire (1st Hants), meant to land directly at Le Hamel, is forced to spend the morning fighting a German strongpoint farther down the coast, before it advances to

▼ *British troops pour ashore on Gold Beach on D-Day. They met little resistance from the German defenders.*

▲ *Royal Marine commandos wade ashore. One of them (centre) is carrying a miniature "Wellbike" motorbike.*

take Le Hamel. The battalion is through the town by mid-afternoon, but Le Hamel is not secured until 20:00 hours. The next battalion, the 1st Dorsets, is luckier, and lands without opposition. It is off the beach within 30 minutes, to begin advancing southwest of Le Hamel towards the village of Ryes. The brigade objective is Arromanches, 5km (3 miles) west of the landing beaches. Capturing it is vital: it is to be the anchorage for a Mulberry harbour, which is to start arriving tomorrow.

On the left, the 69th Brigade moves on La Rivière. The strongpoint here is held by an entire battalion of nearly 1000 Osttruppen (Eastern troops), but it has taken serious damage from the pre-landing bombardment, and is secured by the 5th East Yorkshire Regiment before 10:00 hours. The 69th's battalions, 6th and 7th Green Howards, move south to take German positions at Ver-sur-Mer and then advance onto a ridge near Meuvaines. The brigade's objective to the east is the town of Creully, on the Seulles, to link up with the Canadians from Juno, while to the south it is to advance about 16km (10 miles) through Crépon to secure the Caen–Bayeux road near St Leger.

From 09:50 hours the landing beaches are secure, and follow-up units and armour begin to land. First to arrive are 300 men of 47 Royal Marine Commando. They are to advance west along the coast, bypassing Arromanches to secure Port-en-Bessin, and link up with US V Corps coming from Omaha.

From 11:00 hours, two more brigades begin landing, to take position between the two assault brigades. Moving in behind the 231st is the 56th, which advances southwest towards the River Aure, north of Bayeux. To the east, the 151st Brigade moves through Meuvaines on the flank of the 69th, towards the Caen–Bayeux road west of St Léger. The infantry is supported by tanks of the 8th Armoured Brigade. During the day, getting the tanks over the landing beaches proves difficult and 100 become bogged down in clay, to be swamped by the rising tide. But the brigade has at least three battalions in action by D-Day afternoon. They are soon joined by lead elements of the 7th Armoured Division – the Desert Rats. Meanwhile, D-Day afternoon sees the arrival of the 50th Division

◄ *More British commandos disembark from their transport craft. Note how some are carrying bicycles for transport.*

◄ An injured British soldier is stretchered off to a medical post by his comrades to receive attention.

commander, Major-General D.A.H. Graham, and the establishment of the divisional headquarters at Meuvaines.

At about 16:00 hours, a German battle group of the 352nd Division from Bayeux – two infantry battalions supported by an anti-tank battalion – launches a counterattack on the 69th

▼ British troops and commandos file past a Bren gun carrier armoured vehicle (left) and a Churchill tank (right).

Brigade near Bazenville, southwest of Crépon. It is beaten off, with heavy German losses, and the 69th continues south, to end the day around the villages of Rucqueville and Coulombs. It is still about 3km (2 miles) short of St Léger and the Caen–Bayeux road.

By late afternoon, the 1st Hants has arrived at the outskirts of Arromanches. At first bypassing the town, it captures a radar station on the eastern headland intact. With that, and a nearby gun battery, secure, companies prepare to move on the town. In the words of Major Mott, B Company: "We expected tanks to stand by, but they never came,

so we went in and were met by a dog, which seemed to be German. His masters followed with a white flag. Arromanches was surprisingly full of French people as we had heard they would all be evacuated and out came flowers, tricolors and Union Jacks." To the east, 47 (RM) Commando has fought its way through La Rosière, and ends the day dug-in on the high ground of Point 72, which is 1.6km (1 mile) south of Port-en-Bessin.

Along the rest of the front, the 56th Brigade has dug-in 3km (2 miles) short of Bayeux, despite the fact that the German LXXXIV Corps has no reserves to defend it. Farther east, the 151st has also stopped short of its objective, and ends the day still 3km (2 miles) north of the Caen–Bayeux road. Despite this seeming lack of urgency in some areas, on the right flank the 69th secures Creully by nightfall and links up with the 7th Canadian Brigade from Juno.

By the end of D-Day, the Gold lodgement area covers nearly 13 square kilometres (5 square miles), and the whole of the 50th Division – nearly 25,000 men – are ashore. The division's right has been secured with the arrival of the Canadians, but the left flank is still open, and there is no sign of the US forces. Losses in some battalions have been heavy, with the 1st Hants having suffered some 270 casualties out of the 700 who landed.

June 6
JUNO BEACH

The Canadians landed behind schedule on Juno, and struggled against the rising tide and submerged mines. Many of the first-wave landing craft were lost as a result. Intense street fighting took place in Courseulles as the 12th SS Panzer Division approached the beachhead.

07:35 & 07:45 HOURS, *H-HOURS*

At 05:58 hours, Task Force J, under the command of Commodore Geoffrey Oliver, moves out of the cleared channels and begins to assemble 11km (7 miles) from Juno Beach. At about 06:15 hours, the two lead convoys carrying the assault brigades of the 3rd Canadian Division, British I Corps, begin loading troops into landing craft.

As with Gold Beach, the Juno assault sectors are wide enough to allow a two-brigade front of almost 10km (6 miles). On the right, aiming for sector Mike, is the 7th Brigade: the Royal Winnipeg Rifles, the Regina Rifle Regiment, and 1st Battalion, Canadian Scottish Regiment. On the left, heading for sector Nan, is the 8th Brigade: the Queen's Own Rifles of Canada, the French-Canadian Régiment de la Chaudière, and the North Shore (New Brunswick) Regiment. The 7th Brigade is to land either side of the River Seulles, west of Courseulles, while the 8th Brigade will land 1.6km (1 mile) east, in an area from Bernières-sur-Mer to St Aubin-sur-Mer. To the east of the

▼ *Canadian troops coming ashore onto Juno Beach from various landing craft, including LCI (Landing Craft, Infantry) and LCT (Landing Craft, Tank).*

◄ *The wreckage of a Republic P-47 Thunderbolt, which crashed while giving air support to troops landing on Juno.*

8th Brigade, men of 48 (RM) Commando (of the 4th Special Service Brigade) will land at St Aubin-sur-Mer and advance east along the coast about 3km (2 miles) to Lion-sur-Mer. Here they will link up with the rest of the brigade, consisting of 41 (RM) Commando, landing at Sword Beach.

The German defences, manned by units of the 716th Infantry Division, are concentrated in the towns, farms and villas dotted across the flat landscape.

The beaches themselves are defended with minefields, anti-tank ditches and the occasional bunker, and to break through this thinly held defensive line, British I Corps is relying on the specialist armour of the 79th Armoured Division. As had been planned for Gold Beach, squadrons of DD (Duplex-Drive) tanks will motor in at H-5 minutes to engage enemy strongpoints, followed at H-Hour by one LCT (Landing Craft, Tank) group on each landing sector.

Each group carries three teams of the innovative "Hobart's Funnies" to smash through to the beach road. AVREs (Armoured Vehicles, Royal Engineers) carrying fascines and light bridges, make crossings over sea walls and anti-tank ditches, after which flails move ahead and clear the minefields, leaving the way open for armoured bulldozers to cut new roadways. Any enemy bunkers still causing trouble are engaged by AVREs firing petard charges: big, low-velocity demolition bombs, nicknamed "flying dustbins" by the tank crews. The assault infantry will land at H+5 minutes and, protected by the armour, move straight inland.

Unfortunately, conditions at sea and the coastal geography spoil the timetable. The need for the tide to

JUNE 6, JUNO BEACH

▲ *Dead German troops left behind by British commandos as they battled through the area.*

cover rocks on the approach to the Nan Sector means that H-Hour for the 8th Brigade is delayed by 10 minutes, to 07:45 hours. The late arrival of landing craft across the Channel puts the H-Hour for both sectors back another 10 minutes. As the LCA (Landing Craft, Assault) move from the line of departure towards the beaches, 7th Brigade will be landing at 07:45

hours and 8th Brigade at 07:55 hours. The delays mean that the landing craft are motoring towards beach obstacles that are already being covered by the tide: engineers will not have enough time to clear paths through them before the arrival of follow-on assault waves. As a result, the LCA and their infantry companies take heavy losses. One wave loses 20 out of 24 craft, while out of one company of the Regina Rifles only 49 men make it to the beach. In all,

▼ *The British battleship HMS Rodney adds her weight of shells to the Allied pounding of enemy positions.*

90 craft of all types are lost during the day. Heavy seas also disrupt the landings of the DD tanks. Some are delivered as close inshore as 915m (1000yds) by LCT and arrive 20 minutes in front of the infantry, while others are launched 4575m (5000yds) offshore and motor up the beach 20 minutes after H-hour.

Despite the difficulties, the Canadian infantry secure Juno in a series of actions consisting, in the first hours, in house-to-house fighting to clear Courseulles, Bernières and St Aubin.

◄ *Troops of the 4th British Special Service Brigade near the town of St Aubin-sur-Mer.*

the Queen's Own Rifles land in front of the Bernières strongpoint without any armoured support. They have to scale the 3m (10ft) sea wall and assault the defences on their own with little more than their personal weapons and grenades. Naval gunfire assists, but the Queen's Own is not through the village until 09:30 hours, and it remains under partial German control until noon.

This delay, together with the rising tide and the uncleared beach obstacles, creates serious congestion in the Nan sector. Le Régiment de la Chaudière begins to land at 08:30 hours, and is still on the beach, waiting to move through Bernières, at 14:00 hours. More seriously, the follow-up brigade, the 9th, which is to march inland and take the strategically vital Carpiquet airfield, west of Caen, does not begin to land until 10:50 hours. It is unable to move from Bernières until 16:00 hours – too late to secure its D-Day objective. This failure will have serious repercussions for the British Second Army in the coming weeks, as the the enemy re-inforces the town with panzers.

Nevertheless, there is some progress around Bernières. By noon, the first self-propelled artillery regiments are ashore and in action, while the division commander, Major-General Keller, lands and establishes his HQ at about 13:00 hours. By mid-afternoon, to the south of the town, the lead companies of the Chaudière Regiment are 6km (4 miles)

On the right, in Mike sector, the Winnipeg Rifles are in action on the Seulles by 08:00 hours. The regiment secures the river bridge and west bank opposite Courseulles, and then moves south and southwest, towards Banville and Ste Croix, with the object-ive of Creully and a link-up with the British from Gold. On the east bank of the Seulles, the lead companies of the Regina Rifles are onshore by 08:15 hours, moving east towards Courselles, while AVREs set to work and, by 09:00 hours, have two lanes cleared inland for the follow-up waves. Over the next two hours, the Regina Rifles secure Courseulles in a systematic

attack, clearing 12 pre-planned sectors. By 11:00 hours, the regiment is moving south towards Reviers. Here, it regroups to await the tanks of the 6th Armoured Regiment (1st Hussars) in order to continue the advance to Bretteville l'Orgueilleuse on the Caen–Bayeux Road. With Courseulles secure, the 1st Canadian Scottish Regiment, ashore by 09:30 hours, presses inland and begins marching across country towards Ste Croix to reinforce the Winnipeg Rifles.

In Nan sector, the 8th Brigade runs into trouble at Bernières and St Aubin. On the brigade right, at Nan White, the DD tanks and the AVREs are late, so

▼ *Defences such as this barbed wire were designed to hinder the Allies.*

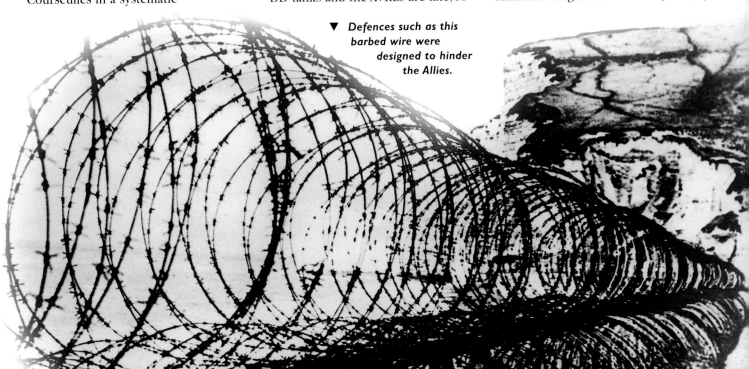

▲ *A Canadian soldier peers down the road as Allied armour clears the route ahead of enemy troops.*

inland and in control of Beny-sur-Mer on the Bernières–Caen road.

At Nan Red, the North Shore Regiment tries to secure the brigade's left-flank objectives at St Aubin, with 48 (RM) Commando. The plan is for the Canadians to secure St Aubin before the commandos land at the east end of the village (08:45 hours). Unfortunately, the pre-landing bombardment has missed St Aubin entirely, and German defences are still intact when the Canadians arrive. The North Shore Regiment is fighting house to house as commandos begin to land. Enfiladed by fire from a German strongpoint in St Aubin, the commandos are pinned down under a sea wall and high earth cliff, suffering heavy casualties. They take most of the day getting off the beach and fighting their way into the neighbouring village of Langrune-sur-Mer, instead of racing along the coast. They secure the area only by nightfall, with the help of Canadian armour. Their losses are severe, with over 100 dead, while patrols return from Lion-sur-Mer with news that the coast east towards Sword is still in German hands and that there is no sign of 41 Commando.

The Canadian advance from Juno slows down as the day goes on. This is partly due to congestion on the beach, but also to the German resistance at strongpoints along the coast and a series of small counterattacks, notably by the 726th Regiment at Ste Croix and the 736th Infantry Regiment at Tailleville, south of St Aubin.

To the west, by 17:00 hours the Winnipeg Rifles are consolidating positions around Creully, and have made contact with the British from Gold Beach. Farther south, the 7th Brigade is digging in around Le Fresne-Camilly. A few tanks are reported to have advanced as far as Bretteville l'Orgueilleuse on a reconnaissance mission, but, being unsupported, have had to withdraw. The 9th Brigade, meanwhile, which has been advancing down the Bernières–Caen road, reached Bény-sur-Mer at 19:00 hours, but has halted at dusk around Villons-les-Buissons, 5km (3 miles) short of the British to the east, and nearly 8km (5 miles) short of Caen to the south. On the beaches, the division has landed 21,500 men, 3200 vehicles and 2540 tonnes (2500 tons) of supplies, while follow-on units, including the lead elements of the 51st (Highland) Division, are already on shore in preparation for the landings on D+1.

▶ *Troops of the British 13/18th Hussars move through Lion-sur-Mer. The damage to the buildings shows there was heavy fighting earlier in the day.*

EYEWITNESS ACCOUNT

AFTERMATH OF ST AUBIN

By a survivor from 48 (RM) Commando
"One thing we had to do was to clear up the St Aubin beach. It was a shocking sight. Many corpses, some of them badly dismembered, were lying among the rest of the debris of the assault: wrecked and burnt-out tanks; equipment and stores of every sort, scattered on the beach or drifted up along the water's edge; wrecked landing craft broached-to on the beach or in the sea among the beach obstacles. Three of our landing craft were still there, wrecked and abandoned; I never heard what the squadron's casualties were in men. Among all this, several French women were walking about, picking up what tinned food they could find – incredibly they had small children with them, who gazed with indifferent curiosity on the shattered corpses, the broken equipment and the scattered tins of food."

Extract from: "Haste to the Battle", by Lt. Col. James Moulton, quoted in "D-Day Then and Now", edited by Winston G. Ramsey: Battle of Britain Prints International, 1995.

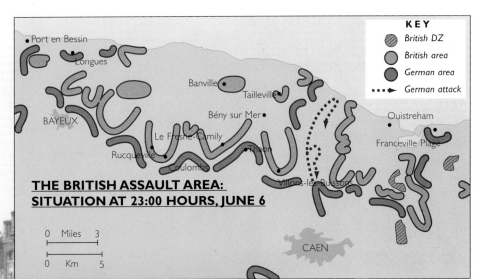

KEY
- British DZ
- British area
- German area
- German attack

Port en Bessin
Longues
Banville
Tailleville
BAYEUX
Bény sur Mer
Ouistreham
Le Freshe-Camily
Franceville Plage
Rucqueville
Tinton
Coulombs
Villons-les-Bussons
CAEN

THE BRITISH ASSAULT AREA:
SITUATION AT 23:00 HOURS, JUNE 6

| 0 | Miles | 3 |
| 0 | Km | 5 |

▲ The general situation on the ground in the British sector at 23:00 hours, June 6, 1944. Despite sizeable gains during the first day, there was to be determined resistance farther inland.

▼ Outside Lion-sur-Mer, men of the 13/18th Hussars get some rest and a chance to eat during a lull in the battle.

June 6 SWORD BEACH

At 05:30 hours, the LCA (Landing Craft, Assault) of Task Force S, commanded by Rear-Admiral Arthur G. Talbot, are in the water 11km (7 miles) offshore, and assault companies of the British 3rd Division begin to embark. Their objectives are sectors Queen White and Queen Red, halfway between Lion-sur-Mer to the west and the port town of Ouistreham, and the Orne estuary, to the east. Although the Sword landing area is over 10,970m (12,000yds) wide, only parts of Queen beach have been selected for landing. This is because of low cliffs to the west in sector Peter and a steep beach in front of sector Roger. This means the landing area for the 3rd Division is 1370m (1500yds) wide, allowing only a limited front of one brigade, consisting of two assault battalions. It also means a gap of over 3km (2 miles) between the landings on Sword and the Canadians at Juno.

Making the assault is the division's 8th Brigade. On the right, Queen White will be stormed by the 2nd Battalion, East Yorkshire Regiment (East Yorks); on the left, Queen Red will be taken by

▼ *Huddling together behind a bank of sand, Allied troops take cover from German snipers and machine guns on Sword Beach.*

T he landings on Sword initially went well: Free French commandos took the town of Ouistreham, by 13:30 hours British commandos under Lord Lovat had seized Hermanville and General Feuchtiger's 21st Panzer Division was repulsed. However, the stated objective, Caen, remained in German hands.

▼ *After jumping from a Landing Craft, Infantry, Allied troops wade chest-high though the Channel surf to Sword Beach.*

the 1st Battalion, South Lancashire Regiment (South Lancs). In support will be DD (Duplex-Drive) tanks of the 13/18 Royal Hussars and the AVREs (Armoured Vehicles, Royal Engineers) of the 5th Assault Regiment, RE.

Guided into position by the midget submarine *X-23*, 6400m (7000yds)

from sector Peter, the first assault waves are closing in on the beach at 06:30 hours. LCTs (Landing Craft, Tanks) carrying the DD tanks are in the lead, but rough seas mean that the tanks have to be launched at 4575m (5000yds). The LCT carrying the AVREs quickly catch them up, and soon the

▲ *Pushing inland, the first elements of the Sword Beach assault group reach the town of Hermanville-sur-Mer.*

June 6, Sword Beach

landing craft are weaving past the DDs, attempting not to run them down. At least one tank is struck and sinks.

Behind the armour, the troops in the LCA are suffering from mixture of sea-sickness and fear, but morale remains high. One major in the East Yorks even reads a patriotic speech to his men from Shakespeare's play *Henry V*.

At 06:45 hours, 72 self-propelled guns in LCTs, coming in behind the troops, begin a "run in shoot" at 9145m (10,000yds) to suppress enemy targets along the beach. They augment other fire-support craft now in action, which

▶ *Two soldiers from the South Lancashire Regiment look on as an M4 Sherman tank reconnoitres ahead.*

include three LCG (Landing Craft, Gun) and five multi-rocket-launching LCT(R). Their fire continues for the next 30 minutes, lifting just before the first AVREs hit Queen Red (07:20 hours) to begin clearing four routes off the beach. The first DD tanks arrive soon afterwards. Despite the crowded boat lanes and a rough sea, 28 out 40 tanks make it safely onto the beach and go straight into action. By 07:45 hours, all the German positions are silenced.

The East Yorks and South Lancs are on the beach by 07:30 hours, as per the schedule. The initial assault succeeds, but not far from the beach the East Yorks, coming from Queen Red, run into German resistance at

strongpoint WN 20, near la Breche, and the landing schedule for Sword begins to slip. The strongpoint, around some beachside villas, has 20 positions and is equipped with a 75mm gun, mortars, anti-tank guns and at least eight machine guns. The East Yorks spend two hours attacking it, delaying the advance east to Ouistreham. To the right, the South Lancs move off Queen White, and secure the only road leading inland, towards Hermanville-sur-Mer.

From 08:30 hours a second wave of assault units begins to land at Queen

▼ *Reinforcements land on the Normandy coast to support the first assault groups. In the background, half a dozen LCI (Landing Craft, Infantry) disgorge troops.*

▶ *Dead soldiers from the British and Commonwealth 3rd Division lie where they fell on Sword Beach.*

Red. These are commandos of the 1st Special Service Brigade (1st SSB), under the command of Lord Lovat. First to land are No. 4 Commando and 170 Free French marines of No.10 (Inter-Allied) Commando, led by Commandant Philippe Kieffer. Both units head east to capture German strongpoints in Ouistreham. They are followed by 41 (RM) Commando, part of 4th Special Service Brigade (4th SSB), which has been landing at Juno. They take the coast road west, to attack through Lion-sur-Mer, and to link up with the 4th SSB and form a united bridgehead with the Canadians. Thirty minutes later, the rest of Lovat's brigade begin to land, played ashore by piper Bill Millin. Led by No. 6 Commando, 1st SSB (with Lovat among the forward units), marches through 8th Brigade, heading southeast through Colleville towards Bénouville and a link-up with the paratroopers of the 6th Airborne Division, east of the Orne.

Meanwhile, reinforcements, which include the 8th Brigade's 1st Suffolk Regiment (Suffolks) and 3rd Division's follow-on brigades (185th, 9th and the 27th Armoured), are on their way. The

Suffolks land at 11:00 hours, with the first objective of taking Colleville.

By mid-morning, the South Lancs have secured Hermanville, while the East Yorks have made it to the southern outskirts of Ouistreham. On the right, the Marines of 41 Commando have run into trouble on the eastern outskirts of Lion-sur-Mer and are trying to push their way in with armoured support.

Back on the beach, three brigades are trying to land over two beach sectors and move inland over one surfaced road to their assembly areas at

▼ *Looking dishevelled and defeated, German prisoners of war are brought in by men of the 13/18th Hussars.*

EYEWITNESS ACCOUNT

THE JOURNEY INTO SWORD

On board the converted American freighter "Battleaxe"

" ... dawn was just breaking and as we looked out over the rough seas we could see a huge red glow on the horizon. This must be France. A destroyer speeding by about 8 miles from us struck a mine and blew up, scattering wreckage in all directions. At 3.30 [03:30 hours] we queued up with our trays for breakfast of porridge, two hard-boiled eggs, four rounds of white bread and butter and jam and a mug of tea. We gave our rifles the once-over, filled the magazines and made sure our ammunition and grenades were ready for use. At 4.45 the word came over the loudspeaker for us to get dressed [for battle]. At 4.50 the captain told us he could see the French coast – a blazing inferno with the Navy shelling it and the RAF bombing it. Then came the order 'Marines of ALC 23 lower away'. Slowly the winches began to turn and we slid down the ship's side and bumped into the stormy sea. We were then 7 miles from shore. We made ourselves as comfortable as possible, some sitting, some standing but all singing. New songs and old – sentimental – patriotic and ballads but we all sang." (*Private Stanley Gardner, 1st Suffolks, 8th Brigade*)

Extract from "Monty's Iron Sides: A History of the British 3rd Division", by Patrick Delaforce, Stroud, Gloucestershire: Alan Sutton, 1995.

Hermanville. The result is heavy congestion, holding up the division's advance south for at least three hours. In the grand plan, 185th Brigade was supposed to be in Caen by midnight; but at noon the brigade is still in Hermanville, 11km (7 miles) to the north, waiting for the arrival of tank support. Finally, brigade commanders lose patience, and its lead battalion, the 1st King's Shropshire Light Infantry (KSLI), starts south towards Beuville.

Farther east, the advance also stalls around Colleville. South of the village the Suffolks come up against a strongpoint codenamed Hillman, a battalion HQ of the 736th Infantry Regiment.

This huge redoubt is 550m (600yds) wide. It has 12 gun emplacements, concrete walls 2.7m (9ft) thick, a double belt of barbed wire 3.6m (12ft) wide and a minefield. It is manned by over 300 men. Allied planners have ignored it, so Hillman has not been hit by either naval or air bombardment, despite being in the direct line of the advance on Caen. It takes the Suffolks until 20:00 hours to take it, with the help of a squadron of tanks, two batteries of artillery and engineers.

South of Hermanville, during the afternoon, a battery of German 88s of the 21st Panzer Division at Périers halts

▼ *Additional vehicles and equipment for the 13/18th Hussars are moved onto the beach, ready for the push inland.*

◄ *Carrying reinforcements for the 6th Airborne Division, which landed on the night of June 5/6, Allied gliders swoop in to land as nightfall approaches on D-Day.*

armour of the Staffordshire Yeomanry. 21st Panzer loses about 10 tanks but presses on, this time making a flanking move north to Périers, where Battle Group Oppeln expects the battery of German 88s to be in position. To its surprise, the guns have been withdrawn, and a squadron of British tanks now dominates the town from Périers Ridge to the east. Again, the Germans take losses and withdraw. Meanwhile, farther west, Battle Group Rauch has moved north unopposed, into the gap between Juno and Sword.

By 19:00 hours, panzers are in Lion-sur-Mer, and for two hours the Allied invasion front is split in two. However, the German forces cannot exploit the position. Colonel Rauch, the battle group commander, knows he has no support and is faced by a vast invasion fleet. At 21:00 hours, hundreds of Allied gliders are seen overhead, and Rauch, assuming their objective to be Caen, decides to pull back to around Bieville. The gliders are, in fact, reinforcements for the 6th Airborne Division; but the sight of their arrival is enough to end the only chance the Germans will have to throw the Allies back into the sea.

By nightfall, nearly 29,000 troops have landed at Sword, and the D-Day objectives to the east have been largely secured: Ouistreham and the mouth of the Orne are in Allied hands, and Lovat's commandos have crossed the river into 6th Airborne's area and are in position around Le Plein. A battalion of the 185th Brigade (2nd Warwickshire Regiment) has reached the Orne at Blainville and is preparing to move into Bénouville in support of the paratroopers holding the bridges.

Elsewhere, the situation at Sword needs radical improvement. On the right flank, the commandos are not yet through Lion-sur-Mer, while the 8th and 9th Brigades are stuck outside Hermanville and Périers, having failed to advance since early afternoon. There are also no signs of the Canadian forces from Juno. To the south, the 185th Brigade has dug-in 6km (4 miles) short of Caen. There has already been one German panzer attack to hold the town, and more are certainly to come. Caen – an invasion objective – is already looking a hard nut to crack.

the division's advance. Instead of clearing them out, the 185th Brigade sticks to its D-Day task and bypasses the village, heading south through Beuville to Biéville, 6.4km (4 miles) north of Caen, which it reaches at 16:00 hours. By now, tanks of the 27th Armoured Brigade have made it through the Hermanville traffic jams and are operating in the division area south to the 185th's positions. Their arrival does not come a moment too soon; it is now that the 21st Panzer Division launches the only German armoured counterattack of D-Day.

Faced with what is, by now, clearly a major Allied landing, the 21st Panzer mobilizes three battle groups. One moves on the paratroopers on the Orne, while the other two, with 70 Mk IV tanks, move north of Caen. The first attack on the 3rd Division, around Biéville, is stopped by the anti-tank guns of the KSLI and supporting

June 7-12 1944

The days after the D-Day landings were ones of frustration for the Allies. As the beachhead was consolidated it appeared that the Allied armies would be able to drive inland with relative ease. But organizational and logistical difficulties slowed the advance, and the German High Command at last began to respond to the landings. Though Allied aerial superiority meant the beachhead was secure, a lot of hard fighting lay ahead.

WEDNESDAY, JUNE 7 (D+1)

OPERATION NEPTUNE

From the early hours of the morning U-boats from the Biscay ports and Brittany make a bid to break into the English Channel and attack the Western Task Force lying off the American sector. They are stopped by patrol aircraft of Coastal Command, which through D+1 make 22 contacts and put in seven attacks. *U-955* is confirmed sunk and five other boats are believed damaged. Nevertheless, their attempts to break into the English Channel continue.

On the eastern flank of the invasion fleet, off Sword Beach, the main attack threat comes from the German Air Force based in the Le Havre/River Seine area. To counter this the Eastern Task Force and Task Force S is flanked by the Trout Line: a line of warships and armed landing craft extending 10km (six miles) out to sea from the Orne estuary. This includes Landing Craft, Flak; Landing Craft, Gun and the so-called Eagle Ships, which are converted vessels, many formerly civilian – including one aged paddle steamer – fitted with a large array of anti-aircraft guns.

These defences do not stop an air attack on HMS *Bulolo*, the headquarters ship of Task Force G. At 06:00 hours she is hit by a bomb. The vessel is saved and she continues to direct landings on Gold Beach.

◀ *Merchant ships were deliberately scuttled to provide makeshift breakwaters for the vessels unloading on the beach.*

▲ German air crew "bombing up" a Ju-88. The Luftwaffe was still able to threaten Allied invasion plans and shipping.

AIR CAMPAIGN, *NORMANDY*

The Allied air forces are faced with increased German air activity throughout D+1. About 250 sorties are made by German fighters over the beachheads, while there are 50 fighter-bomber attacks on the Sword area. The most serious of these, made by a lone FW 190, hits a beach sector supply dump and blows up 450,000 litres (100,000 gallons) of fuel and 400 tonnes (406 tons) of ammunition. Secondary explosions continue through most of the day.

Luftflotte (Air Fleet) 3 also orders the medium bombers of IX Fleigerkorps (IX Air Corps) into the battle from their bases in northern France. Tonight 130 bombers, including Ju-88s, Ju-188s and Do-217s, half the Fleigerkorps' strength, attack the invasion fleet but are driven off by anti-aircraft fire and night-fighters.

Allied fighters continue to cover the beachheads with a fighter screen, while offensively the priority is to attack road and rail bridges to the south and west of Normandy over the Loire and Seine

rivers. This is to delay the arrival of German reinforcements. But the weather is now deteriorating as the meteorologists predicted on Sunday, and low cloud levels are keeping aircraft at their bases in England. Allied air chief Leigh-Mallory records in his diary: "The weather has interfered with my air programme all day and is seriously upsetting me. The German army is being re-inforced and I cannot bomb the reinforcements in daylight."

On a positive side, airfield construction has already begun at the beachhead. The first is an emergency landing strip at Laurent-sur-Mer off Omaha due for completion on D+2. It will be joined by another 89 airfields scheduled for construction by the end of June.

COMMANDERS, *BRITISH AND US*

General Montgomery, on his way to join 21st Army tactical HQ almost doesn't make it to France. HMS *Faulknor* gets lost in the Channel and ends up in the early hours positioned

▲ After landing, Allied engineers set about constructing makeshift airfields for fighters to provide close air support.

off the Cotentin Peninsula. Dawn sees the destroyer back on course to Juno.

By 06:00 hours the *Faulknor* is with the invasion fleet, and General Bradley is aboard for his first command conference with Montgomery. Dominating their meeting is Omaha Beach and the position of General Gerow's V Corps. As far as is known the bridgehead at Omaha is barely 1.6 km (1 mile) deep and V Corps is still in danger of being pushed back into the sea. The decision is made to give Collins's VII Corps at Utah a new set of priorities. Instead of its headlong drive to Cherbourg, VII Corps is to concentrate its efforts south towards Isigny and Carentan to take the pressure off Omaha and to link up with Gerow. Collins is also to concentrate on getting his forces west of the Merderet River with the aim of reaching the west coast of the Cotentin at Lessay and cutting off Cherbourg from any German reinforcements. Elsewhere, the priorities are to link the British and American beachheads around Port-en-Bessin, close the gap between Juno and Sword and take Bayeux

▼ Numbers of Ju-88s were gradually depleted by Allied bombing raids on airfields and factories.

JUNE 7, D+1

▶ *An aerial view of Allied gliders that landed on D-Day. They look to have had a fortunate landing in a clear field.*

and Caen. Now the Allies are ashore the primary concern is to secure and expand the bridgehead, to allow the space for the follow-up divisions to land and deploy at a faster rate than the Germans can reinforce.

In England, General Eisenhower and Admiral Ramsay leave forward SHAEF HQ at Southwick House to tour the assault area. By 08:00 hours they are on board HMS *Apollo* and on their way across the Channel. Eisenhower's first visit is to General Bradley on board the cruiser USS *Augusta*. He then visits Montgomery on HMS *Faulknor*. Eisenhower's main concern is that the build-up of men and equipment at the beachhead is already behind schedule. Only a quarter of the 14,500 tonnes (14,732 tons) of supplies and 7000 of the planned 14,000 vehicles due by D+1 are ashore, while the total number of troops scheduled – 107,000 – is 20,000 short. As the sea in the Channel is becoming rougher by the hour, it is difficult to see how this situation can be improved. However, the commander of the Eastern Task Force, Admiral Vian, has one solution and orders his LSTs to ground on the beaches and unload their stores directly on to the

beach. Eisenhower is back in Portsmouth by 20:00 hours for meetings with Leigh-Mallory and Spaatz.

THE BUILD-UP

Lead units of the British 7th Armoured Division (of XXX Corps) and 51st (Highland) Division (of I Corps) are arriving at Juno. In the American sector, the 2nd Infantry Division and lead elements of the 2nd Armored Division, both part of US V Corps, begin to land at Omaha. On Utah, lead units of the 90th Division land.

MULBERRY HARBOURS

At 12:30 hours the first convoys of the Gooseberry blockships arrive off Omaha Beach at St Laurent and Gold at Arromanches. They will be scuttled bow to stern to produce 8km (5 miles) of breakwaters. The first to go down is the Alynbank. The Gooseberries are joined during the day by the first of the concrete Bombardons that are sunk to form the outer breakwaters. These measures will prove to be important during the coming days.

▼ *American Landing Ship, Tanks (LSTs) transport ever more men and materiel onto the Omaha beachhead. After beaching themselves, they needed to wait for high tide to leave the area.*

GERMAN DEFENCES

After being taken by surprise on June 6, today the German Army in France begins to organize for battle. OB West divides the front into two. Seventh Army has the western sector from the Cotentin to Bayeux, Panzer Group West has the eastern sector from Bayeux to the River Dives. Seventh Army orders II Parachute Corps from Brittany into the Cotentin with three divisions, the 17th SS Panzergrenadier, 77th Infantry, and 3rd Parachute Division. Panzer Group West assigns I SS Panzer Corps to the Caen area. Of the three panzer divisions which come under its command during the day, 21st Panzer is already heavily engaged defensively east and north of Caen, units of 12th SS are arriving west of the town and attacking north towards the Canadians, and Panzer Lehr is 139km (87 miles) to the southwest around Chartres.

Panzer Lehr's commander, General Fritz Bayerlein, is ordered to move his division immediately for an attack west of Caen tomorrow, despite the general's objections that a move in daylight risks Allied air attack. Over the next 24 hours, Panzer Lehr comes under repeated Allied bombing and loses 130 trucks and fuel tankers, 84 self-propelled guns and halftracks and 5 tanks before it even reaches the battle front.

THE BEACHHEAD, *UTAH*

On the right flank, moving north along the coast of the Cotentin, two regiments of the 4th Division fail to capture two large German gun emplacements at Crisbecq and Azeville.

In the centre, a large pocket of German resistance around Turqueville south of St Mère-Eglise, is removed.

North of St Mère-Eglise the German 1058th Regiment renews its counterattack down the Montebourg road. Reinforced with an infantry battalion, 10 self-propelled guns and artillery, it reaches as far as the outskirts of the village before American tanks make a flanking attack on Neuville and force it back.

West of St Mère-Eglise, at 08:00 hours, the German 1057th Regiment launches a counterattack across the Merderet River at the La Fiere crossing, but is stopped by a company of the 505th Parachute Infantry.

To the south, on the north bank of the Douve River near Carentan, two regiments of the 101st Airborne, the 506th and 501st, kill or capture an entire battalion of German paratroopers of the 6th Parachute Regiment. Out of a unit of nearly 1000, only 25 Germans escape.

During the day, after new instructions from First Army, VII Corps headquarters assigns the task of capturing Carentan to the 101st.

AIRBORNE ASSAULT, *US SECTOR*

Over the Cotentin, the last American glider operations of the invasion begin at about 07:00 hours. Two hundred gliders in four waves deliver reinforcements and supplies to the 82nd and 101st Airborne; the last drop taking place at about 09:00 hours which lands

▲ *Private Boyle of the 6th Durham Light Infantry displays the holes in his helmet caused by shell fragments during battle.*

two infantry battalions to the 101st. In contrast to the chaos on D-Day morning, this drop, made in daylight, delivers 90 percent of the two battalions safely, and by 10:30 hours they are assembled and moving against German positions.

THE BEACHHEAD, *OMAHA*

In the western part of the bridgehead, regiments of the 29th Division, the 115th and 116th, spend most of the day consolidating their positions and clearing out pockets of German defenders. After securing St Laurent the 115th moves southwest towards Lôuvieres and Montigny, while the 116th, supported by the newly arrived 175th Regiment moves along the coast over the bluffs of the Pointe de Raz to try and relieve the Rangers on the Pointe-du-Hoc. By noon they are at St. Pierre du Mont, still 914m (1000yds) short of the Pointe.

Meanwhile, the position of Colonel Rudder's Rangers is perilous. Over a period of 24 hours, counterattacks by the German 914th Regiment have reduced the Ranger force to less than 100 men and have forced them back, until by the afternoon of D+1 they hold a strip of cliff only 182m (200yds) wide. Two landing craft manage to deliver their first fresh supplies of food, water and ammunition, but the Rangers must hold out until the 116th can reach them.

▲ *Having been rounded up on the land, German prisoners are loaded onto transport ships to take them back to holding camps in England.*

From the eastern end of Omaha Beach, two regiments of the 1st Division, the 16th and 18th, are advancing east to clear Colleville and reach the high ground on the River Aure south of Port-en-Bessin.

THE BEACHHEAD, *GOLD*

The British No. 47 (RM) Commando begins its attack on Port-en-Bessin at dawn. The small port is secured during the early hours of D+2. While heavy fighting goes on, contact is made with a company of the US 16th Regiment from Omaha Beach during the afternoon.

Everywhere in the Gold area, the 50th Division is making good progress. By noon, two battalions of the 56th Brigade have entered Bayeux unopposed. To the east the 151st Brigade advances to the southeast of the town and is astride the Bayeux–Tilly Road. On the flank, 69th Brigade has advanced 8km (5 miles) south from Coulombs, crossing the Bayeux–Caen road at St. Leger, capturing Ducy St. Marguerite and joining up with the Canadians south of the road at Bronay.

THE BEACHHEAD, *JUNO*

The 7th Canadian Brigade crosses the Caen-Bayeux at Bretteville l'Orgueville and pushes on to the railway at Bronay. To their left, the 9th Canadian Brigade moves west of Caen through Authie towards Carpiquet and its airfield. The Canadians come under artillery fire which halts the advance. The decision is made to retire to defensive positions north of Authie, but as the withdrawal begins at about 14:00 hours, the Canadians come under attack by a reinforced panzergrenadier regiment of the 12th SS Panzer Division. This pushes the Canadians back 5km (3 miles) through Authie and Buron to high ground around les Buissons. The 12th SS Panzer Division begins to arrive in force and concentrates west of Caen. The British Second Army has lost another opportunity to close on the town.

THE BEACHHEAD, *SWORD*

North of Caen, the 185th and 9th Brigades renew their advance towards the town through units of the 21st Panzer Division. The 185th Brigade, while holding a battalion at Bieville, makes a flank attack with two battalions on Lébisey, but is held in heavy fighting and forced to withdraw. The 9th Brigade meanwhile attempts to advance southwest. Périers is taken but the advance is halted outside Cambes. The 8th Brigade meanwhile makes a slow advance west of Hermanville.

East of the Orne River, two commandos of the 1st Special Service Brigade attempt to retake the Merville Battery, but the attack fails with resulting heavy losses.

▼ *More German prisoners are rounded up by British soldiers and sent back to the beach holding areas.*

Thursday, June 8 (D+2)

IN THE ENGLISH CHANNEL

During the night, a Liberator of 224 Squadron, Coastal Command piloted by Flying Officer Kenneth Moore, attacks and sinks *U-629* and *U-373* in the space of 30 minutes.

Meanwhile, German air raids on the invasion fleet go on. At 05:15 hours the frigate HMS *Lawford* is sunk, probably by a Henschel Hs 293 radio-controlled glider bomb, launched from the air by a converted Do-217 bomber. This is one of the first times an anti-ship missile has been used in warfare.

German surface vessels are also in action. During the evening the 5th and 9th E-Boat flotillas sortie from Le Havre. They go north into mid-Channel, avoiding the Trout Line and attack a convoy of 17 landing craft, sinking two of them before they disengage.

Due to enemy action SHAEF warns fishermen from across Europe to return to port and remain there until June 15.

▶ *The Henschel Hs 293 radio-controlled glider bomb, the first guided missile in the history of warfare to be used in action on June 8.*

MULBERRY

During the morning the last "Gooseberry" blockships are sunk in position, forming the fixed breakwaters of the two harbours: Mulberry A off St Laurent and Mulberry B off Arromanches. Other elements arrive today having been towed across the Channel by tugs. They include concrete Bombardons - floating breakwaters; "Phoenix" caissons – fixed breakwaters designed to be sunk in position; "Whale" floating piers and "Spud" pier heads. The sea is becoming increasingly rough and the crossing has not been easy. About 40 percent of the "Whales" have been damaged or lost at sea.

COMMANDERS

At Juno Beach, General Montgomery disembarks from HMS *Faulknor* and

▲ *A group of US paratroopers from the 101st Airborne Division in the village of St Marcouf, near Utah Beach. They wait for orders to push on to their next objective.*

joins his tactical headquarters ashore. The HQ has been established at Croix sur Mer, but Monty orders it moved closer to the frontline. By the end of the day it's at Cruelly, 16km (10 miles) west of Caen and only 5km (3 miles) from the battle front, between the British XXX and I Corps. The headquarters remains here until June 22. Contact with SHAEF at Southwick House and 21st Army Group base headquarters in London is maintained by radio, and soon staff officers will be flying over every day as Allied forces advance inland.

JUNE 8, D+2

▶ *The town of St Lô took a heavy pounding from Allied bombers before and during the invasion, as they tried to soften up the German garrison based there.*

In the American sector, the US Ninth Air Force and IX Air Force Service Command establish advance headquarters ashore. They join forward supply units that arrived on D-Day.

GERMAN PRISONERS

The first trainload of German Army prisoners from Normandy, consisting of 364 men, arrives from Southampton at a processing centre at Kempton Park horse race course west of London. From here they will be transferred to permanent camps in the US, Canada and Great Britain.

Six POW camps are scheduled to be set up in Normandy, but at the beginning of the campaign prisoners are kept on the beaches behind wire and shipped over the Channel in LSTs. Estimates by 21st Army Group of the numbers of Germans it will take in Normandy prove to be wildly optimistic. From D-Day to D+9 the estimate is 500 a day, rising to 1000 a day by D+29. In fact by July 29 (D+53) only 12,153 have been captured.

BRITISH HOME FRONT

In London, General Eisenhower holds his first press conference since June 6. A pre-recorded message by the Supreme Commander was broadcast on D-Day, but this is the first time journalists have had the opportunity to question Eisenhower personally about the progress of the new Second Front.

The information they're given is very limited, with Eisenhower voicing no comment or opinion on the progress of the operation so far. What he does say is that what he wants most, and indeed is praying for, is good weather. Bad weather is slowing the build-up across the Channel and preventing Allied aircraft from flying and attacking the German divisions as they close on the bridgehead.

THE BRIDGEHEAD, *UTAH*

On Utah, regiments of the 90th Division come ashore to join the lead elements that have been coming ashore since D+1.

To the north, VII Corps makes another attack to silence the German gun emplacements at Crisbecq and Azeville. This combines with a flanking attack by the 82nd Airborne from the area of St Mère-Eglise with the aim of securing a ridge of high ground from Montebourg to Quineville on the coast.

To the south, units of the 101st Airborne are clearing the Germans from north of the Douve River in preparation for the attack on Carentan. On the road north of the town, the village of St Come-du-Mont is occupied during the day after an attack by four infantry battalions supported by light tanks and a battalion of field artillery. The Germans disengage, cross the river and regroup in Carentan, bringing their forces in the town to two battalions of the 6th Parachute Regiment plus elements of the 1058th Regiment.

By nightfall the 101st has three regiments along the Douve ready for the assault on Carentan.

THE BRIDGEHEAD, *OMAHA*

The US 2nd Infantry Division comes ashore at Omaha. Its lead regiments, the 9th and 38th Infantry, are immediately rushed forward into the centre of V Corps's line between the 29th and 1st Divisions, their first objective being the village of Trévières. The advance is made without heavy weaponry, most of which is still being unloaded.

As preparations are being made to take Carentan, from the east the 29th Division is attacking Isigny to complete

An American paratroop patrol moves cautiously through the churchyard in St Marcouf, using the high stone wall as cover against enemy fire.

the link-up between Omaha and Utah. Leading the advance is the 175th Infantry. By nightfall it is in Isigny itself, and in the process of securing the town.

Elsewhere in the 29th Division area, units of the 115th and 116th Regiments have pushed south across the Isigny–Bayeux road and on high ground overlooking the River Aure. On the coast, the Rangers on the Pointe-du-Hoc are relieved at about midday by a force of the 116th and two companies of tanks.

In the 1st Division's area, regiments are moving south to Formigny on the Isigny–Bayeux road and securing the left flank of the bridgehead, pushing German forces situated around Port-en-Bessin south down the valley of the River Drome.

THE BRIDGEHEAD, *GOLD*

The British 56th Brigade consolidates its position in Bayeux, pushing southwest to block any German advance from St Lô. East of the town, the 151st Brigade advances between the rivers Aure and Seulles, while the 8th Armoured Brigade makes a rapid advance through the 69th Brigade at Coulomb. North of the Bayeux–Caen rail line at Loucelles the tanks engage units of the 12th SS Panzer Division. These are flanked and the 8th Armoured Brigade has advanced as far as Audrieu by nightfall. Its objective is

▼ *A section of prefabricated port under tow across the Channel, heading for the Normandy coastline.*

to clear the east bank of the Seulles River towards Tilly-sur-Seulles.

THE BRIDGEHEAD, *JUNO*

The Canadian advance south of the Caen–Bayeux rail line at Putot-en-Bessin is stopped by a counterattack by regiments of the 12th SS Panzer Division moving west. This is part of a larger operation by I SS Panzer Corps for a two-division drive to the coast to capture Courseulles and split the Allied bridgehead in two. 12th SS is operating with 21st Panzer on the right and elements of Panzer Lehr, which is beginning to arrive southwest of Caen.

Within 24 hours of their arrival at Normandy front, units of the 12th SS are reported to be committing war crimes. Today, for example, seven Canadian prisoners are taken to the headquarters of the 25 Panzergrenadier Regiment and executed.

THE BRIDGEHEAD, *SWORD*

The 9th Brigade continues its attack on Cambes while the 8th Brigade continues to close the gap between Sword and Juno to the west. The enemy facing the 185th Brigade north of Caen remains strong, with units of the 716th Division and the 21st Panzer Division.

East of the Orne, the 6th Airborne Division has attempted to advance south from Herouvillette towards St Honorine la Chardonnerette and Escoville, but has failed under increasing pressure from tanks of the 21st Panzer Division and newly arrived units of the 125th Panzergrenadier Division.

June 9, D+3

Friday, June 9 (D+3)

AIR CAMPAIGN

During the early hours of the morning, 24 Lancaster bombers of 617 Squadron carry out an attack on the Saumur rail tunnel near the River Loire, 200km (125 miles) south of the battle front. Station X at Bletchley Park has decrypted information that the 17th SS Panzergrenadier Division *Götz von Berlichingen* is on the move north by rail and the raid is organized to stop it.

The Lancasters carry one of the biggest weapons in the RAF arsenal, the 12,000lb "Tallboy", ground-penetrating blast bomb. At least 16 "Tallboys" come close to the target and one direct hit seals the tunnel for the rest of the war.

Despite this awesome display of firepower, a panzer battalion of the division is already on its way to face the Americans near Carentan.

IN THE ENGLISH CHANNEL

Admiral Kranke, commanding Navy Group West, has ordered his last remaining destroyers on the French Atlantic coast, *ZH-1*, *Z-24*, *Z-32* and *T-24*, to sortie from the Bay of Biscay to Cherbourg, in an attempt to reinforce his tiny surface fleet in Normandy. In the early hours of this morning during the final leg of their journey from Brest, the four German Navy vessels are intercepted by the Royal Navy's 10th Destroyer Flotilla, pre-warned of their arrival through Ultra. Action begins in the dark at about 01:30 hours, and for

◄ *Dropping depth charges and firing machine guns, a Sunderland Flying Boat attacks a German U-boat.*

▲ *An RAF Mosquito fighter-bomber makes a strafing run at a German U-boat. In this attack, one U-boat was sunk and another severely damaged.*

the next four hours the destroyers fight it out in a running battle. ZH-1 is sunk, *Z-32* is set ablaze and has to beach while the other two German warships, after taking heavy damage, escape back to Brest. From now on Admiral Kranke will have to rely on his E boats.

The U-boats of Group Landwirt are also having a rough time of it. During the day *U-740* is sunk by a Liberator and the decision is made in the face of growing losses to withdraw all boats from the Channel except the six advanced Snorkel types. The remaining

▼ *A convoy of Allied destroyers patrols the sea to the west of the landing beaches, keeping watch for enemy U-boat activity.*

18 boats of the group are stationed in the Bay of Biscay. Meanwhile, five Snorkel boats from Group Mitte in Norway are ordered to the Channel.

Luftflotte (Air Fleet) 3 is also continuing its attacks on the invasion fleet, and from today begins laying sea mines in the Force U area from low-flying aircraft.

MULBERRY

Surveying of the sites for the two harbours is underway as the first "Phoenix" concrete caissons are flooded and sunk in position off the beachhead. Elsewhere along the coast, the small ports of Port-en-Bessin (on Gold) and Courseulles (on Juno) have now been cleared of obstacles and are open to small landing craft.

BRITISH HOME FRONT

The US Joint Chiefs of Staff, General Marshall, Admiral King and General Arnold, fly into England for their scheduled meeting with General Eisenhower. Arriving by train in London their first visit is to the British Chiefs of Staff.

On the same day as the Allied chiefs of staff confer, Winston Churchill is writing to Montgomery with his plans to visit the bridgehead in three days time. Having been thwarted in his attempt to be with the fleet on D-Day, the prime minister is not to be denied a visit to Normandy now the troops are ashore. In good humour he writes: "We do not wish in any way to be a burden to you or your headquarters, or in any way to divert your attention from the battle. All we should require is an ADC or a Staff Officer to show us around. We shall bring sandwiches with us."

AT THE BEACHHEAD

General Bradley comes ashore at Omaha to join the headquarters of the US First Army, which has been established a couple of miles inland from the former Ranger positions on the Pointe-du-Hoc.

Off Omaha, landing ships arrive carrying the bulk of the US 2nd Armoured Division, which has been at sea since June 7. Vehicles and tanks begin to be unloaded immediately and are moved to the division assembly area around Mosles, on the Bayeux–Isigny road east of Formigny.

Over St Mère-Eglise, meanwhile, C-47s of the IX Troop Carrier Command begin a small series of drops to keep regiments of the 82nd Airborne supplied. The drops go on for the next four days.

In the British sector the first Graves Registration Unit (GRU) comes ashore. In one of the rare logistics failures of the invasion, manufacturers have failed to deliver 10,000 metal crosses on time, and the GRUs have to improvise wooden crosses

▲ An RAF ground crew load a 12,000lb "Tallboy" bomb into the bomb bay of a Lancaster II.

with the help of the British Army's Royal Engineers.

THE BATTLE FRONT, *UTAH*

While the 82nd Airborne is holding down the centre of the Utah bridgehead along the Merderet River east of St Mère-Eglise, VII Corps is pushing four regiments north from its right flank towards Montebourg in a line from the river to the coast.

German resistance, though, is stiffening and a new defence line held by three regimental battle groups and units from three infantry divisions has been established west from Quinéville, blocking the main road to Montebourg from St Mère-Eglise.

VII Corps makes its first attack left of the road, and by the end of the day

▼ *Troops from the* **Hitlerjugend** *Division man their 75mm PAK 40 anti-tank gun. The PAK 40 was a highly effective weapon, capable of knocking out all Allied armour.*

has pushed back the Germans at Magneville and Escouville, though the regiments engaged suffer heavy losses.

On the right, the advance is being held up by the German garrisons at Crisbecq and Azeville, which for the last two days have withstood attacks by battalions of the 22nd Infantry. Today, the regiment concentrates its efforts on Azeville. As the Crisbecq position is hit with artillery fire, a fresh battalion approaches Azeville from the west, its weaker point. After breaching the wire and minefield the blockhouse is attacked, the German garrison eventually dislodged after a lucky shot from a flamethrower detonates an ammunition store. Though Crisbecq still remains in German hands, the capture of Azeville at least opens up the route to Quinéville.

To the south, on the Douve River, the 101st Airborne is advancing on Carentan. Its attack on the town will begin tonight. The plan is for a flanking manoeuvre upriver by the 327th Glider Infantry on the left that will take it through Brevands to attack Carentan from the east, and at the same time link up with

V Corps units coming from Isigny. At the same time paratroopers of the 501st, 502nd and 506th will come down the road from the north, cross the river and then flank the town from the northwest.

OMAHA

The 29th Division having secured Isigny yesterday and having secured its right on the River Vire, begins to advance south with the 175th and 115th Infantry. From the beachhead, the 115th finds crossing points over the flooded River Aure and advances on Colombiere. On its right, the 175th fights its way through La Foret from Isigny and by nightfall is between Lison and la Fortelai, having crossed the Bayeux–Carentan rail line. Meanwhile, patrols of the 29th Division and the 101st Airborne meet at the River Vire.

In the 1st Division area, German resistance on the left flank is collapsing and by the end of the day 26th Infantry is 6km (4 miles) southwest of Bayeux around Agy, with the British 56th Brigade on its left and the US 18th Infantry on its right astride the Bayeux rail line.

While the flank divisions of V Corps are making good progress, in the centre, the 38th and 9th Regiments, still lacking most of their mortars, machine guns and artillery, are held

at Trévières all day by the remnants of the German 352nd Division.

GOLD

The 8th Armoured Brigade secures Audrieu during the morning. A battalion of the 151st Brigade – the 8th Durham Light Infantry – is brought up in support and advances a mile south to St Pierre on the right bank of the Seulles opposite Tilly. This rapid advance by the 50th Division has left its lead brigades in a salient near Tilly, and there are reports of growing concentrations of German armour nearby.

JUNO AND SWORD

There are now believed to be three panzer divisions north of Caen, the 12th SS, Panzer Lehr and 21st Panzer, blocking a direct advance on the town. General Montgomery therefore decides on an attack on the flanks by two of Second Army's follow-up divisions. On the left, the 51st Division will move from the Juno area to east of the Orne. There it will support 6th Airborne and attack south to Cagny, 10km (6

▶ *With a "potato masher" stick grenade to one side, a German paratrooper hidden in a foxhole awaits the Allies.*

miles) southeast of Caen. On the right, the 7th Armoured Division (XXX Corps) will advance through Tilly to Villers-Bocage and then to Noyers southwest of Caen on the Avranches road, which will be its route east. The operation is codenamed Perch and is scheduled to begin tomorrow.

The arrival of the 51st Division east of the Orne cannot come too soon for the 6th Airborne. This morning Ranville comes under heavy artillery fire, and a battle group of the 21st

▲ *US soldiers grab some food, whilst the fire set on the hillside in the background is intended to smoke out any snipers.*

Panzer moves up from the southwest for another counterattack. In a two-pronged sweep the battle group strikes Longueval and Herouvillette, but both attacks are driven off, with the help of 3rd Division artillery.

▲ *A German paratrooper anti-aircraft battery crew on the lookout for Allied aircraft in Normandy.*

SATURDAY, JUNE 10 (D+4)

THE BATTLE FRONT, *UTAH*

On the right flank of the bridgehead the advance north has stalled after the capture of Azeville yesterday. The 22nd Infantry is meant to attack Quinéville but is still being held by German positions at Crisbecq.

To the west of the Montebourg–St Mère-Eglise Road, the 8th Infantry advance north of Escouville and cross the Montebourg–le Ham road but are stopped short of the rail line. To the left of the 8th Infantry, the paratroopers of the 505th advance west towards Le Ham, but are stopped half a mile short.

In the centre of the bridgehead, for the last four days the 82nd Airborne has been trying to cross the swamps surrounding the flooded Merderet River, with the aim of relieving its units isolated on the west bank since D-Day and beginning VII Corps's delayed advance to cut the Cotentin Peninsula. Action concentrates around the village of la Friere and a causeway running to the south of it. Two battalions are needed to force a crossing, and by the end of today the division has five battalions on the roads running west facing Germans concentrations in the villages of Amfreville, Le Motey and Haute-Gueutteville.

Meanwhile, in the attack on Carentan, a causeway crossing was also proving an obstacle to the paratroopers of the 101st Airborne. The flank advance on the left by the 327th Glider Infantry has gone well, though, and all its battalions were across the Douve at Brevands by midday, with lead patrols in contact with units of the 175th Infantry from Isigny during the

▼ *Commandos set out to capture a German gun position. Once a gun site had been captured, all the enemy equipment would be destroyed to avoid recapture.*

▲ *British Sherman tanks of the 13/18th Hussars move cross-country in pursuit of German forces.*

afternoon. On the right flank, a battalion of the 502nd Parachute Infantry spent all day under fire trying to thread its way down the causeway and across its four bridges. By midnight the battalion had companies across the last bridge but was still faced by German positions across the road north of the town.

OMAHA

In the centre of the V Corps bridge-head, the 2nd Division succeeds in taking Trévières in the early hours of the morning. The remains of the German 352nd Division is withdrawn to a new defence line northwest of St Lô, allowing the 2nd Division to make an advance of over 8km (5 miles), to a position south of the woods of the Fôret de Cérisy. On the 2nd Division's left, the 1st Division holds a line facing southeast along the Bayeux–St Lô road. At its furthest point, V Corps's lodgement area is now 11km (7 miles) deep, a vast improvement on the dire situation on Wednesday, D+1.

GOLD

XXX Corps begins the opening moves of Operation Perch. West of Caen, between the Seulles and Aure rivers, the 7th Armoured Division follows the road south from Bayeux and by 06:30 hours has a brigade in contact with Germans at Buceels 3.2km (2 miles) north of Tilly. In support of the advance, Royal Navy warships begin to target German positions to the south and west. South of Tilly, the village of

▼ *A British Sherman tank crew take some well-earned rest, having been in support of infantry holding the bridge at Benouville for four days.*

June 10, D+4

Hottot comes under bombardment from the battleship HMS *Nelson,* which drops 16in shells on it from 30km (18.75 miles), while to the west, Lingeveres draws the attention of the cruiser HMS *Orion*. By nightfall the 7th Armoured has Buceels almost secured, while on the division's left, Juaye Mondaye on the Aure has been taken.

Meanwhile, east of the River Seulles, at St Pierre, the 8th Armoured Brigade comes under heavy counterattack, but has succeeded by the end of the day in holding the northern end of the village.

SWORD

The 51st (Highland) Division is on the move from the Juno area to concentrate east of the River Orne. It is to form the left flank of Operation Perch, but the division is behind schedule. Only two of its three brigades have landed so far, and the division will not be in a position to

▼ *German anti-aircraft gunnery crews rush to their battle stations on hearing the air-raid alarm.*

begin its advance south from the Herouvillette area until June 13 (D+7).

East of the Orne, the Germans are keeping up the pressure on the 6th Airborne Division. At 09:00 hours German infantry begin to advance on Ranville, but they are not supported by armour and are driven off. In

▲ *Off the Ile de Batz, a beached German destroyer is left a smouldering hulk after Allied fighter-bombers attacked it with rockets and bombs.*

the centre of the 6th Airborne's positions along the ridge near Breville and St Come, Lovat's 1st Special Service Brigade and the 3rd Parachute Brigade come under attack from units of the German 346th Division supported by self-propelled artillery guns. These positions are in range of the 6in guns of the cruiser HMS *Arethusa*, which help defeat the attack during the afternoon.

▲ *Opening its massive bomb bay, a B-17 Flying Fortress drops thousands of pounds of bombs onto enemy targets below.*

AT THE BEACHHEAD

The US 9th Infantry Division begins to land at Utah, while units of the US 30th Infantry Division begin to land at Omaha. There are now 10 US Army Divisions in Normandy.

In the British sector at St Croix-sur-Mer, north of Cruelly, the RAF opens its first airfield. This is the first RAF base to operate in France since 1940 and begins work today with the refuelling of three squadrons of RCAF Spitfires.

AIR CAMPAIGN

Ultra intelligence identifies the location of Panzer Group West's mobile headquarters, 19.2km (12 miles) south of Caen at the Chateau le Cain. At 21:00 hours, four squadrons of Typhoons sweep in to rocket the area and are followed by four squadrons of B-24 Mitchells dropping 500lb bombs. The raid devastates the headquarters, killing 18 staff officers, including the chief of staff General von Dawans and injuring the commander General Geyr

von Schweppenburg. Panzer Group West ceases to exist as an operational headquarters and is pulled back to Paris. Command of the sector now passes to I SS Panzer Corps.

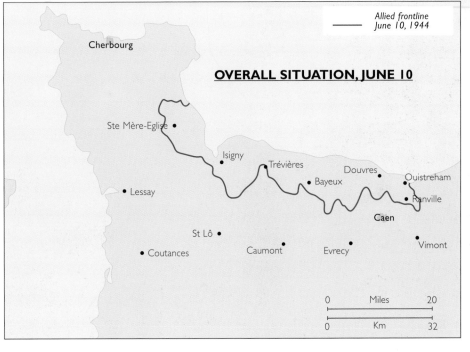

Allied frontline
June 10, 1944

OVERALL SITUATION, JUNE 10

Cherbourg

Ste Mère-Eglise

Isigny

Trévières

Douvres

Ouistreham

Bayeux

Ranville

Lessay

Caen

St Lô

Vimont

Coutances

Caumont

Evrecy

| 0 | Miles | 20 |
| 0 | Km | 32 |

▲ *The situation on the morning of June 10, 1944, showing the depth of the Allied beachhead only four days after the invasion. From here onwards, however, the fighting would get harder.*

SUNDAY, JUNE 11 (D+5)

AT THE BEACHHEAD

General Montgomery gives a press conference to journalists at his tactical headquarters at Cruelly; his first since the invasion.

MULBERRY

Two "Whale" floating roadways are under construction in Mulberry A off Omaha beach. Mulberry A is ahead of schedule. It is not due to be operational until June 24 (D+18), but in fact unloads its first LST on 17 June (D+11).

THE BATTLE FRONT, *UTAH*

On VII Corps's right flank, the Germans still hold Quinéville and control a stretch of coast 5km (3 miles) to the south of it, allowing their artillery to keep up a bombardment on Utah Beach. The 22nd Infantry attack on Quinéville has stalled, and the frontline from Montebourg to the coast is only thinly held by the 12th Infantry and the 22nd on its right. Reinforcements are needed, and the arrival of the 9th Division yesterday gives the corps commander, General Gerow, options to put a fresh regiment on the 22nd's right to make a drive up the coast while another attack goes in on Quinéville.

Along the Merderet River, the 82nd Airborne is now supported by the 90th Division, which advanced its two lead regiments over the river crossings from St Mère-Eglise yesterday morning. The 90th's original task was to drive north on the 4th Division's left to capture

▲ *General Sir Bernard Montgomery (centre) visits a recently captured small port on the French coast.*

Cherbourg, but now it is to add its weight to the drive west to cut the peninsula. By nightfall, the division's 357th Regiment is through Le Motey and Amfreville on the St Mère-Eglise–Carteret road and is attacking Les Landes. On its left, the 358th Regiment is at the road junction of Pont-l'Abbe.

At Carentan the German garrison is being reinforced. Two Ost battalions have arrived from LXXXIV Corps and the surviving defenders of Isigny have arrived. To the south, lead units of the

17th SS Panzergrenadier Division are preparing a counterattack. LXXXIV Corps must hold Carentan to stop the link-up of the two American bridgeheads and to prevent an advance southwest through Périers to Coutances, which would outflank St Lô.

Meanwhile the regiments of the 101st are closing in on the town. By midnight the 502nd Parachute Infantry

▶ *An M4 Sherman Firefly. Equipped with a 17lb gun, it was arguably the most effective Sherman during the war.*

▲ *Round a ruined wall in the Normandy village of St Mauvieu, Allied troops move cautiously to avoid snipers and booby-traps.*

has three battalions across the causeway to the north, but has taken so many casualties over the past 24 hours it is withdrawn and replaced by the 506th. On the left, the 327th Glider Infantry has now completed its flanking march and is on the eastern outskirts of Carentan along the Taute River, astride the rail line and the Isigny road. The assault will begin before dawn tomorrow reinforced by the 501st Parachute Infantry, advancing on the left of the 327th, and the tanks of the 41st Armored Infantry Regiment (part of the 2nd Armored Division from Omaha) coming down the Isigny road. To coordinate the operation, all units are reorganized into a single task force commanded by Brigadier-General McAuliffe of the 101st Airborne.

OMAHA
In the 29th Division area, units of the 175th and 115th Infantry are now in position along the Elle River south of Isigny. On their left regiments of the 2nd and 1st Divisions are regrouping

▲ *Scouts from the British 5/7th Gordon Highlanders watch for enemy movement in the woods at Bois-de-Bevent.*

south and west of the Fôret de Cérisy after their rapid gains of yesterday.

Their lack of progress today is a mistake. Had the two divisions advanced they would have moved into a 16km (10-mile) gap north of Caumont between the Panzer Lehr Division attacking the British at Tilly, south of Bayeux, and the remnants of the 352nd Division northeast of St Lô.

The only German unit in the area over the last 24 hours has been a reconnaissance battalion of the 17th SS Panzergrenadier Division. Today this battalion is reinforced by a regiment of the 3rd Parachute Division on the right of the 352nd, but the Caumont Gap still remains largely undefended.

GOLD

The 7th Armoured Division continues its advance between the rivers Aure and Seulles towards Tilly, but its advance is slowing. The British are now entering the Bocage country with its thick hedgerows that are proving difficult obstacles for tanks but natural defensive positions for the Germans. XXX Corps has brought up infantry

▼ *Fighting through the dense Bocage countryside of northern France, US soldiers moving along a pathway bob and weave as they try to avoid enemy fire.*

brigades in support, and today the 7th Armoured organizes two tank and infantry groups to renew the advance. One attacks Tilly, the other Lingevres to the west on the Tilly–Balleroy road.

At Tilly, the infantry fight its way in, but the tanks are held on the outskirts. By nightfall the British have pulled back to positions to the north, and the Germans still have the village in their possession. At Lingevres, by nightfall the second battle group has advanced as far as woodland to the north, but its position is not secure, and after dark the Germans put in a counterattack. This is beaten off, but the Germans regroup and launch another attack at about midnight. On the road west from Lingevres, units of the 50th Division have captured the crossroads at La Belle Epine by the end of the day.

On the 7th Armoured's right flank, northeast of the St Pierre, there is fighting all day between le Haut d'Audrieu and

Cristot. The 69th Brigade, of 50th Division, tries to attack east to Cristot only to be held and counterattacked by units of the 12th SS Panzer Division.

JUNO

On the left of the 69th Brigade, the 3rd Canadian Division takes advantage of the move from St Pierre to strengthen its position south of Bronay and Putot-en-Bessin, after holding off the counterattacks by the 12th SS on June 8. The 2nd Canadian Armoured Brigade, supported by the Queen's Own Rifles, are pushed forward in a hurriedly conceived attack that reaches as far as Le Mesnil Patry. Here, the Canadians are caught between German positions around Cristot and St Mauvieu and subjected to tank and anti-tank fire that inflicts heavy infantry casualties and destroys 37 tanks.

After the action around Le Mesnil, this part of the front stabilizes for the next two weeks. The 3rd Canadian Division will not go on the offensive again until Operation Epsom on June 26 (D+20) while the 12th SS, now under constant

▲ *Propped up against the rubble of a destroyed building, a British soldier of the Durham Light Infantry opens fire with his Bren light machine gun.*

Allied air attack, is forced on to the defensive west of Carpiquet.

SWORD

After yesterday's heavy counterattack on the 3rd Parachute Brigade at Breville, the frontline here is reinforced by the 5th Black Watch of the 51st Division's 153rd Brigade. The battalion attacks Breville but is met with heavy German fire that inflicts 200 casualties. To the south the remainder of 153rd Brigade advances south in preparation for Operation Perch, and by the end of the day has secured Touffreville, north of the Caen rail line.

GERMAN DEFENCES

Von Rundstedt and Rommel meet in conference in Paris to discuss the serious situation now facing Seventh Army. Their conclusions are sent in two separate reports to Hitler.

Both reports state plainly that units are on the defensive everywhere from the River Orne to the Vire, and because of a lack of infantry, armoured units are holding the line and are unable to counterattack in strength. More infantry is needed in Normandy to consolidate the front and free the panzers. Operations should be concentrated on the Americans in the Cotentin to defend Carentan, Montebourg and Cherbourg. Only then should the weight of the attack be switched east to the British at Caen. The two officers identify four areas of Allied superiority that may disrupt these plans:

1 Control of the air: "From the long-term point of view this superiority of the enemy air forces will paralyze all movement and control of the battle, and make it impossible to conduct operations."

2 The domination of much of the front by the firepower of Allied warships.

3 The material superiority of the Allied forces." . . . the spirit and morale [of our] troops are good, but the material superiority of the Anglo-Americans must in the long run have its effect on any troops."

4 The strength and flexibility of the Allied airborne and parachute troops.

Hitler's response is a rejection of the "Cotentin first" proposal. The danger of a breakout by the British through Caen to Paris is too great. The panzer divisions will therefore concentrate around Caen. Hitler will accept no large-scale tactical retreats to form new defensive lines in northern France, stating in his now infamous remark: "Every man shall fight and die where he stands."

▼ *Men of the 23rd Hussars warily search trees looking for snipers. Even one good sniper could hold up a sizeable force in the right conditions.*

June 12, D+6

AT THE BEACHHEAD

The battle at the beachhead is now becoming one of logistics. A race is on to land fresh troops and supplies faster than the Germans can bring in reinforcements. To increase the unloading capacity over Utah, another two beach sectors have been opened at Sugar Red and Roger White. This nearly triples the capacity of Utah from 1500 tonnes (1524 tons) a day to 4000 tonnes (4064 tons).

On Omaha, Mulberry A nears completion at St Laurent. Meanwhile, army and navy engineers have cleared the mines and battlefield debris and laid heavy steel mesh over the beach to convert these former killing grounds into hards; landing ramps for the DUKW amphibious trucks and Rhino ferries that shuttle between the shore and the transport vessels, that are now protected from rough seas by the Gooseberry breakwaters.

On Gold the lead brigades of the 49th (West Riding) Division begin to land a day late because of bad weather. The division is assigned to XXX Corps.

COMMANDERS

D+5 is a day of high-level official visits to the bridgehead. The US Joint Chiefs of Staff, Generals Marshall, Arnold and Admiral King, conclude their visit to the European Theatre of Operations with a tour of the American sector, accompanied by General Eisenhower. The party comes over in the destroyer USS *Thomson* from Portsmouth and lands at St Laurent on Omaha and is met by General Bradley. The tour takes them to Bradley's headquarters and then on to Utah by sea, the road through Isigny still being too close the front line. The visit lasts until late afternoon.

The British sector sees the arrival of Winston Churchill and Field Marshal Sir Alan Brooke, Chief of the Imperial General Staff. The prime minister left Portsmouth at 08:00 hours in the destroyer HMS *Kelvin* and lands at 11:00 hours at Courselles on Juno to be met by General Montgomery. The party then visits Montgomery's headquarters at Cruelly for lunch before visiting General Dempsey's

▼ *Fresh off their transport ships, Allied tanks and troops filter through the town of Reviers on their way to the front.*

Second Army Headquarters and the Mulberry harbour at Arromanches. The prime minister returns to Courseulles and is on his way back to England by late afternoon.

THE BATTLE FRONT, *UTAH*

General Gerow, commanding VII Corps, orders 9th Division's 39th Regiment to join the 22nd Infantry in the attack on Quinéville. So far the 22nd has been trying to do the job on its own.

Moving into position on the right of the 22nd Infantry, the 39th's 2nd and 3rd Battalions move east towards the coast. They find Crisbecq unoccupied, but Fontenay-sur-Mer is garrisoned and is only captured after a fight. The 1st Battalion takes the beach road advancing on Fort St Marcouf.

North of Fontenay, the 22nd Infantry takes fortifications at Ozeville, allowing the 12th Infantry to advance east of Montebourg. By the end of the day the 12th is across the Montebourg road and is on high ground around Les Fieffes Dancel. The German defence line between Montebourg to Quinéville is cracking, but Montebourg itself remains in German hands and its garrison is being reinforced with light tanks and an infantry battal-

LOGISTICS

KEEPING THE ARMIES RUNNING

To provide enough fuel for the vehicles, armour and aircraft during the first two weeks of Overlord, the Eastern Task Force alone transported a 286,400-litre (63,000-gallon) reserve of petrol, oil and lubricant (POL) on D-Day. By D+6 (12 June) this reserve had grown and the British bridgehead had a stockpile of 4.6 litres (1 million gallons) of POL representing a two-day supply for every vehicle ashore. From D+6 petrol began to be landed ashore direct from deep-draught tankers through "Tombola" pipelines and stored in bulk storage tanks, one of which was constructed at Port en Bessin.

ion. A probing attack into Montebourg from the south by the 8th Infantry is called off during the day when the strength of the enemy garrison is discovered.

West of the River Merderet, the 90th Division and regiments of the 82nd Airborne continue to advance slowly against German opposition now desperate to hold open the roads to Cherbourg. To the south, rapid advances are made across the River Douve by the 82nd Airborne's 508th Parachute Infantry, which attacks before dawn across the river towards Baupte to link with the right flank of the 101st Airborne around Carentan. The German battalion holding the sector flees on first contact and the 508th advances 6.4km (4 miles) to Baupte meeting no resistance, and by 08:00 hours has reached the village.

In Carentan, the defending German garrison, surrounded on three sides by American troops, receives some support after OB West orders a supply drop flown in – the first time the Germans have attempted to do this in Normandy. Before dawn, 18 tonnes (18.28 tons) of artillery and small arms ammunition is dropped by parachute. It arrives too late to affect the outcome of the battle because the garrison commander, Major von der Heydte, has already ordered his men to withdraw south to new defence line.

Overnight, Carentan is prepared for the final American assault by coming under sustained bombardment by naval and land-based artillery. By 02:00

▲ *Allied ships offload supplies onto waiting trucks at Mulberry B, one of the prefabricated artificial harbours. Mulberry B at Arromanches was used extensively.*

hours the 506th Parachute Infantry are on the move from the causeway, making a flanking march to the west and taking position on Hill 30 which dominates the road southwest to Périers. By 05:00 hours the hill is finally secure and the regiment's 2nd Battalion is ordered into the town. As it fights its way in from the south, the 327th Glider Infantry attacks over the Taute River from the east, supported on its left by the 501st which flanks to the town to the south, reaching Hill

30. By 08:00 hours Carentan is in American hands.

The 506th and 501st now try to sustain the momentum of the attack by advancing from Hill 30 on the line of the Périers road, southwest. Both regiments are stopped within a few hundred yards by von der Heydte's new defence line. During the night the First Army receives information that the Germans are preparing to launch a counterattack in force. General Bradley orders V Corps to have a battalion of tanks and armoured infantry between Isigny and Carentan by dawn to stop it.

▼ *The German garrison at Carentan was attacked by the Allies from three sides during a four-day battle, putting up some stiff resistance against the odds.*

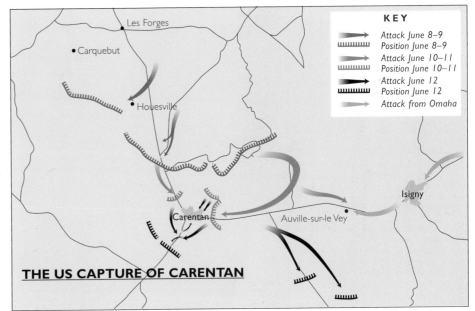

THE US CAPTURE OF CARENTAN

KEY

Attack June 8–9
Position June 8–9
Attack June 10–11
Position June 10–11
Attack June 12
Position June 12
Attack from Omaha

Les Forges
Carquebut
Houesville
Carentan
Auville-sur-le Vey
Isigny

JUNE 12, D+6

▶ A quick-reaction force patrol of the 101st Airborne Division sweeps through the area looking for the snipers that shot their comrades.

OMAHA

The 2nd and 1st Divisions renew their attacks to the south and west of the Fôret de Cérisy and advance into the Caumont Gap. On the far left of the 1st Division, the 18th and 26th Infantry regiments, which are moving in support of the British 7th Armoured Division's attack on Villers-Bocage, advance about 6.4km (4 miles) against little resistance and are across the Caumont-St Lô road by the end of the day. The 26th Infantry is in position on the northern outskirts of Caumont, but waits for dawn to begin an assault to clear out companies of the 2nd Panzer Division. South of the forest, the 2nd Division's 9th Infantry moves in support and occupies a ridge near Liteau.

West of the forest, the 2nd Division's 23rd Infantry with the 115th Infantry of the 29th Division on its right begin a slow advance southwest towards St Lô. German resistance intensifies as the Americans move deeper into the bocage. The 115th makes an advance of about 2700m (3000yds) during the morning, but has to withdraw to avoid being surrounded and cut off. The attack on St Lô has been slowed to a halt by the end of its first day.

GOLD

The 7th Armoured Division's advance on Villers-Bocage has been held north of Lingevres and Tilly by Panzer Lehr, which holds strong positions between the rivers Aure and Seulles. Taking ad-

vantage of the gap that has opened in the German line around Caumont, tonight 7th Armoured moves its line of advance. Leaving the infantry of the 50th Division to hold the road between La Belle Epine and St Pierre, at 22:00 hours 7th Armoured crosses the Aure and outflanks Panzer Lehr to the west. Meeting little opposition, the advance reaches Livy, 3km (2 miles) northeast of Caumont and only five miles east Villers Bocage, where its lead brigade halts for the night.

SWORD

East of the Orne, the German 346th Infantry Division intensifies its counterattacks around Breville and forward British positions at St Come. At 15:00 hours, after a three hour bombardment men of the 5th Black Watch and paratroopers of the 3rd Parachute Brigade in St Come are attacked by an infantry battalion of the 858th Regiment supported by assault guns. Holding out in woods and a chateau, the British are reinforced by tanks and a battalion of Canadian paratroopers. The battle goes until 21.00 hours when the Germans withdraw to Breville which the British promptly start shelling. General Gale, commander of the 6th Airborne, decides to counterat-

tack immediately and at 22:00 hours the understrength 12th Battalion of the 5th Parachute Brigade and a squadron of tanks advances east from Amfreville and attacks Breville. By midnight the paratroopers have taken the village, but the cost is appallingly high. Out of 160 officers and men engaged, the 12th Battalion has taken 141 casualties. The German 858th Regiment has also suffered heavily, its 3rd Battalion having only 146 men left out of 564.

◀ As Churchill continues his tour of the front, enemy planes fly over chased by Allied fighters and engaged by AA guns. Winston undoubtedly enjoyed the show.

The capture of Carentan on June 12 links all the invasion beachheads for the first time and extends the Allied bridgehead into a continuous front 80km (50 miles) long and up to 19km (12 miles) deep. From D+7 the fighting in Normandy revolves around four objectives. In the American sector they are the Port of Cherbourg, the west coast of the Cotentin Peninsula, and St Lô. In the British sector, the key target is the town of Caen.

US VII Corps reaches Barneville on the west coast of the Cotentin on June 18, sealing off Cherbourg, which falls after a five-day battle on June 27. The US First Army now concentrates its efforts on St Lô, beginning an attack on July 3 that does not succeed until July 18.

Meanwhile, the British Second Army mounts two major operations to take Caen from the north and west: Epsom on June 30 and Charnwood on July 8. Both attempts fail, and on July 18 General Montgomery tries again, launching Operation Goodwood to the east. Caen, a D-Day objective, finally falls, but the British are held a few miles south along the Bourgebus Ridge and fail to exploit Goodwood into a breakout.

The US First Army has better fortune on July 25 when Operation Cobra drives a route out of the Cotentin through Coutances. On July 31 Avranches falls, and on August 1 the US Third Army, commanded by General Patton, is activated. In eight days the Third Army advances west into Brittany, east to Le Mans, and south to the Loire River. The Allies now have their breakout.

On August 8, the Canadian First Army launches Operation Totalize from Caen to Falaise. At the same time, Patton switches his advance north through Alençon. A vast pincer movement has now enveloped the German Seventh Army in the Falaise Pocket, and 23 divisions are in danger of annihilation. The US First Army closes the pocket on August 21 with the capture of Argentan. The Allies capture 50,000 prisoners and estimate they have destroyed at least 5000 tanks and armoured vehicles. The German Army in Normandy, now reduced to a battered remnant of 30,000 men, is in full retreat across the River Seine and leaves behind it an estimated 400,000 killed since D-Day.

▼ *Among the ruins of a French town, US troops clear a path for the trucks of the "Red Ball Express".*

INDEX

Italic page numbers indicate illustrations.

INDEX